Lecture Notes in Computer Science   11322

Commenced Publication in 1973
Founding and Former Series Editors:
Gerhard Goos, Juris Hartmanis, and Jan van Leeuwen

More information about this series at http://www.springer.com/series/7410

Cas Cremers · Anja Lehmann (Eds.)

Security Standardisation Research

4th International Conference, SSR 2018
Darmstadt, Germany, November 26–27, 2018
Proceedings

 Springer

Editors
Cas Cremers (iD)
CISPA-Helmholtz-Zentrum (i.G.)
Saarbrücken, Germany

Anja Lehmann
IBM Research Zurich
Rüschlikon, Switzerland

ISSN 0302-9743   ISSN 1611-3349   (electronic)
Lecture Notes in Computer Science
ISBN 978-3-030-04761-0   ISBN 978-3-030-04762-7   (eBook)
https://doi.org/10.1007/978-3-030-04762-7

Library of Congress Control Number: 2018962149

LNCS Sublibrary: SL4 – Security and Cryptology

This Springer imprint is published by the registered company Springer Nature Switzerland AG
The registered company address is: Gewerbestrasse 11, 6330 Cham, Switzerland

Preface

The 4th Conference on Security Standards Research (SSR 2018) was held during November 26–27, 2018, in Darmstadt, Germany. The purpose of this conference is to discuss the many research problems deriving from studies of existing standards, the development of revisions to existing standards, and the exploration of completely new areas of standardization. Additionally, SSR aims to be a platform for exchanging knowledge between academia and industry to improve the security of standards.

Overall, there were 16 submissions to SSR 2018, out of which nine were accepted. On average, submissions were reviewed by four Program Committee members. The accepted papers cover a range of topics in the field of security standardization research, including cryptographic evaluation, standards development, analysis with formal methods, potential future areas of standardization, and improving existing standards.

The conference program also featured four invited talks:

- Karthikeyan Bhargavan (Inria, France)
  "Verified Cryptography for Verified Protocols"
- Andreea Gulasci (CEN, Belgium)
  "European Security Challenges – What Role for Standards?"
- Andreas Huelsing (TU Eindhoven, The Netherlands)
  "(To Be) Standardized Hash-Based Signature Schemes"
- Tanja Lange (TU Eindhoven, The Netherlands)
  "The Standardization Ecosystem: A Fertile Ground for Bad Ideas and Backdoors"

We would like to thank all the people who contributed to the success of SSR 2108. First, we thank the authors for submitting their work to our conference. We heartily thank the Program Committee, and also the external reviewer, for their careful and thorough reviews. Thanks must also go to the shepherds for their expert guidance and helpful advice for improving papers. Finally, we are grateful to Marc Fischlin for hosting SSR 2018 at TU Darmstadt, and thank Jean Paul Degabriele and Andrea Püchner for their support with the conference organization.

October 2018

Cas Cremers
Anja Lehmann

SSR 2018

4th Conference on Security Standardisation Research

November 26–27, 2018, Darmstadt, Germany

Program Chairs

Cas Cremers   CISPA – Saarbrücken, Germany
Anja Lehmann   IBM Research – Zurich, Switzerland

General Chair

Marc Fischlin   TU Darmstadt, Germany

Program Committee

Steve Babbage   Vodafone, UK
Liqun Chen   University of Surrey, UK
Jean Paul Degabriele   TU Darmstadt, Germany
Antoine Delignat-Lavaud Microsoft Research, UK
Orr Dunkelman   University of Haifa, Israel
Cedric Fournet   Microsoft Research, UK
Britta Hale   Norwegian University of Science and Technology,
                             Norway
Harry Halpin   Inria, France
Tibor Jager   Paderborn University, Germany
John Kelsey   NIST, USA
Markulf Kohlweiss   University of Edinburgh, UK
Stephan Krenn   AIT Austrian Institute of Technology, Austria
Xuejia Lai   Shanghai Jiaotong University, China
Tancrède Lepoint   SRI International, USA
Peter Lipp   Graz University of Technology, Austria
Atul Luykx   Visa Research, USA
Catherine Meadows   Naval Research Laboratory, USA
David Naccache   ENS, France
Valtteri Niemi   University of Helsinki, Finland
Kenneth Paterson   Royal Holloway, University of London, UK
Eric Rescorla   Mozilla, USA
Matt Robshaw   Impinj, USA
Phillip Rogaway   University of California, Davis, USA
Mark Ryan   University of Birmingham, UK
Kazue Sako   NEC, Japan
Peter Schwabe   Radboud University, The Netherlands
Tom Shrimpton   University of Florida, USA

Contents

hacspec: Towards Verifiable Crypto Standards

Karthikeyan Bhargavan[1], Franziskus Kiefer[2]([✉]), and Pierre-Yves Strub[3]

[1] INRIA, Paris, France
karthikeyan.bhargavan@inria.fr
[2] Mozilla, Berlin, Germany
mail@franziskuskiefer.de
[3] École Polytechnique, Palaiseau, France
pierre-yves@strub.nu

Abstract. We present hacspec, a collaborative effort to design a formal specification language for cryptographic primitives. Specifications (specs) written in hacspec are succinct, easy to read and implement, and lend themselves to formal verification using a variety of existing tools. The syntax of hacspec is similar to the pseudocode used in cryptographic standards but is equipped with a static type system and syntax checking tools that can find errors. Specs written in hacspec are executable and can hence be tested against test vectors taken from standards and specified in a common format. Finally, hacspec is designed to be compilable to other formal specification languages like F*, EASYCRYPT, Coq, and cryptol, so that it can be used as the basis for formal proofs of functional correctness and cryptographic security using various verification frameworks. This paper presents the syntax, design, and tool architecture of hacspec. We demonstrate the use of the language to specify popular cryptographic algorithms, and describe preliminary compilers from hacspec to F* and to EASYCRYPT. Our goal is to invite authors of cryptographic standards to write their pseudocode in hacspec and to help the formal verification community develop the language and tools that are needed to promote high-assurance cryptographic software backed by mathematical proofs.

1 Introduction

Cryptographic algorithms such as those standardized by organizations like the NIST, IETF, and the ISO, are written with a focus on clarity, ease of implementation, and interoperability. To this end, standards authors employ a combination of carefully edited text, precise mathematical formulas, and pseudocode. Many standards include test vectors and some even include reference code written in popular languages like C or python. Each standard is looked over by dozens of experts before publication and then closely vetted by the developer community during implementation and deployment.

Standards vs. Implementations. Despite this care, implementing cryptographic standards remains challenging and error-prone for a variety of reasons.

© Springer Nature Switzerland AG 2018
C. Cremers and A. Lehmann (Eds.): SSR 2018, LNCS 11322, pp. 1–20, 2018.
https://doi.org/10.1007/978-3-030-04762-7_1

First, the mathematical structure used in a cryptographic algorithm may be easy to specify but hard to implement correctly and efficiently. For example, most elliptic curve standards such as [2], require modular arithmetic over large prime fields, but implementing bignum arithmetic efficiently and correctly is hard, leading to numerous subtle bugs that are hard to find simply by testing.[1]

Second, the specification of an algorithm in a standard may not account for side-channel attacks that require specific countermeasures to be implemented. For example, the natural way to implement the AES standard [13] leads to cache-timing attacks [6] that are hard to protect against without significantly changing the main routines of the algorithm [17].

Third, standards typically do not specify the interface (API) through which applications may use the cryptographic algorithm in practice. For example, the SHA-2 specification [10] specifies how a message can be hashed in one pass, but does not describe the incremental hashing interface that is commonly used, and which can be quite error-prone to implement [19].

Fourth, the security guarantees and assumptions of a cryptographic algorithm are often subtle and easy to misunderstand, leading to dangerous vulnerabilities. For example, the GCM [12] and ECDSA [15] specifications both require unique nonces but the use of bad randomness and incorrect configuration has led to real-world implementations that repeat nonces, leading to practical attacks [8,11].

These are just a few of the reasons why there is often a substantial gap between a cryptographic standard and its implementations. It is hard to close this gap just with testing since cryptographic algorithms often have corner cases that are reached only with low probability and some properties like side-channel resistance and cryptographic security are particularly hard to test. Instead, we advocate the use of formal methods to mathematically prove that an implementation meets the standard and protects against side channels as well as programmatically check expected cryptographic security guarantees of the spec.

Formal Verification of Cryptography. A wide range of verification frameworks have been proposed for the analysis of cryptographic algorithms and their implementations. The Software Analysis Workbench (SAW) can verify C and Java implementations for input-output equivalence with specifications written in Cryptol, a domain-specific language for specifying cryptographic primitives [22]. The Verified Software Toolchain can be used to verify C implementations against specifications written in Coq [4]. HACL* is a library of modern cryptographic algorithms that are written in F*, verified against specifications written in F*, and then compiled to C [23]. Fiat-Crypto generates efficient verified C code for field arithmetic from high-level specifications embedded in Coq [14]. Vale can be used to verify assembly implementations of cryptography against specifications written in Dafny or F* [9]. Jasmin is another crypto-oriented assembly language verification tool with a verified compiler written in Coq [3]. EASYCRYPT can be used to build cryptographic game-based security proofs for constructions and protocols written in a simple imperative language [5]. The Foundational

---

[1] See, for example, this bug in a popular Curve25519 implementation https://www.imperialviolet.org/2014/09/07/provers.html.

Cryptography Framework (FCF) mechanizes proofs of cryptographic schemes in Coq [20]. CryptoVerif can be used to develop machine-checked proofs of cryptographic protocols written in the applied pi calculus [7].

In order to benefit from any of these verification frameworks, the first step is to write a formal specification of the cryptographic algorithm. Since each framework uses its own specification language, this step can be tedious, time-consuming, and error-prone. Furthermore, the resulting formal specification is often tailored to suit the strengths of a particular verification framework, making it difficult to check the conformance of the specification with the standard or to compare it with other formal specifications.

Ideally, the published standard would itself include a formal-enough reference specification from which these tool-specific specs could be derived. Indeed, standards bodies have considered incorporating formal languages in the past. Since 2001, the IETF has a guideline on the use of formal languages in standards, which sets out sensible requirements, such as "The specification needs to be verifiable".[2] Nevertheless, the use of formal languages in cryptographic standards has not caught on, probably because authors did not see a significant benefit in exchange for the time and effort required to write formal specifications.

In this paper we propose hacspec, a new domain-specific formal language for cryptographic algorithms that we believe is suitable for use in standards. The language comes equipped with syntax and type checkers, a testing framework, and several verification tools. Hence, standards authors can use it to formalize, test, and verify pseudocode written in hacspec before including it in the standard. Furthermore, the language provides a common front-end for various cryptographic verification frameworks, so that proofs in these frameworks can be precisely compared and composed.

The authors believe that it is vital for a cryptographic standard to not only specify the mathematical algorithm describing the standard but also to allow engineers to implement the specification securely. In order to securely implement a specification it is important to make sure that the implementation is correct, i.e. that the implementation is functionally equivalent to the specification. This is especially important for highly optimized implementations that are hard to verify manually. The mechanisms proposed in this paper allow to prove this correctness property. The proposed tools further allow to prove cryptographic properties of the specified algorithm as well as security properties of an implementation. While these additional proofs do not necessarily belong into a specification of an algorithm, it makes the specification the single document of reference when implementing the algorithm or examining its security.

hacspec is designed in order to keep the barriers of entry low by being very close to what some specification authors use already and most engineers, mathematicians, and researchers are familiar with. Because of the design and additional benefits hacspec offers the authors believe that hacspec has a good chance to get adopted by specification authors.

---

[2] https://www.ietf.org/iesg/statement/pseudocode-guidelines.html.

Contributions and Outline. The design of hacspec originates from discussions at the HACS workshop[3] held alongside the Real-World Crypto conference 2018. The workshop participants included crypto developers for many major crypto libraries as well as researchers behind many popular verification frameworks. Together, we sought to achieve a balance between developer usability and ease of formal verification. This paper is the realization and continuation of the discussions and outcomes of that group.

We present hacspec in Sect. 2, a new specification and verification architecture for cryptographic standards. We describe the syntax of the hacspec language and show how it can be used to write cryptographic specifications on some examples in Sect. 3. We present compilers from hacspec to F* and EASYCRYPT and show how the resulting specifications are used as verification targets in formal proofs in Sects. 5.1 and 5.2. Finally, we present our current status and ongoing work in Sect. 6. Everything described in this paper is implemented and available in the hacspec git repository.[4]

2   Architecture and Design Goals

Figure 1 depicts the proposed architecture of hacspec and design workflow. In the remainder of this section we describe each component and its design goals. In subsequent sections, we will describe in more detail how our current tool-set realizes these goals, and we will present preliminary results.

A New Specification Language. hacspec is a new domain-specific language for cryptographic algorithms that aims to build a bridge between standards authors and formal verification tools. Consequently, the language needs to be familiar to spec writers, mathematicians, and crypto developers alike, but with precise semantics that can be easily translated to various formal specification languages.

We chose to design hacspec as a subset of python (version 3.6.4) since python syntax is already used as pseudocode in various standards, e.g. [16,18], and hence is familiar to standards authors and crypto developers. Python is especially well suited for this task since it is an imperative language that supports native bignums (arbitrary-size integers) and has an expressive type annotation syntax. As we will see in Sect. 3 we restrict and enhance the python syntax in many ways to enable compilation to typed formal specifications.

Scope and Limitations. Although hacspec may eventually be used as a starting point for specifying cryptographic protocols and APIs, we emphasize that capturing anything other than cryptographic algorithms is out of scope for hacspec at this point. By focusing only on cryptographic algorithms, we believe we obtain a simpler syntax and are able to design more usable tools. Also note that the language as defined in Sect. 3 currently does not allow to use more advanced concepts such as higher-order functions. Because it would increase the

---

[3] https://hacs-workshop.github.io/.

[4] https://github.com/hacs-workshop/hacspec/.

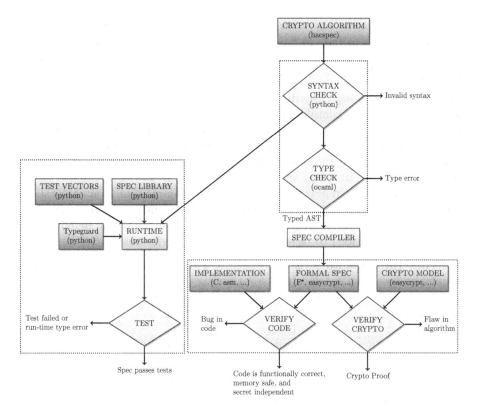

Fig. 1. hacspec specification and verification architecture. Authors of cryptographic standards write their algorithm in hacspec, aided by the syntax and type checker. They can then test their specs by executing the spec in python (along with an implementation of the builtin library). They can also use spec compilers to generate formal specifications in languages like F*, EASYCRYPT, etc., that can in turn be used as the basis for verifying the correctness of various implementations, or for proving the cryptographic security guarantees of the algorithm.

complexity of the compiler, more advanced features — while planned — are left for future work.

Syntax and Type Checking. Since specifications written in hacspec are meant to be used as a basis for formal proofs, it is important that the specs themselves are correct. We propose several static and run-time tools that can find common programming errors in hacspec specifications.

First, we provide a syntax checker written in python that can find simple errors and reject specifications that use python features or control structures that are not supported by our domain-specific language. Second, we use a run-time type checker plugin for python called TypeGuard to find type errors in hacspec specifications. Using these two tools, authors who only have python on their system can already author and check hacspec specifications.

As a third tool, we also provide a static type checker for hacspec written in OCaml which can find violations of the annotated types at compile time. In addition to finding type errors, this typechecker generates a typed abstract syntax tree (AST) that is then used as a basis for our spec compilers.

Running and Testing Specifications. A key goal of hacspec is that the specifications should be executable. hacspec specifications are already written in a subset of python but they use many domain-specific types and data structures. We provide a library written in python that implements these builtin types and data structures, so that the specification can be run by a standard python interpreter and tested against test vectors.

Hence, a hacspec can also be seen as a reference implementation of the standard that can be used to guide other implementations and test them for correctness. However, these specs should clearly not be used in real-world deployments as they are not intended to be side-channel free or performant.

Verifying Implementations. The hacspec language is designed to support compilation to formal specifications for a variety of verification frameworks. We present a compiler from hacspec to F* in Sect. 5.1 and show that specifications generated by this compiler can be used to verify implementations written in Low*, a subset of F* that can be compiled to C.

We also envision compilers from hacspec to Cryptol and Coq models that can serve as formal specifications for verifying code written in C, Java, and assembly, using the SAW, Fiat-Crypto, VST, and Jasmin verification frameworks.

Verifying Cryptographic Security. Formal specifications compiled from hacspec can also be used as the basis for cryptographic proofs. We present a compiler from hacspec to EASYCRYPT in Sect. 5.2 and show how such specifications can be used to prove that a construction meets its cryptographic security guarantees under precise assumptions on its underlying primitives. Hence, we intend for hacspec to provide a starting point for mechanized cryptographic proofs of standards. We also envision compilers that can generate specifications for other cryptographic verification frameworks like FCF [20].

3   The hacspec Language

In this section, we will describe the syntax of hacspec language. As we shall see in Sect. 3.2 this syntax is already adequate to write cryptographic algorithms. But for developer convenience we also provide a builtin library that contains a number of commonly-used types, constants, operators, and functions. This library is described in Sect. 3.3.

3.1   hacspec Syntax

The full syntax of hacspec is depicted in Table 1, divided in terms of values, expressions, types, statements, and specs.

Table 1. hacspec syntax: values, expressions, types, statements, and specifs. For types, constants, functions, and operators provided by the builtin library, see Sect. 3.3.

Values v ::=	`n`	*integer constants*
	`| True | False`	*boolean constants*
	`| '...' | "..."`	*string constants*
	`| (v1,...,vn)`	*tuple constant*
	`| array([v1,...,vn])`	*array constant*
Expressions e ::=	`v`	*values*
	`| x | m.x`	*local and global variables*
	`| (e1,...,en)`	*tuple construction*
	`| array([e1,...,en])`	*array construction*
	`| array.length(e)`	*array length*
	`| e[e0]`	*array access*
	`| e[e0:e1]`	*array slice*
	`| e(e1,...en)`	*function call*
	`| e1 binop e2`	*builtin binary operators*
	`| unaryop e`	*builtin unary operators*
Types t ::=	`int, str, bool`	*basic types*
	`| tuple_t(t1,...tn)`	*tuples*
	`| vlarray_t(t)`	*variable-length array*
	`| x`	*user-defined or builtin type*
	`| x(t1,...,tn,e1,...,em)`	*builtin type application*
Statements s ::=	`x: Type = t`	*type declaration*
	`| x: t`	*variable declaration*
	`| x = e`	*variable assignment*
	`| x binop= e`	*augmented variable assignment*
	`| (x1,..,xn) = e`	*tuple matching*
	`| x[i] = e`	*array update*
	`| x[i] binop= e`	*augmented array update*
	`| x[i:j] = e`	*array slice update*
	`| if e:`	*if-elif-else conditional*
	`    s1...sn`	
	`  elif e:`	
	`    s1'...sn'`	
	`  else`	
	`    s1''...sn''`	
	`| for i in range(e):`	*for loop*
	`    s1...sn`	
	`| break`	*break from loop*
	`| def x(x1:t1,...,xn:tn) → t:`	*function declaration*
	`    s1 ... sn`	
	`| return e`	*return from function*
	`| from x import x1, x2,..., xn`	*module import*
Specs σ ::=	`s1...sn`	*sequence of statements*

Values. Specifications in hacspec define computations over values. The simplest values are arbitrary-size integers, booleans, and strings. Integer constants can be written in decimal, binary, octal, or binary; booleans are True or False; string constants begin and end with quotes (" or '). The builtin library defines additional constants. The two main data structures used in hacspec are tuples and arrays. Tuple constants are written (v1,...,vn), parentheses are optional, and array constants are written array([v1,...,vn]).

Expressions. Expressions represent purely functional computations that yield values without any side-effects. Expressions include values as well as tuples and arrays constructed with a sequence of expressions (evaluated left to right). Variables (x) may be local or global; global variables may be qualified by a module name (e.g. array.empty). Global variables may only be assigned once when they are initialized; thereafter they are read-only.

Arrays can be accessed in two ways: a[i] reads the i'th element of an array a; a[i:j] copies a slice of the array a from index i (inclusive) to index j (exclusive) into a fresh array and returns the result.

A function call, written f(e1,...,en), calls the function f that may be user-defined or from the builtin library. A special case of builtin functions are unary and binary infix operators (e.g. arithmetic operators like +, bitwise operators like <<, and comparison operators like ==).

Functions in hacspec are call-by-value, the arguments to the function are first evaluated, then the resulting values are *copied* into the arguments of the function, and then the function is called with these arguments. The function itself may allocate and modify local state, as we will see below, but all this state is deallocated when the function returns; only the output of the function remains. Consequently, function calls are *observationally pure*, i.e. they have no side effects and hence can be treated as pure functions that return a fresh result.

Notably, all hacspec expressions produce a fresh value: even when an expression evaluates to an array, the resulting value is a fresh array value, not a pointer into or an alias to some other array.

Types. The basic types in hacspec are integers (int), booleans (bool), and strings (str). Types can be parameterized, that is, they are defined as functions over both types and values; such parametric types can be instantiated by applying them to specific types and expressions x(t1,...,tn,e1,...,em). Two special cases of such parametric types are tuples and arrays. Each n-tuple has a type tuple_t(t1,...,tn), where the first component has type t1, the second has type t2, and so on. Arrays have type vlarray_t(t), where the contents of the array have type t. These are called variable-length arrays since their length is only known at run-time.

As we will see, the builtin library defines more types and type constructors for writing refinement types, which can be used to annotate and check specs for more advanced logical properties.

Statements. A hacspec specification is a sequence of statements, each of which defines a global constant, a type, or a function. Such statement sequences are written one on each line (hence with a newline as a separator), with the indentation of each line indicating the block that the statement belongs to. This syntactic convention, taken from python, simplifies and unclutters the specification by removing the need for block and statement separators.

All variables must be declared before use; thus the statement x:t declares a new variable x that has type t, whereas the statement x:t = e declares and initializes x that has type t to the value obtained by evaluating e. New type abbreviations are defined by writing x:Type = t; by convention all user-defined type names are suffixed by _t (e.g. vlarray_t).

Local variables can be modified with an assignment x = e or an augmented assignment, e.g. x += e, which applies a binary operator before assignment. Note, however, that global variables in a specification are constant; they are assigned a value at initialization time and never change thereafter. Within a function body, we can read global variables and the function arguments, but we may only modify declared function-local variables.

Arrays held in local variables can be modified by the statement x[i] = e, which constructs a new array value by setting the i'th value in the current value of the array x to the result of evaluating e and writes this new array value into x. We may also modify a slice of an array by writing x[i:j] = e, which copies the array value resulting from evaluating e into the indicated slice of array x.

Conditional expressions and for-loops are standard, except that we allow the use of elif to combine an else with a subsequent if, and we allow the use of break to escape from a loop early. Each branch of a conditional, and each loop body is itself a sequence of statements, one on each line and indented appropriately.

Functions are defined with types annotating their arguments and results: def f(x1:t1,...,xn:tn) → t declares a new function called f with n arguments x1,...,xn with types t1,...,tn, and returns a result of type t. The body of the function is a sequence of statements; notably, the statement return e returns from the function with the evaluation of e as the result.

Each specification has a name (the name of the file in which it resides) and a sequence of statements that defines a cryptographic algorithm. Specifications can refer to other specifications by importing selected variables from the other specification into its own namespace by writing e.g. from otherspec import function1.

3.2   Example: Poly1305

Using the syntax defined above we can now write specifications like the Poly1305 MAC algorithm [1]. An excerpt of this hacspec, showing the core polynomial computation, appears in Spec 1.

The first 5 lines define the field of integers modulo the prime $p = 2^{130} - 5$. Line 1 declares and initializes the global variable p. The functions fadd (Lines 2–3) and fmul (Lines 4–5) define addition and multiplication in the field (modulo p). Both functions take two arguments of type int and return an int.

The function poly evaluates a polynomial over the prime field at a particular field element and returns the result. A polynomial of degree n is represented by an array of integers, where the 0'th element of the array contains the n'th

Spec 1. Poly1305 hacspec

```
1   p:int = 2 ** 130 - 5
2   def fadd(x:int, y:int) -> int:
3       return (x + y) % p
4   def fmul(x:int, y:int) -> int:
5       return (x * y) % p
6
7   def poly(text:vlarray_t(int), key:int) -> int:
8       result: int = 0
9       for i in range(array.length(text)):
10          result = fmul(key,fadd(result, text[i]))
11      return result
```

coefficient, the $(n-1)$'th element contains the first coefficient, and the coefficient with degree 0 is assumed to be 0.

In the Poly1305 MAC algorithm, this array of coefficients is an encoding of the plaintext (text), and the value at which it is being evaluated is the MAC key (key). The body of the poly function first declares the local variable result of type int and initializes it to 0. It then iterates over the length of text with a for-loop. The loop body (Line 10) updates the value of result by multiplying (fmul) the key with the sum (fadd) of the previous result and the i-th coefficient in text. Thus, for a text of size n, this function computes the field element:

$$\text{key}^n \cdot \text{text}[0] + \text{key}^{n-1} \cdot \text{text}[1] + \ldots + \text{key} \cdot \text{text}[n-1] \text{ modulo p}.$$

3.3 The Builtin Library

hacspec comes with a builtin library that implements many common functionalities needed by cryptographic algorithms. The full list of provided functions and types can be found in the hacspec documentation.[5] While it is possible to write specs entirely with the syntax defined in Table 1, the builtin library makes writing precise specs easier and simplifies compilation and formal proofs.

The set of cryptographic primitives (specs) implemented while working on hacspec (see Sect. 6 for details on the currently implemented primitives) can be used as well but are not provided as a library right now.

Modular Arithmetic. As we saw in Spec 1, cryptographic algorithms often rely on arithmetic modulo some (large, not necessarily prime) integer. The builtin library defines a type called natmod_t(n), representing natural numbers modulo n (the set $\{0, \ldots, n-1\}$). It also defines modular arithmetic operations +, -, *, ** (addition, subtraction, multiplication, exponentiation) on values of this type.

Hence, using the natmod_t type, we can rewrite the Poly1305 specification as shown in Spec 2. We first define a type felem_t for the field elements (naturals

---

[5] https://hacs-workshop.github.io/hacspec/docs/.

modulo p). We can then directly use * and + for field operations, without needing to define fadd and fmul. Furthermore, the spec is now more precise: it requires that the arguments of poly are in the prime field and guarantees that the result of polynomial evaluation is a field element, and violations of this post-condition can and should be checked in the spec and its implementations.

Spec 2. Poly1305 hacspec using the builtin library

```
1  p = nat((2 ** 130) - 5)
2  felem_t = natmod_t(p)
3  def poly(text:vlarray_t(felem_t), key:felem_t) -> felem_t:
4      result = natmod(0,p)
5      for i in range(array.length(text)):
6          result = key * (result + text[i])
7      return result
```

Machine Integers. A special case of natmod_t(n) are integers of a certain bit-length, i.e. when n is of the form 2^l. In particular, many cryptographic algorithms are defined over machine integers like unsigned 32-bit integers, which correspond to natmod_t(2 ** 32). The builtin library defines types for commonly used machine integers like uint8_t, uint16_t, uint32_t, uint64_t, and uint128_t as well as an arbitrary-length unsigned integer type uintn_t(n). These integers provide the usual arithmetic operators like natmod_t but further provide bitwise operators ^, |, &, <<, >> (xor, or, and, left-shift, right-shift) and the unary operator ~ (bitwise negation). In addition, the library defines functions for rotating machine integers, and converting between integers of different sizes.

Byte-Arrays, Vectors, and Matrices. The library defines abbreviations for several commonly-used variants of arrays. For example, the type array_t(t,l) represents arrays of type t and length l, a special case of the vlarray_t(t) type. The type vlbytes_t represents variable-length byte-arrays (vlarray_t(uint8_t)), which are commonly used as inputs and outputs of cryptographic algorithms. The corresponding fixed-length byte-array type is bytes_t(l). These byte-array types provide library functions that convert byte-arrays to and from arrays of machine integer values; for example, the functions bytes.from_uint32s_le and bytes.to_uint32s_le inter-convert byte-arrays and uint32_t arrays, interpreted in little-endian order.

Another useful special case of arrays are vectors (vector_t(t,l)), which represent fixed-length arrays of numeric types. The content of a vector is either an integer (int), or natmod_t(n), or uintn_t(l), or another vector type. The advantage of using vectors is that they offer pointwise arithmetic operators (+, -, *, **), as well as standard functions like dot-products. We can build multi-dimensional vectors as vectors of vectors, but the builtin library provides a special type matrix_t(t,rows,cols) for two-dimensional vectors, for which it defines matrix-vector and matrix-matrix multiplication functions.

Type Abbreviations, Refinements, and Contracts. For the most part, specification authors can use just the types in the standard library to write their specs and use local type abbreviations when needed, for clarity, like the `felem_t` type in Spec 2. However, in many cases we may want to define a more specific type that represents a subset or a *refinement* of an existing type. The builtin library already provides commonly used refinements, like `nat_t` (integers ≥ 0), `pos_t` (integers > 0) and `range_t(s,e)` (integers from `s` to $e - 1$). In addition, it provides a construct for users to define their own refinement types.

The type `refine_t(t,f)` takes a type `t` and a predicate `f` from type `t` to `bool`, and returns a new type that represents values of type `t` that satisfy `f`. Elements of this new type can be implicitly converted to elements of type `t` but not vice-versa. Refinement types can be used to encode arbitrary logical invariants and are extensively used in verification frameworks like $F^\star$ and Coq. When a refinement type is used on a function argument, it becomes a pre-condition for calling the function; when it is used in the result type, it becomes a post-condition guaranteed by the function. Since refinement predicates can be arbitrarily complex, checking refinement types is not always easy. We show how these types can be checked at run-time, using the python plugin Typeguard, or can be verified statically with powerful verification tools like $F^\star$.

Not all function specifications can be written using refinements. For example, refinements cannot specify how the result of a function relates to its arguments. We are experimenting with a general contract mechanism for hacspec, implemented as annotations, that can fill this gap.

4   Checking and Executing **hacspec**

We expect the hacspec language to be used at two levels. Standards authors and cryptographic researchers may write a hacspec for a new cryptographic algorithm and include it as pseudocode in a standard or in a research paper. They would like to easily check their spec for syntax and basic type errors and test it for correctness errors. For such users we provide tools written in python so that they do not need to install or learn any new tool to be able to achieve their goals.

More advanced users will want to check their hacspec for deeper properties, ranging from logical invariants to cryptographic security. They may also want to verify that an implementation of the algorithm, written in C or assembly, is correct with respect to the hacspec. For these users, we provide a syntax and static type checker, and compilers to various verification frameworks. To run these tools, one must install OCaml as well as the target verification tool. Note that verifying existing implementations requires a compilation target such as cryptol or VST that do not exist yet.

In this section, we describe our tool-set for checking and running hacspec and highlight the main challenges in implementing these tools.

4.1   Syntax and Static Type Checking

Since hacspec is a subset of python, specification authors used to python may be tempted to use python features that are not supported by our domain-specific language. To check that a hacspec is valid we have built a python tool called *hacspec-check* that is part of the hacspec python package. This checker enforces the syntax in Table 1; it finds and points out invalid expressions, types, and statements, and forbids the use of external values and functions that are not included in the builtin library.

The syntax checker only ensures that the type annotations in a hacspec have the right syntax, it does not check that the code is type-correct. We wrote an additional tool in OCaml that statically enforces the hacspec type system. It requires that all variables be declared before use, and that they are used in accordance with their declared type. This tool does not perform any inference, but still, it must account for basic types (like int), builtin types (like uint32_t), and parameterized types (like array_t(t,l)). The checker also knows and enforces the types for all the builtin operators and functions in the builtin library. In particular, the type-checker prevents aliasing of mutable data structures like arrays, by ensuring that two array variables never point to the same array value — when assigning an array variable, the assigned value must be a fresh copy of an array.

4.2   Executing hacspec with Run-Time Checks

Because hacspec uses python syntax it can be directly executed using the python runtime. We provide a python implementation, called speclib.py, for the builtin library. To make hacspec easy to use for spec authors the library and the hacspec-check command line tool are bundled in the hacspec python package.[6] After installing this package, the spec author can include the standard library: from hacspec.speclib import * and write and run specifications.

Our python library uses python classes to implement the various types and type constructors: natmod_t, uintn_t, array_t, etc. Each class defines the relevant unary and binary operators (e.g. +) for a type by overloading the corresponding python "magic" methods (e.g. __add__) in that class. We define each of these operator methods to first check that the left and right expressions are both of the expected type, before calculating the result and casting it to the expected return type. Python also allows us to define custom getters and setters for arrays using the standard syntax (e.g. a[1] += b[1]), and we overload these methods to check that the array and the assigned values have a consistent type, and that all indexes are within bounds, before executing the expected array access operation. Vectors and matrices are sub-classes of arrays but are provided with point-wise binary operators that are subject to further checks.

Although python allows a rich type annotation syntax (allowing arbitrary expressions to compute types), it does not itself check these types. However, there are various tools and plugins that can check type annotations statically or at runtime. For example, mypy[7] can perform basic static type checking, but unfortunately it does not not support everything needed by hacspec, e.g., generic types, custom types, or type aliases. Instead, we use run-time type checking with

---

[6] https://pypi.org/project/hacspec/.

[7] http://www.mypy-lang.org/.

typeguard[8], which allows spec authors to quickly get feedback on the correctness of their used types without having to use an additional execution environment.

Typeguard checks functions that are annotated with the @typechecked decorator for conformance to their declared types. We annotate all the functions in our builtin library and hence require that they be used correctly. The same is required from all user-written hacspec functions. In addition to the checks built into Typeguard, our library functions themselves perform a variety of builtin semantic checks that can detect common coding errors in hacspec specifications. For example; Every array access is bound-checked to make sure that it is not over- or under-running the array; When modifying array elements type checks ensure that only compatible values are added; Arithmetic operations ensure that only operands of appropriate bit-lengths and moduli are used, e.g., rotate and shift functions ensure that the shift values are positive and not greater than the integers bit-length; Using refinement types ensures that the type is correct and within the refined value range.

For each specification we encourage authors to provide an extensive test-suite as a list of positive and negative test vectors. These should include all the test-vectors provided in the standard but also other test-suites, such as those provided by NIST[9] or open-source projects like Wycheproof[10]. Running tests on the code with run-time type-checking can make the execution very slow but provides higher assurance in the spec. Our specs can also be tested in an optimized mode that disables these run-time type-checks.

5   Verifying **hacspec**

For advanced users, we describe two verification tools we are currently building for hacspec: one for verifying implementations using F* and the other for building cryptographic proofs in EASYCRYPT. Both tools are based on the typed AST, generated by the hacspec static type-checker.

5.1   F* Compiler

F* is a general-purpose programming language targeted at building verified software [21]. In particular, it has been used to build a verified cryptographic library called HACL* [23]. For each cryptographic algorithm HACL* includes an optimized stateful implementation written in a subset of F* called Low*. Code written in this subset can be compiled to C code and hence used within cryptographic protocol implementations, such as TLS libraries.

---

[8] https://github.com/agronholm/typeguard/.

[9] https://csrc.nist.gov/Projects/Cryptographic-Algorithm-Validation-Program.

[10] https://github.com/google/wycheproof.

The Low* implementation of each algorithm is verified for functional correctness against a formal specification written in F*. Unlike the implementation, the specification is pure and total; i.e. it cannot have any side-effects and must always terminate. In addition to correctness, Low* code is also proved to be memory safe and have secret independent execution time, i.e. it does not branch on secret values or access memory at secret addresses.

HACL* includes hand-written specifications for all the algorithms in the library. Our goal is to replace these specifications with those written in hacspec and to make it easier for new HACL* specifications to be compiled from hacspec. To this end we develop a compiler from hacspec to F* specifications.

First, we implement the hacspec builtin library as an F* module (SpecLib.fst), so that the compiled F* specifications can also have access to all the types and functions used in the source specification. This library module defines hacspec types like int, natmod_t, vlarray_t etc. in terms of the corresponding types in the F* standard library. In particular, hacspec arrays (vlarray_t(t)) are implemented as immutable sequences (seq t) in F*. We implement all unary and binary operators using function overloading in F*.

Then, we implement a translation from hacspec specifications to F* modules that syntactically transforms each value, expression, and statement to the corresponding syntax in F*. For example, the Poly1305 specification in Spec 2 translates to the F* specification in Spec 3. The main syntactic change in the F* version is that all statements that modify local variables get translated to pure expressions (in a state-passing style) that redefine the local variables (using scoped let-expressions) instead of modifying them. For loops are translated to an application of the higher-order repeati combinator, which applies a function a given number of times to the input.

Spec 3. Poly1305 hacspec using the builtin library

```
1  let p : nat = (2 ** 130) - 5
2  type felem_t = natmod_t(p)
3  let poly (text:vlybtes_t) (key:felem_t) : felem_t =
4      let result = natmod(0, p) in
5      repeati (length text)
6              (fun i result -> key * (result + text.[i]))
7              result
```

In addition to the syntactic translation of the code, the F* compiler translates hacspec refinement types to refinement types in F*, so that the F* typechecker can verify all of them statically using an SMT solver.

In a typical workflow the standard author writes a hacspec for a cryptographic algorithm, translates it to F*, and typechecks the result with F* to find progamming errors. The crypto developer then writes an optimized implementation of the algorithm in Low* and verifies that it is memory-safe, secret independent, and that it conforms to the specification derived from the hacspec. For example, a Low* implementation of Poly1305 would first need to implement the modular arithmetic in natmod_t with prime-specific optimized bignum arithmetic. The developer would then typically write a stateful version of poly that modified the result in-place. Proving that this implementation matches the specification is a challenging task, but one made easier by libraries of verified code in HACL*.

5.2   EasyCrypt Compiler

EASYCRYPT is a proof assistant for verifying the security of cryptographic constructions in the computational model. EASYCRYPT adopts the code-based approach [5], in which security goals and hardness assumptions are modeled as probabilistic programs (called experiments or games) with unspecified adversarial code. EASYCRYPT uses formal tools from program verification and programming language theory to rigorously justify cryptographic reasoning.

EASYCRYPT is composed of several ingredients: (i) a simply-typed, higher-order, pure functional language that forms the logical basis of the framework; (ii) a probabilistic While language that allows the algorithmic description of the schemes under scrutiny; and (iii) programming language logic. These logic include a probabilistic, relational Hoare logic, relating pairs of procedures; a probabilistic Hoare logic allowing one to carry out proofs about the probability of some event during the execution of a procedures; and an ordinary (possibilistic) Hoare logic.

The compiler from hacspec to EASYCRYPT is composed of two phases. First, the types and procedures are translated from the hacspec syntax to the relevant EASYCRYPT constructions. Since EASYCRYPT enjoys a simply-typed language discipline, nearly all refinements have to be pruned during this phase. However, we have some special support for types that depend on fixed values: in that case, we define a generic theory that encloses the dependent type and use the EASYCRYPT theory cloning for generating instances of that type for some fixed values. This translation relies on a EASYCRYPT library that mirrors speclib. When the translator detects that a procedure is pure, deterministic and terminates (w.r.t. the EASYCRYPT termination checker), this one is translated directly as a logical operator. In all other cases, hacspec procedures are translated to While-based EASYCRYPT ones. Some constructions ares not supported by the current compiler. For example, EASYCRYPT does not allow the definition of recursive procedures and inner procedures and we currently simply reject them. We plan to modify the compiler so that it encodes these constructs as valid EASYCRYPT programs.

In a second phase, top-level refinements (i.e. refinements that apply to the arguments or result types of a procedure) are translated into EASYCRYPT statements using the probabilistic Hoare logic. We give, in Spec 4, the Poly1305 specification in Spec 2 translated to EASYCRYPT.

Spec 4. Poly1305 hacspec using the builtin library

```
1   op p : int = 2 ^ 130 - 5.
2
3   clone import NatMod as FElem_p with op size <- p.
4
5   module Spec = {
6     proc poly(text : byte array, key : felem_t) : felem_t = {
7       var result = FElem.zero, i;
8       i = 0; while (i < Array.length text) {
9         result = key * (result + FElem.mk (Byte.to_int (text.[i])));
10        i = i + 1;
11      }
12      return result;
13    }
14  }.
```

From that point, it is then possible to use EASYCRYPT to prove these statements, hence verifying the soundness of the hacspec refinements directly in EASYCRYPT. However, we expect developers to follow a two-tier workflow. First, developers can use the F* compiler of Sect. 5.1 and derive the correctness of the refinements using the F* type-checker. Because both F* and EASYCRYPT work on the same specification by construction (they are obtained from the compilation of the same hacspec procedure), this step enforces that the refinements that are translated as Hoare statement into EasyCrypt are sound. In a second step, developers could take advantage of EASYCRYPT to prove the security of the obtained primitives. Indeed, EASYCRYPT comes with all the necessary materials (relational probabilistic logic, libraries of standard cryptographic games, experiments & arguments) for the study of cryptographic primitives in the computational model, using the now standard game-hopping technique. For example, in addition to Poly1305, one could also write in hacspec the Chacha20 encryption scheme, obtain their EASYCRYPT counter-part, and prove in the same system that they provide a secure AEAD (Authenticated Encryption with Associated Data) scheme. This, along with the verified Low* implementation of Chacha20-Poly1350, would lead to an efficient and formally proven secure AEAD scheme.

Note that by the different nature of the two involved languages (hacspec & EASYCRYPT), the obtained EASYCRYPT specification might not be in total adequacy with EASYCRYPT idioms. However, using EASYCRYPT relational logic, one can start by first proving that the hacspec specifications simulate a handwritten, more natural, EASYCRYPT one. Although this requires more work to link the EASYCRYPT proofs to the hacspec specifications, it gives a formal link between the two.

6   Evaluation, Conclusion, and Future Work

To evaluate hacspec we implemented several standardized cryptographic algorithms using only the builtin library. Table 2 summarizes the specifications we currently have written and tested in hacspec as well as their F* version if available. Even more complex algorithms such as Kyber or the SHA2 and SHA3 function families (with all their variants including SHAKE), as well as combined algorithms like the AES-GCM and ChaCha20-Poly1305 AEAD can be written in less than 300 lines of hacspec. (The combined AEAD algorithms in Table 2 list the lines of code for the combination of cipher and MAC as well as the combined lines of code of cipher and MAC.) Modern algorithms that are designed to have rather straight-forward implementations like Poly1305 or Curve25519/Curve448 can be implemented in 50 to 70 lines of code. This shows that hacspec allows concise specifications of common cryptographic algorithms.

The last column in Table 2 lists the lines of F* code that is produced when compiling the hacspec code. Not all specs can be compiled to F* at this point because some hacspec constructs are not fully supported by the compiler yet. The hash algorithms SHA2, SHA3, and Blake2 for example use inner functions for concise handling of multiple digest lengths, which can not be properly compiled to F* at the moment.

Table 2. Specifications written in hacspec

hacspec	Category	Standard	LoC	F* LoC
speclib	Library	-	849	213
AES	Symmetric Cipher	NIST FIPS 197	190	210
GCM	MAC	NIST SP 800-38D	61	46
AES-GCM 128	AEAD	NIST SP 800-38D	47 + 251	-
Chacha20	Symmetric Cipher	IETF RFC 7539	87	89
Poly1305	MAC	IETF RFC 7539	43	37
Chacha20-Poly1305	AEAD	IETF RFC 7539	45 + 130	-
SHA-2	Hash	NIST FIPS 180-2	192	-
SHA-3	Hash	NIST FIPS 202	193	-
Blake2	Hash	IETF RFC 7693	162	-
Curve25519	ECDH	IETF RFC 7748	87	100
Curve448	ECDH	IETF RFC 7748	69	63
P256	ECDH/Signature	NIST SP 800-56A	102	-
Ed25519	Signature	IETF RFC 8032	182	-
RSA-PSS	Signature	IETF RFC 8017	151	-
Kyber	Post-Quantum KEM	NIST PQ Challenge	285	-
Frodo	Post-Quantum KEM	NIST PQ Challenge	192	-
WOTS+	One-time Signature	IETF RFC 8391	134	-

Conclusion. In this paper we described the goals and architecture of hacspec, a new specification language for cryptographic algorithms. We defined hacspec as a domain-specific language with minimal syntax that can be interpreted by the python runtime. We showed that together with a builtin library hacspec allows to write succinct specifications of cryptographic algorithms. To allow spec authors to use hacspec without much effort we provide an implementation of the builtin library in python and a tool to check the spec syntax. To verify specs written in hacspec we showed how to compile specs to F* and EASYCRYPT. This enables formal proofs of correctness of code with respect to the spec, proves of protection against side channels and memory issues, as well as cryptographic security proves.

Future Work. The compiler and builtin library are still in early stages and are likely to evolve over time. Additional library features such as function contracts are in development. The goal of this work is to describe the current state of hacspec and invite spec authors to use it and give feedback to guide future development of the hacspec language, the builtin library, and tooling. We would like to see more compilers to other formal languages such as cryptol and Coq to allow formal proofs of specifications using hacspec in those frameworks.

Acknowledgments. We would like to thank all participants of the HACS workshop that made this work possible. hacspec is an ongoing project with a number contributors in addition to the the the authors.

Online Materials
hacspec source code: https://github.com/hacs-workshop/hacspec/
hacspec builtin library documentation: https://hacs-workshop.github.io/hacspec/docs/
hacspec mailing list: https://moderncrypto.org/mailman/listinfo/hacspec.

References

1. ChaCha20 and Poly1305 for IETF Protocols. IETF RFC 7539 (2015)
2. Elliptic Curves for Security. IETF RFC 7748 (2016)
3. Almeida, J., et al.: Jasmin: high-assurance and high-speed cryptography. In: Proceedings of the 2017 ACM SIGSAC Conference on Computer and Communications Security, CCS. pp. 1807–1823. (2017, to appear). https://acmccs.github.io/papers/p1807-almeidaA.pdf
4. Appel, A.W.: Verified software toolchain. In: Goodloe, A.E., Person, S. (eds.) NFM 2012. LNCS, vol. 7226, pp. 2–2. Springer, Heidelberg (2012). https://doi.org/10.1007/978-3-642-28891-3_2
5. Barthe, G., Dupressoir, F., Grégoire, B., Kunz, C., Schmidt, B., Strub, P.-Y.: EasyCrypt: a tutorial. In: Aldini, A., Lopez, J., Martinelli, F. (eds.) FOSAD 2012-2013. LNCS, vol. 8604, pp. 146–166. Springer, Cham (2014). https://doi.org/10.1007/978-3-319-10082-1_6
6. Bernstein, D.J.: Cache-timing attacks on AES. Technical report (2005)
7. Blanchet, B.: A computationally sound mechanized prover for security protocols. IEEE Trans. Dependable Secure Comput. **5**, 193–207 (2007)
8. Böck, H., Zauner, A., Devlin, S., Somorovsky, J., Jovanovic, P.: Nonce-disrespecting adversaries: practical forgery attacks on GCM in TLS. In: 10th USENIX Workshop on Offensive Technologies (WOOT 2016). USENIX Association, Austin (2016). https://www.usenix.org/conference/woot16/workshop-program/presentation/bock

9. Bond, B., et al.: Vale: verifying high-performance cryptographic assembly code. In: Proceedings of the USENIX Security Symposium, August 2017
10. US Department of Commerce, National Institute of Standards and Technology (NIST): Federal Information Processing Standards Publication 180-4: Secure Hash Standard (SHS) (2012)
11. Courtois, N.T., Emirdag, P., Valsorda, F.: Private key recovery combination attacks: on extreme fragility of popular bitcoin key management, wallet and cold storage solutions in presence of poor RNG events. Cryptology ePrint Archive, Report 2014/848 (2014). https://eprint.iacr.org/2014/848
12. Dworkin, M.: Recommendation for Block Cipher Modes of Operation: Galois/-Counter Mode (GCM) and GMAC. NIST Special Publication 800-38D (2007)
13. Dworkin, M.J., Barker, E.B., Nechvatal, J.R., Foti, J., Bassham, L.E., Roback, E., Dray Jr., J.F.: Advanced Encryption Standard (AES). NIST FIPS-197 (2001)
14. Erbsen, A., Philipoom, J., Gross, J., Sloan, R., Chlipala, A.: Simple high-level code for cryptographic arithmetic - with proofs, without compromises. In: Proceedings of the IEEE Symposium on Security and Privacy 2019, S&P 2019, May 2019. http://adam.chlipala.net/papers/FiatCryptoSP19/
15. Institute, A.N.S.: Public Key Cryptography for the Financial Services Industry: The Elliptic Curve Digital Signature Algorithm. ANSI X9.62-1998 (199)
16. Josefsson, S., Liusvaara, I.: Edwards-Curve Digital Signature Algorithm (EdDSA). RFC 8032 (Informational), January 2017. 10.17487/RFC8032. https://doi.org/10.17487/RFC8032. https://www.rfc-editor.org/rfc/rfc8032.txt
17. Käsper, E., Schwabe, P.: Faster and timing-attack resistant AES-GCM. In: Clavier, C., Gaj, K. (eds.) CHES 2009. LNCS, vol. 5747, pp. 1–17. Springer, Heidelberg (2009). https://doi.org/10.1007/978-3-642-04138-9_1
18. Langley, A., Hamburg, M., Turner, S.: Elliptic Curves for Security. RFC 7748 (Informational), January 2016. https://doi.org/10.17487/RFC7748. https://www.rfc-editor.org/rfc/rfc7748.txt
19. Mouha, N., Raunak, M.S., Kuhn, D.R., Kacker, R.: Finding bugs in cryptographic hash function implementations. Cryptology ePrint Archive, Report 2017/891 (2017). https://eprint.iacr.org/2017/891
20. Petcher, A., Morrisett, G.: The foundational cryptography framework. In: Focardi, R., Myers, A. (eds.) POST 2015. LNCS, vol. 9036, pp. 53–72. Springer, Heidelberg (2015). https://doi.org/10.1007/978-3-662-46666-7_4
21. Swamy, N., et al.: Dependent types and multi-monadic effects in F*. In: Proceedings of the 43rd Annual ACM SIGPLAN-SIGACT Symposium on Principles of Programming Languages, POPL 2016, St. Petersburg, FL, USA, 20–22 January 2016, pp. 256–270 (2016). https://doi.org/10.1145/2837614.2837655
22. Tomb, A.: Automated verification of real-world cryptographic implementations. IEEE Secur. Priv. **14**(6), 26–33 (2016)
23. Zinzindohoué, J.K., Bhargavan, K., Protzenko, J., Beurdouche, B.: HACL*: a verified modern cryptographic library. In: Proceedings of the 2017 ACM SIGSAC Conference on Computer and Communications Security, CCS 2017, Dallas, TX, USA, 30 October–03 November 2017, pp. 1789–1806 (2017)

Formal Verification of Ephemeral Diffie-Hellman Over COSE (EDHOC)

Alessandro Bruni[✉], Thorvald Sahl Jørgensen, Theis Grønbech Petersen, and Carsten Schürmann

IT University of Copenhagen, Copenhagen, Denmark
`brun@itu.dk`

Abstract. Ephemeral Diffie-Hellman over COSE (EDHOC) [1] is an authentication protocol that aims to replace TLS for resource constrained Internet of Things (IoT) devices using a selection of lightweight ciphers and formats. It is inspired by the newest Internet Draft of TLS 1.3 [2] and includes reduced round-trip modes. Unlike TLS 1.3, EDHOC is designed from scratch, and does not have to support legacy versions of the protocol. As the protocol is neither well-known nor has been used in practice it has not been scrutinized to the extent it should be.

The objective of this paper is to verify security properties of the protocol, including integrity, secrecy, and perfect forward secrecy properties. We use ProVerif [3] to analyze these properties formally. We describe violations of specific security properties for the reduced round-trip modes. The flaws were reported to the authors of the EDHOC protocol.

1 Introduction

Ephemeral Diffie-Hellman over COSE (EDHOC [1]) is a lightweight authenticated key exchange protocol proposed by Selander et al., part of a family of protocols for Internet of Things (IoT) devices, and intended to be used in conjunction with OSCORE [4]. COSE refers to a proposed IETF Encryption standard [12]. The rationale for designing EDHOC is to provide a lightweight alternative to the TLS handshake standard that can fit in a micro-controller. For this purpose the backwards compatibility features of TLS are an unnecessary obstacle to an efficient implementation. Furthermore, a clean-slate design can help improve performance and also security, by supporting by default Perfect Forward Secrecy (PFS) and following the best practices of the SIGn-and-MAC (SIGMA) family of protocols [5], offering two modes of operation: asymmetric using public identities, and symmetric using both public identities and pre-shared keys.

This work was funded in part through the Danish Council for Strategic Research, Programme Comission on Strategic Growth Technologies under grant 10-092309. This publication was also made possible by NPRP grant NPRP 7-988-1-178 from the Qatar National Research Fund (a member of Qatar Foundation). The statements made herein are solely the responsibility of the authors.

© Springer Nature Switzerland AG 2018
C. Cremers and A. Lehmann (Eds.): SSR 2018, LNCS 11322, pp. 21–36, 2018.
https://doi.org/10.1007/978-3-030-04762-7_2

With this work we provide a formal analysis of the EDHOC protocol, which is currently an Internet Draft on track for standardisation. We analyze the draft version 08 of the specification [1] and uncover hidden assumptions in the use of encrypted payloads in the protocol. In particular, it is possible for an attacker to learn the content of encrypted application data during key exchange in the asymmetric version of the protocol, and to violate perfect forward secrecy of application data for protocol executions in both modes (symmetric and the asymmetric) when the attacker actively interferes with the session establishment. These findings, albeit similar to other instances of SIGMA key establishment protocols [6], are important to prevent potential misuse of the protocol features, and have been incorporated into later revisions of the draft.

Compared with other authentication protocols, for example TLS 1.3 [2], EDHOC is conceptually much simpler, because it implements only the handshake part without certificate handling and it has to run reliably on low energy devices. EDHOC optimizes the number of messages to be exchanged, the length of the message, and the number of encryption, decryption and signing operations.

However, the low complexity of EDHOC should not distract from the security objectives such a protocol must satsify. EDHOC is an authentication protocol that is designed to be deployed on billions of IoT devices, and any security vulnerability in the design of the protocol would be difficult to fix and give adversaries a powerful platform to launch distributed attacks. Thus, we conduct a rigorous and mechanized security analysis of EDHOC, develop a formal model of the respective symmetric and asymmetric modes of EDHOC, and verify them in the protocol verifier ProVerif [3]. Our model allows the former to feed into the latter, i.e. keys established during the asymmetric mode can be used as long-term keys in the symmetric mode. In our formalization, we are able to verify that the protocol preserves *authentication, identity protection, secrecy and integrity of encrypted application data, and perfect forward secrecy of established sessions.*

Related Work. The formal analysis of security standards is an active area of research. Bhargavan et al. [6] present an analysis of the TLS 1.3 draft 18, deriving from a reference implementation both ProVerif and CryptoVerif [7] models; a comprehensive analysis of TLS 1.3 draft 21 has been presented by Cremers et al. [8] using the Tamarin prover [9]. These works have served as an inspiration when analyzing the EDHOC protocol. Also, Meadows presented a formal analysis of the Internet Key Exchange protocol [10] using the NRL protocol verifier, to which EDHOC is related.

Structure of this Paper. The paper proceeds as follows: Sect. 2 presents the EDHOC protocol as of draft version 08; Sect. 3 presents our modeling of the EDHOC protocol in ProVerif and our findings are presented in Sect. 4. Finally, we conclude in Sect. 5.

2   The Protocol

EDHOC is an authenticated key exchange protocol of the SIGMA-I family. It is a three-message exchange between an *initiator (U)* and a *responder (V)* that establishes a Diffie-Hellman shared secret between the two parties. Being a SIGMA-I protocol, each party can check the other identity without revealing it to a passive attacker, and the initiator identity is also protected from an active attacker.

Krawczyk presented the rationale behind the choices of SIGMA in [5], and Canetti and Krawczyk analysed it formally in [11]; we refer the interested reader to those papers for an extended presentation of the general scheme.

Before we dive into presenting the details of EDHOC, we first show the SIGMA-I protocol using authenticated encryption with associated data (AEAD), which we denote with $aead_k^a\{m\}$, using key k, optional authenticated data a and encrypting message m. We use exponentials instead of elliptic curve notation, as this make the paper easier to read. SIGMA-I follows this three-message exchange:

$$
\begin{align}
U &\to V : g^x & (\Sigma 1) \\
V &\to U : g^y, aead_{K_2}\{ID_V, sign_V(g^x, g^y)\} & (\Sigma 2) \\
U &\to V : aead_{K_3}\{ID_U, sign_U(g^y, g^x)\} & (\Sigma 3)
\end{align}
$$

The initiator first generates a fresh ephemeral public key for the session g^x and sends it to the responder in message ($\Sigma 1$); analogously, the responder generates their own ephemeral public key g^y. From the Diffie-Hellman shared secret $(g^x)^y$ they can then derive the two encryption keys K_2 and K_3.[1] K_2 is used to encrypt the public identity ID_V together with the signature by the responder V of the two ephemeral keys (g^x, g^y).

Upon receiving message ($\Sigma 2$), the initiator can also derive K_2 and K_3, check the identity of the responder, and from that produce message ($\Sigma 3$) containing the encrypted signature of (g^y, g^x) and their identity.

Intuitively, the two signatures of message ($\Sigma 2$) and ($\Sigma 3$) ensure that the two parties U and V agree on the ephemeral keys g^x and g^y if they are freshly generated at each run of the protocol. Alternatively, if the concrete protocol reuses ephemeral keys over sessions at the expense of forward secrecy to—like EDHOC for example—save computations, it must include two public nonces in the signature for the agreement to hold. Furthermore, authenticated encryption is critical to bind the knowledge of the Diffie-Hellman shared secret $(g^x)^y$ to the identities of V and U, as both K_2 and K_3 are derived from it; it also protects the responder's identity from a passive attacker, and the initiator's from an active one[2].

2.1   EDHOC with Asymmetric Keys

Figure 1 shows the asymmetric mode of operation for EDHOC. It implements the SIGMA-I protocol with a few added details. On top of the ephemeral

---

[1] See also Figures 1 and 2.

[2] The original SIGMA-I protocol uses a message authentication code (MAC), and then encrypts the signature and the authentication code with a symmetric encryption scheme for identity protection and binding: the use of authenticated encryption here serves this combined purpose.

Diffie-Hellman half-keys—which we now denote as E_U and E_V—EDHOC adds
the following parameters to each session:

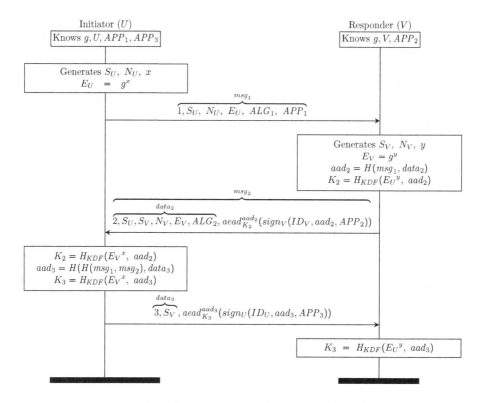

Fig. 1. Model of the asymmetric variant of EDHOC

- the constants 1, 2, and 3 in front of each message used for tagging;
- two session identifiers S_U, S_V that can be reused across sessions (e.g. to resume a previous session using a pre-shared key in the symmetric mode);
- two nonces N_U, N_V that must be fresh for each new session, relieving the requirement to generate fresh Diffie-Hellman half keys each time;
- the parameter ALG_1 that includes the names of all elliptic curves supported for the Diffie-Hellman key agreement, the supported Hashed Key Derivation Functions (HKDF) and authenticated encryption algorithms; similarly, the parameter ALG_2 includes the selected elliptic curve, HKDF and AEAD functions; we use H and $aead$ to denote these two functions, respectively;
- authentication data for each encrypted message (aad_2 and aad_3);
- optionally unencrypted application data APP_1 on the first message, and encrypted application data APP_2 and APP_3.

All messages in EDHOC are encoded using the CBOR Object Signing and
Encryption standard (COSE) [12], which in turn uses the Compact Binary

Object Representation [13], a binary alternative to the more common JSON web format. For the automatic security proof that we discuss in Sect. 3 we chose to abstract away from COSE and leave a mechanization to future work. The algorithm negotiation parameters aim to ensure compatibility with future versions by allowing flexibility in the choice of algorithms, however this being the first edition of the EDHOC standard, it mandates a fixed set of algorithms that are currently deemed secure: ECDH-SS, HKDF-256 [14], AES-CCM-64-64-128, and EdDSA from the COSE standard.

As the EDHOC key establishment protocol is intended to be combined with the OSCORE standard [4], it must derive a new OSCORE session key from the Diffie-Hellman session key, which by construction is ensured to be different from K_2 and K_3 by using the algorithm identifier "EDHOC OSCORE Master Secret" when applying the HKDF function.

Finally, the EDHOC asymmetric key exchange can produce a pre-shared key for further communication that is also ensured to be different from all other keys by using the algorithm identifier "EDHOC PSK Chaining" when applying the HKDF function.

2.2   EDHOC with Pre-shared Symmetric Keys

When two devices have a pre-shared key in EDHOC, either by establishing one through the PSK Chaining mode, or by being deployed with one, they can run the symmetric protocol, shown in Fig. 2.

In the symmetric variant, the public identities of U and V are not used. Instead, the protocol relies on the presence of a pre-shared key PSK between U and V, identified by the value of KID. Overall, the symmetric variant runs similarly to the asymmetric one, except for the following:

- the keys K_i, $i \in \{2, 3\}$ are derived from the Diffie-Hellman shared secret $(g^x)^y$, the authentication data aad_i, and the pre-shared key PSK;
- there is no signature scheme involved to certify the identities of U and V, since their identities are already fixed by the identification of PSK.

Analogously to the asymmetric variant, the symmetric mode of EDHOC should guarantee secrecy of the established session key, authentication, identity protection, perfect forward secrecy, integrity protection of the application data APP_1, and secrecy of the application data APP_2 and APP_3.

However, since the pre-shared keys identify the two parties that share them, and are in turn identified by the KID parameter, even a passive attacker can link multiple sessions pertaining to the same two principals by observing KID. The standard at its current revision suggests that party U and V anonymize KID to avoid this attack, though it does not specify how the two parties should realize such anonymization. We will see next that the guarantees for the two variants of the protocol are in fact slightly different, not just regarding the claims of identity protection, but also regarding the claims of perfect forward secrecy, and integrity and secrecy protection of application data.

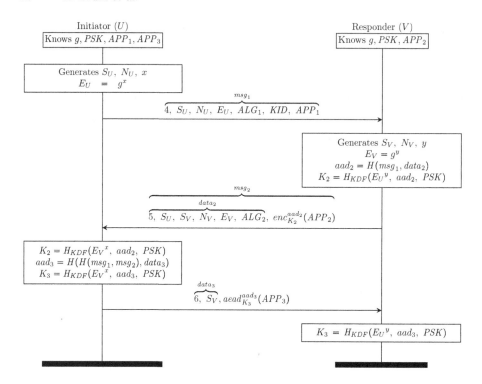

Fig. 2. Model of the symmetric variant of EDHOC

2.3 Properties

The current draft describes the security guarantees in Sect. 8 (Security Considerations) [1]. Here we summarize the security claims of the original text and integrate them with the results that we prove in our models, which we present Sect. 4.

Perfect Forward Secrecy. EDHOC, being part of the SIGMA-I family of protocols, should provide secrecy of the established session keys for past sessions, even when the long term keys are leaked. We check this for the session key derived for the OSCORE protocol. The same does not apply to K_2, as we discuss later.

Identity Protection. Thanks to the use of authenticated encryption, EDHOC protects the initiator's identity from an active adversary, and the responder's identity from a passive adversary. However in symmetric variant reusing the same key identifier *KID* allows a passive attacker to correlate multiple sessions.[3]

---

[3] As discussed in Sect. 2.2, draft 08 warns against the reuse of *KID*, but does not prescribe a standard mechanism to avoid such reuse.

Protection of Application Data. Sect. 8 of the EDHOC draft 08 makes the following claims regarding the protection of application data:

> Party U and V must make sure that unprotected data and metadata do not reveal any sensitive information. This also applies for encrypted data sent to an unauthenticated party. In particular, it applies to APP_1 and APP_2 in the asymmetric case, and APP_1 and KID in the symmetric case.

And further down in the section:

> Party U and V must make sure that unprotected data does not trigger any harmful actions. In particular, this applies to APP_1 in the asymmetric case, and APP_1 and KID in the symmetric case. Party V should be aware that replays of EDHOC msg_1 cannot be detected unless previous nonces are stored.

Our claim is that these sentences do not reflect the actual guarantees that EDHOC offers. In fact, disregarding the issue on KID that we already discussed, all application data is protected in some way, though *the guarantees vary* between APP_1, APP_2 and APP_3, *according to how far the protocol has progressed*, according to *the variant* of the protocol that is being considered—being it *symmetric or asymmetric*—and finally also depending on whether we are checking for *integrity, secrecy or perfect forward secrecy*.

Table 1 summarizes the guarantees of EDHOC. The columns in this table identify the following guarantees: *Secrecy* denotes whether a specific piece of application data is guaranteed to be a secret between the two parties at the time it is sent; *Secrecy (at completion)* denotes whether the secrecy claim can be made if the protocol reaches completion; *PFS* denotes whether the protocol maintains secrecy of application data even in case that the long term keys are revealed; *PFS (at completion)* denotes whether the secrecy of a piece of application data is guaranteed in the case that the long term keys are revealed if the protocol reaches completion; finally *Integrity* denotes whether the other party can check the authenticity of a particular piece of application data, similarly *Integrity (at completion)* refers to whether the integrity of said application data can be trusted if the protocol completes successfully. For each case, the table shows a check mark if the particular piece of application data has the desired property, a cross if the property doesn't hold, and a dash where not relevant (i.e. secrecy of unencrypted data).

Note that the integrity of APP_1 is guaranteed if the protocol completes successfully. Furthermore, the standard does not clearly specify what "unprotected data" actually means, referring to APP_2 as unprotected data for the asymmetric variant, even though it is encrypted, while not for the symmetric case. As we will see, the guarantees that we get from APP_2 are rather interesting: one can rely on APP_2 being secret only at protocol completion in both the symmetric and the asymmetric case; when an active attacker interferes with the protocol run (and thus the protocol fails to reach completion), the attacker can obtain APP_2 for the asymmetric variant, but not for the symmetric one. However if the long

Table 1. Secrecy, PFS and integrity of application data.

Variant	Data	Secrecy	(at completion)	PFS	(at completion)	Integrity	(at completion)
Asymmetric	APP_1	–	–	–	–	✗	✓
	APP_2	✗	✓	✗	✓	✓	✓
	APP_3	✓	✓	✓	✓	✓	✓
Symmetric	APP_1	–	–	–	–	✗	✓
	APP_2	✓	✓	✗	✓	✓	✓
	APP_3	✓	✓	✓	✓	✓	✓

term keys are leaked, there is an active attack for APP_2 also in the symmetric variant of the protocol, where the attacker interferes with the transmission of message 1 by injecting their own ephemeral key, and then learn the content of APP_2 when the long-term pre-shared key is leaked. This can however be avoided if the protocol reaches completion and hereby validating the authenticity of both principals.

Understanding the subtleties of these guarantees is a rather non-trivial task. In fact we advocate that the standard should claim that APP_2 is not confidential in both variants of the protocol, and to avoid potential implementation mistakes, the authors have decided to move APP_2 outside the encryption. On the other hand one can rely on the integrity of both APP_1 and APP_2 when the protocol reaches completion, which allows to relax the claims of EDHOC draft 08. That data can be used to perform irreversible actions, but only at the transmission of the third message.

3   Modeling EDHOC in Proverif

We model EDHOC in ProVerif [3], a symbolic protocol verifier supporting unbounded number of sessions and with support for Diffie-Hellman equational theories. ProVerif's logical foundation is the applied π-calculus [15], which we introduce and explain alongside our presentation of the EDHOC models. The four processes of Figs. 4 and 5 represent the Initiator and Responder roles of the protocol, in the symmetric and asymmetric variants, respectively. We consider a unified model where the asymmetric and the symmetric variants run in parallel, with unbounded numbers of principals and instances of each principal, that interact in any combination with each other. Furthermore, all long term private keys and pre-shared keys are revealed after the protocol has completed.

The Equational Theory and Adversary Model. By working on the symbolic Dolev-Yao model [16], we abstract away from concrete cryptographic primitives and their representation. Instead, we assume that the cryptographic primitives are "perfect", following common practice when working with ProVerif [17].

The Dolev-Yao model puts the attacker in control of the communication channel: it can intercept all communication between the honest principals, drop and inject messages, construct and decompose them using the known cryptographic primitives, and generate new secrets (keys, nonces etc.). It is a powerful adversary, though its capabilities end there: The Dolev-Yao attacker cannot decrypt messages without the proper keys, invert hash functions, etc. For the purpose of an efficient analysis, several defining features attributed to real cryptographic constructions are simply ignored, for example the extensionality of hash functions or the malleability of encryption schemes.

Let us thus define the symbols that model our cryptographic primitives, along with their arities:

$$\{ aeadEncrypt/3, aeadDecrypt/3, decrypt/2, pk/1, sign/2, verify/2$$
$$id/1, HKDF/4, empty/0, getAlgorithm/1, hash/1, g/0, exp/2 \}$$

and the equations that hold between them:

$$\{ aeadDecrypt(aeadEncrypt(x, y, aad), y, aad) = x,$$
$$decrypt(aeadEncrypt(x, y, aad), y) = x,$$
$$verify(sign(x, y), pk(y)) = x,$$
$$getAlgorithm(HKDF(x, aad, y, algID)) = algID,$$
$$exp(exp(g, x), y) = exp(exp(g, y), x) \}$$

The first equation implements the symmetric authenticated encryption scheme with associated data (*aead* in the protocol presentation): when a message is decrypted with key y the authentication data *aad* is also verified. The second equation models decryption without verifying the authenticity of the message. The third equation models a public signature scheme, where the signature of a message x with the private key y can be checked with the corresponding public key. The function H_{KDF} derives a key from the Diffie-Hellman shared secret, some authentication data, an optional symmetric key (we use the symbol *empty* to denote a missing key), and the algorithm—or purpose—for which it will be used. The function *getAlgorithm* is used to retrieve the algorithm identifier, and distinguish between keys with different purposes. This is a modelling artefact to aid termination of the tool, avoiding loops that re-insert pre-shared keys between parties that already ran the symmetric protocol (see lines 42–44 of the listing in Fig. 5). No equation is defined for the hash function *hash*, since it is irreversible. Finally, the last equation models the commutative property of Diffie-Hellman groups.

The equations that we introduced so far are useful for the sake of automated verification: all but the last one are subterm convergent, and hence can be interpreted from left to right leading to a decidable equational theory; the last one can also be handled as a special case by ProVerif [18].

The main process is defined in Fig. 3. It puts in parallel multiple replicated sub-processes ($P \mid Q$ represents the two processes P and Q running in parallel, and the bang operator ! represents unbounded copies of the same process).

The first process produces the identities of the unbounded principals: a fresh host U and their secret key skU are created in lines 2–3, using the **new** construction. The public key is constructed through the **let** binding and assigned to pkU in line 4. Finally, lines 5 and 6 output on the secret channel s the tuple

```
1 process
2   (!new U: host;
3       new skU: skey;
4       let pkU = pk(skU) in
5       out(s, (U, skU, pkU)); out(s, (U, skU, pkU));
6       out(c, (pkU)); phase 1; out(c, skU) ) |
7   (!in(s, (U:host, skU:skey, pkU:pkey));
8       in(s, (V:host, skV:skey, pkV:pkey));
9       new random: bitstring;
10      let PSK = HKDF(g, random, empty, EDHOC_PRESHARED) in
11      out(s2, (U, V, PSK)); out(s2, (U, V, PSK)); phase 1; out(c, PSK) ) |
12  (!in(s, (U:host, skU:skey, pkU:pkey));
13      in(s, (V:host, skV:skey, pkV:pkey));
14      (initiatorAsym(U, V, skU, pkU, pkV) |
15        responderAsym(V, U, skV, pkV, pkU)) ) |
16  (!in(s2, (U:host, V:host, PSK:key));
17      (initiatorSym(U, V, PSK) |
18        responderSym(V, U, PSK)) )
```

Fig. 3. Main ProVerif process

(U, skU, pkU), then output the public key pkU on the public channel c, and through the use of the **phase** construct reveal the secret key skU after the protocol ended, that will later be used for checking Perfect Forward Secrecy.[4]

The replicated process in lines 7–11 models the out-of-bounds registration of pre-shared keys for the symmetric variant of the protocol: it inputs the principals U and V from the secret channel s, generates a fresh random value $random$ and creates the pre-shared key PSK in line 10, which is output in line 11 on another secret channel $s2$ that maintains the mapping between the two principals and their shared key. Also PSK is output on the public channel in phase 1.

Finally, lines 12 through 18 of Fig. 3 call the asymmetric and symmetric variants of the protocol—shown in Figs. 1 and 2—after binding the relevant data through the secret channels s and $s2$. We will not describe in detail those processes, as they closely follow the presentation of Sect. 2 and we hope the reader is by now acquainted with the language. We will however present their salient features.

3.1 Asymmetric Variant

Starting with the asymmetric variant of EDHOC in Fig. 4, the initiator process is parameterized by their own identity U and that of the responder V it is supposed to talk to, along with their private skU and corresponding public key pkU,

---

[4] The use of **phase** is a ProVerif-specific extension to the Applied Pi-calculus, which intuitively disables a process in a later phase to interact with processes from previous phases, though the attacker's information is carried through phases. For a more detailed description of how phases work, we refer to the ProVerif manual [3].

1 **let** *initiatorAsym*(*U*: *host*, *V*: *host*, *skU*: *skey*, *pkU*: *pkey*, *pkV*: *pkey*) =
2   **new** *x*: *exponent*; **let** *E_U* = *exp*(*g*, *x*) **in new** *S_U*: *bitstring*;
3   **new** *N_U*: *nonce*; **new** *APP_1A*: *bitstring*; **new** *APP_3A*: *bitstring*;
4   **event** *startInitiatorA*(*U*, *V*, *E_U*, *APP_1A*, *APP_3A*);
5   **let** *msg_1*: *bitstring* = (*T1*, *S_U*, *N_U*, *E_U*, *APP_1A*) **in**
6   **out**(*c*, *msg_1*); **in**(*c*, *msg_2*: *bitstring*);
7   **let** (*data_2*: *bitstring*, *COSE_ENC_2*: *bitstring*) = *msg_2* **in**
8   **let** (=*T2*, =*S_U*, *xS_V*: *bitstring*, *N_V*: *nonce*, *xE_V*: *G*) = *data_2* **in**
9   **let** *aad_2*: *bitstring* = *hash*((*msg_1*, *data_2*)) **in**
10   **let** *K*: *G* = *exp*(*xE_V*, *x*) **in**
11   **let** *K_2*: *key* = *HKDF*(*K*, *aad_2*, *empty*, *EDHOC*) **in**
12   **let** *signature_2*: *bitstring* = *aeadDecrypt*(*COSE_ENC_2*, *K_2*, *aad_2*) **in**
13   **let** (=*idR*(*pkV*), =*aad_2*, *APP_2A*: *bitstring*) = *verify*(*signature_2*, *pkV*) **in**
14   **event** *midInitiatorA*(*U*, *V*, *xE_V*, *APP_2A*);
15   **let** *data_3*: *bitstring* = (*T3*, *xS_V*) **in**
16   **let** *aad_3*: *bitstring* = *hash*((*hash*((*msg_1*, *msg_2*)), *data_3*)) **in**
17   **let** *signature_3*: *bitstring* = *sign*((*idI*(*pk*(*skU*)), *aad_3*, *APP_3A*), *skU*) **in**
18   **let** *K_3*: *key* = *HKDF*(*K*, *aad_3*, *empty*, *EDHOC*) **in**
19   **let** *COSE_ENC_3*: *bitstring* = *aeadEncrypt*(*signature_3*, *K_3*, *aad_3*) **in**
20   **let** *msg_3*: *bitstring* = (*data_3*, *COSE_ENC_3*) **in**
21   **out**(*c*, *msg_3*);
22   **event** *endInitiatorA*(*U*, *V*, *xE_V*, *APP_2A*).
23
24 **let** *responderAsym*(*V*: *host*, *U*: *host*, *skV*: *skey*, *pkV*: *pkey*, *pkU*: *pkey*) =
25   **new** *y*: *exponent*; **let** *E_V*: *G* = *exp*(*g*, *y*) **in new** *S_V*: *bitstring*;
26   **new** *N_V*: *nonce*; **new** *APP_2A*: *bitstring*; **new** *APP_2A'*: *bitstring*;
27   **event** *startResponderA*(*U*, *V*, *E_V*, *APP_2A*);
28   **in**(*c*, *msg_1*: *bitstring*);
29   **let** (=*T1*, *xS_U*: *bitstring*, *xN_U*: *nonce*, *xE_U*: *G*, *APP_1A*: *bitstring*) = *msg_1* **in**
30   **let** *data_2*: *bitstring* = (*T2*, *xS_U*, *S_V*, *N_V*, *E_V*) **in**
31   **let** *aad_2*: *bitstring* = *hash*((*msg_1*, *data_2*)) **in**
32   **let** *signature_2*: *bitstring* = *sign*((*idR*(*pk*(*skV*)), *aad_2*, *APP_2A*), *skV*) **in**
33   **let** *K*: *G* = *exp*(*xE_U*, *y*) **in**
34   **let** *K_2*: *key* = *HKDF*(*K*, *aad_2*, *empty*, *EDHOC*) **in**
35   **let** *COSE_ENC_2*: *bitstring* = *aeadEncrypt*(*signature_2*, *K_2*, *aad_2*) **in**
36   **let** *msg_2*: *bitstring* = (*data_2*, *COSE_ENC_2*) **in**
37   **out**(*c*, *msg_2*); **in**(*c*, *msg_3*: *bitstring*);
38   **let** (*data_3*: *bitstring*, *COSE_ENC_3*: *bitstring*) = *msg_3* **in**
39   **let** (=*T3*, =*S_V*) = *data_3* **in**
40   **let** *aad_3*: *bitstring* = *hash*((*hash*((*msg_1*, *msg_2*)), *data_3*)) **in**
41   **let** *K_3*: *key* = *HKDF*(*K*, *aad_3*, *empty*, *EDHOC*) **in**
42   **let** *signature_3*: *bitstring* = *aeadDecrypt*(*COSE_ENC_3*, *K_3*, *aad_3*) **in**
43   **let** (=*idI*(*pkU*), =*aad_3*, *APP_3A*: *bitstring*) = *verify*(*signature_3*, *pkU*) **in**
44   **event** *endResponderA*(*U*, *V*, *xE_U*, *APP_1A*, *APP_3A*);
45   **let** *signature_2'*: *bitstring* = *sign*((*idR*(*pkV*), *aad_2*, *APP_2A'*), *skV*) **in**
46   **let** *COSE_ENC_2'*: *bitstring* = *aeadEncrypt*(*signature_2'*, *K_2*, *aad_2*) **in**
47   **let** *msg_2'*: *bitstring* = (*data_2*, *COSE_ENC_2'*) **in**
48   **out**(*c2*, *msg_2'*);
49   **let** *PSK* = *HKDF*(*K*, *hash*(*msg_3*), *empty*, *EDHOC_PSK_Chaining*) **in**
50   **out**(*s2*, (*U*, *V*, *PSK*)).

Fig. 4. Asymmetric protocol

as well as the responder public key pkV. A dual set of parameters is provided to the responder process to put them in communication.

The use of $id(pkU)$ and $id(pkV)$ is perhaps noteworthy: these are constructed using the private constructor id, and then used to check whether the attacker has learned the identity of one of the principals in the protocol. Even though the attacker has access to all public keys, they cannot construct these terms themselves, hence they need to learn them from the protocol. This allows to check whether the attacker can learn the identity of the each principal by checking if the attacker can obtain the information created with either of the two functions: $id(pkU)$ or $id(pkV)$.

In order to check agreement properties, the initiator and responder processes are annotated with the events $startInitiatorA$, $midInitiatorA$, $endInitiatorA$ and $startResponderA$, $endResponderA$, respectively. The lack of a corresponding $midResponderA$ is due to the first message being unprotected by any cryptographic mechanism, therefore the agreement at that point will trivially not hold.

In order to check whether the secrecy and PFS hold after the completion of the protocol, a duplicate of message two is created in the lines 45 through 48 of Fig. 4. This message will be sent on a different channel that the processes do not listen to but the attacker does. It is hereby possible to check if the attacker can obtain the application data of message 2 after the completion of the protocol.

Finally, at the end of the responder process on line 49 of Fig. 4, a pre-shared key PSK' is generated from the Diffie-Hellman shared secret, and then inserted into channel $s2$, which serves as a key-store for U and V.

3.2 Symmetric Variant

Figure 4 shows the symmetric variant of the protocol. It is parameterized by the identities of the hosts and the pre-shared key PSK that is used to establish the session. Like for the asymmetric variant, it is annotated with events that mark various steps of the protocol, with a lack of a *mid*-event for the responder. Also the events for the privacy of the initiator and responder are missing in this case, since the symmetric variant does not use at all public keys.

To check the secrecy and PFS properties after the completion of the protocol, the symmetric version similar to the asymmetric version creates a duplicate of the second message in the lines 39–41 of Fig. 4.

Similarly to the asymmetric version, the responder process is also responsible for inserting a new pre-shared key PSK' derived from the Diffie-Hellman secret in lines 42–44, making use of the "EDHOC PSK Chaining" mode of the standard. Note the conditional in line 42: in our model we do not allow inserting a key derived using "EDHOC PSK Chaining" from one that was itself derive using the same technique. Doing so leads to the tool not terminating.

```
1  let initiatorSym(U: host, V: host, PSK: key) =
2    new x: exponent; let E_U: G = exp(g, x) in new S_U: bitstring;
3    new N_U: nonce; new APP_1S: bitstring; new APP_3S: bitstring;
4    event startInitiatorS(U, V, E_U, APP_1S, APP_3S);
5    let msg_1: bitstring = (T4, S_U, N_U, E_U, APP_1S) in
6    out(c, msg_1); in(c, msg_2: bitstring);
7    let (data_2: bitstring, COSE_ENC_2: bitstring) = msg_2 in
8    let (=T5, =S_U, xS_V: bitstring, xN_V: nonce, xE_V: G) = data_2 in
9    let aad_2: bitstring = hash((msg_1, data_2)) in
10   let K: G = exp(xE_V, x) in
11   let K_2: key = HKDF(K, aad_2, PSK, EDHOC) in
12   let (APP_2S: bitstring) = aeadDecrypt(COSE_ENC_2, K_2, aad_2) in
13   event midInitiatorS(U, V, xE_V, APP_2S);
14   let data_3: bitstring = (T6, xS_V) in
15   let aad_3: bitstring = hash((hash((msg_1, msg_2)), data_3)) in
16   let K_3: key = HKDF(K, aad_3, PSK, EDHOC) in
17   let msg_3: bitstring = (data_3, aeadEncrypt(APP_3S, K_3, aad_3)) in
18   out(c, msg_3);
19   event endInitiatorS(U, V, xE_V, APP_2S).
20
21 let responderSym(V: host, U: host, PSK: key) =
22   new y: exponent; let E_V: G = exp(g, y) in new S_V: bitstring;
23   new N_V: nonce; new APP_2S: bitstring; new APP_2S': bitstring;
24   event startResponderS(U, V, E_V, APP_2S);
25   in(c, msg_1: bitstring);
26   let (=T4, xS_U: bitstring, N_U: nonce, xE_U: G, APP_1S: bitstring) = msg_1 in
27   let data_2: bitstring = (T5, xS_U, S_V, N_V, E_V) in
28   let aad_2: bitstring = hash((msg_1, data_2)) in
29   let K: G = exp(xE_U, y) in
30   let K_2: key = HKDF(K, aad_2, PSK, EDHOC) in
31   let msg_2: bitstring = (data_2, aeadEncrypt(APP_2S, K_2, aad_2)) in
32   out(c, msg_2); in(c, msg_3: bitstring);
33   let (data_3: bitstring, COSE_ENC_3: bitstring) = msg_3 in
34   let (=T6, =S_V) = data_3 in
35   let aad_3: bitstring = hash((hash((msg_1, msg_2)), data_3)) in
36   let K_3: key = HKDF(K, aad_3, PSK, EDHOC) in
37   let (APP_3S: bitstring) = aeadDecrypt(COSE_ENC_3, K_3, aad_3) in
38   event endResponderS(U, V, xE_U, APP_1S, APP_3S);
39   let COSE_ENC_2': bitstring = aeadEncrypt(APP_2S', K_2, aad_2) in
40   let msg_2': bitstring = (data_2, COSE_ENC_2') in
41   out(c2, msg_2');
42   if(getAlgorithm(PSK) = EDHOC_PRESHARED) then
43   let PSK' = HKDF(K, hash(msg_3), PSK, EDHOC_PSK_Chaining) in
44   out(s2, (U, V, PSK')).
```

Fig. 5. Symmetric protocol

4   Security Properties

In this Section, we present the definitions used to check the properties that we claim in Sect. 2.3, in terms of ProVerif queries.

Identity Protection Against an Active Adversary. The protocol reveals the identity of the initiator against an active adversary if the attacker can obtain the term $idI(pkU)$ for any public key pkU registered to an honest party. Likewise, the protocol reveals the identity of the responder from an active adversary if the attacker can obtain the term $idR(pkU)$ for any public key pkU registered to an honest party. As we expect, ProVerif confirms that the identity of the initiator kept private, whereas the identity of the responder is revealed.

Secrecy of Data, Perfect Forward Secrecy. We measure secrecy and perfect forward secrecy of APP_2 and APP_3. That is, we check whether the attacker is able to obtain the application data from the second and the third message of the protocol, in both the symmetric and asymmetric variants. In the asymmetric variant, we find that APP_2 is not secret unless the session completes, while APP_3 is secret. These properties are maintained for completed sessions even after revealing the long-term keys. In the symmetric variant, APP_2 is secret (but not after revealing the long-term keys with incomplete sessions), and APP_3 is secret even after revealing long-term keys. These results match our claims on Table 1 for the columns "Secrecy" and "PFS" as well as their corresponding "(at completion)" columns.

Strong Authentication. In our model, all correspondence agreements between the initiator and the responder hold. Note that in both versions, when the initiator U ends the protocol, or even when they receive the second message, we have no assurance that the responder intended to talk to U, thus we leave freedom of choice for another U' on these correspondence checks. This is obviously acceptable: because of the unprotected nature of the first message the responder has no way to check the identity of the initiator until it reaches the end of the protocol. This is reflected by the other side of the correspondence, that matches in all parameters, including the application data. Hence we can confirm the integrity of all application data at the completion of the protocol, and also the integrity of APP_2 when the initiator receives it, in both cases. However since the responder is not certain of the identity of the initiator when sending APP_2, that payload should not contain any information about that is confidential for them.

5   Conclusion

The EDHOC protocol is the result of a clean slate design of an authentication protocol for IoT devices that is light weight, easy to implement, and that does not have any legacy modes. The protocol is currently under consideration for standardization, with the next step being to prove the standardization body that the protocol is secure. In this work, we describe a formal analysis of the protocol in the symbolic model using the ProVerif tool. We have identified security issues and hidden assumptions, which have led to further refinements of the EDHOC protocol. ProVerif has been an excellent tool to conduct this work, although, our model had to be carefully engineered, not to get in trouble with the well-known over-approximations that ProVerif models entail. In general we would recommend that any protocol that is used in security sensitive domains and considered for standardization should be modelled using formal methods and verified using mechanized reasoning tools, such as ProVerif.

Future Work. The protocol has been analyzed alone, whereas it is intended to be used in conjunction with other protocols, including the secure data transport standard "Object Security for Constrained RESTful Environments" (OSCORE [4]), for which EDHOC creates an explicit context (i.e. session keys). Protocol composition is not automatically guaranteed, and is an active area of research in the theory of protocol security. Even though it is reassuring to know that the OSCORE session key is never used nor is derivable from an EDHOC key (though it is derivable from the Diffie-Hellman exchange), it would be interesting to conduct a formal analysis of those standards that are meant to be used in conjunction. Other involved standards that would require further analysis would be the CBOR binary format [13], and the COSE [12] standard of encryption formats, which are used by EDHOC for formatting messages, and mimick the JSON web standard and JOSE encryption standard that sits on top of it. Furthermore, since the protocol is at its first version and only mandates the use of algorithms that are currently deemed secure, we have not modelled downgrade attacks. It will be helpful to extend this model to consider downgrade attacks, once new versions of the EDHOC are released.

The next iteration of the EDHOC protocol, draft 09 [19], has incorporated our findings, and the authors decided to move away from encrypting the application data contained in the second message, in an effort to simplify the protocol and offer weaker—but clearer—security guarantees. This work has provided useful input to the designers of EDHOC, and the authors intend to evolve the models with the evolution of the standard, so as to provide useful input and higher assurance on the correctness of its design.

References

1. Selander, G., Mattsson, J., Palombini, F.: Ephemeral Diffie-Hellman over cose (EDHOC) (2018). https://tools.ietf.org/html/draft-selander-ace-cose-ecdhe-08. Accessed 10 May 2018
2. Rescorla, E.: The Transport Layer Security (TLS) Protocol Version 1.3. Internet-Draft draft-ietf-tls-tls13-28, Internet Engineering Task Force (2018, Work in Progress)
3. Blanchet, B., Smyth, B., Cheval, V., Sylvestre, M.: Proverif 2.00: automatic cryptographic protocol verifier, user manual and tutorial (2018)

4. Selander, G., Mattsson, J., Palombini, F., Seitz, L.: Object Security for Constrained RESTful Environments (OSCORE). Internet-Draft draft-ietf-core-object-security-13, Internet Engineering Task Force (2018, Work in Progress)
5. Krawczyk, H.: SIGMA: the 'SIGn-and-MAc' approach to authenticated Diffie-Hellman and its use in the IKE protocols. In: Boneh, D. (ed.) CRYPTO 2003. LNCS, vol. 2729, pp. 400–425. Springer, Heidelberg (2003). https://doi.org/10.1007/978-3-540-45146-4_24
6. Bhargavan, K., Blanchet, B., Kobeissi, N.: Verified models and reference implementations for the TLS 1.3 standard candidate. In: 2017 IEEE Symposium on Security and Privacy (SP), pp. 483–502. IEEE (2017)
7. Blanchet, B.: Cryptoverif: Computationally sound mechanized prover for cryptographic protocols. In: Dagstuhl seminar Formal Protocol Verification Applied, vol. 117 (2007)
8. Cremers, C., Horvat, M., Hoyland, J., Scott, S., van der Merwe, T.: A comprehensive symbolic analysis of TLS 1.3. In: Proceedings of the 2017 ACM SIGSAC Conference on Computer and Communications Security, pp. 1773–1788. ACM (2017)
9. Meier, S., Schmidt, B., Cremers, C., Basin, D.: The TAMARIN prover for the symbolic analysis of security protocols. In: Sharygina, N., Veith, H. (eds.) CAV 2013. LNCS, vol. 8044, pp. 696–701. Springer, Heidelberg (2013). https://doi.org/10.1007/978-3-642-39799-8_48
10. Meadows, C.: Analysis of the internet key exchange protocol using the NRL protocol analyzer. In: Proceedings of the 1999 IEEE Symposium on Security and Privacy, pp. 216–231. IEEE (1999)
11. Canetti, R., Krawczyk, H.: Security analysis of IKE's signature-based key-exchange protocol. In: Yung, M. (ed.) CRYPTO 2002. LNCS, vol. 2442, pp. 143–161. Springer, Heidelberg (2002). https://doi.org/10.1007/3-540-45708-9_10
12. Jim Schaad, A.C.: CBOR object signing and encryption (COSE) (2010). https://tools.ietf.org/html/rfc8152. Accessed 10 May 2018
13. Bormann, C.: Concise binary object representation (CBOR) (2013). https://tools.ietf.org/html/rfc7049. Accessed 10 May 2018
14. Krawczyk, D.H., Eronen, P.: HMAC-based Extract-and-Expand Key Derivation Function (HKDF). RFC 5869 (2010)
15. Abadi, M., Blanchet, B., Fournet, C.: The applied pi calculus: mobile values, new names, and secure communication. J. ACM **65**, 1:1–1:41 (2018)
16. Dolev, D., Yao, A.: On the security of public key protocols. IEEE Trans. Inf. Theory **29**, 198–208 (1983)
17. Blanchet, B.: Modeling and verifying security protocols with the applied pi calculus and proverif. Found. Trends Priv. Secur. **1**, 1–135 (2016)
18. Schmidt, B., Meier, S., Cremers, C., Basin, D.: Automated analysis of Diffie-Hellman protocols and advanced security properties. In: 2012 IEEE 25th Computer Security Foundations Symposium (CSF), pp. 78–94. IEEE (2012)
19. Selander, G., Mattsson, J., Palombini, F.: Ephemeral Diffie-Hellman Over COSE (EDHOC). Internet-Draft draft-selander-ace-cose-ecdhe-09, Internet Engineering Task Force (2018, Work in Progress)

Experimental Evaluation of Attacks on TESLA-Secured Time Synchronization Protocols

Kristof Teichel[1]([✉]) and Gregor Hildermeier[2]

[1] Physikalisch-Technische Bundesanstalt,
Bundesallee 100, 38116 Braunschweig, Germany
kristof.teichel@ptb.de
[2] Technische Universität Braunschweig, 38092 Braunschweig, Germany

Abstract. There is an increasingly relevant class of protocols that employ TESLA stream authentication to provide authenticity for one-way time synchronization. For such protocols, an interdependency between synchronization and security has been found to theoretically enable attackers to render the security measures useless. We evaluate to what extent this attack works in practice. To this end, we use a tailor-made configurable testbed implementation to simulate behaviors of TESLA-protected one-way synchronization protocols in hostile networks. In particular, this lets us confirm vulnerabilities to the attack for two published protocols, TinySeRSync and ASTS. Our analysis also yields a set of countermeasures, with which in-development and future specifications can potentially use TESLA to successfully secure one-way time synchronization.

Keywords: (One-way) time synchronization protocols · TESLA Authentication · Experimental attack analysis · ASTS · TinySeRSync

1 Introduction

Time synchronization has been a crucial mechanism since the creation of the first computer networks. In many settings, clock synchronization failure or manipulation is unacceptable. With an increasing focus on security in recent years, the demand for authenticity in time synchronization protocol specifications has increased. A mechanism called "Timed Efficient Stream Loss-tolerant Authentication" (TESLA) [10,11], which employs delayed key disclosure, has been adopted for providing authenticity for one-way time synchronization protocols. TESLA is attractive because it meets a combined challenge: it supplies well-scaling authentication in systems with large numbers of slaves and mostly one-way communication flow, but at the same time offers the speed of symmetric cryptography. However, a potential attack vector has been discovered in which, under certain circumstances, the authenticity provided by TESLA can be compromised entirely when it is used to protect one-way time synchronization [16].

© Springer Nature Switzerland AG 2018
C. Cremers and A. Lehmann (Eds.): SSR 2018, LNCS 11322, pp. 37–55, 2018.
https://doi.org/10.1007/978-3-030-04762-7_3

Our main focus in this paper is the question to what extent this attack is relevant in practice, on standardized protocol specifications.

At least two published protocols have already made use of TESLA-based authentication mechanisms to secure time-related messages: the "Secure and Resilient Time Synchronization protocol" [15] (TinySeRSync) and the "Agile Secure Time Synchronization protocol" (ASTS) [17], both of which were developed for wireless sensor networks. Furthermore, the network time synchronization community is reviewing how to apply TESLA in ongoing specification work. The Institute of Electrical and Electronics Engineers describes a TESLA-based security scheme in the upcoming version of its Precision Time Protocol [1] specification. The Internet Engineering Task Force has been discussing TESLA's use for the broadcast mode of the Network Time Protocol [9] in the context of the ongoing Network Time Security specification [13,14]. The European Space Agency is building TESLA protection into the Open Service Message Authentication scheme [5] of Galileo, the European global Navigation satellite system. Thus, depending on how these specifications turn out, TESLA-protected one-way synchronization might in the future be employed on billions of devices.

The complexity that arises from the combination of TESLA with time synchronization procedures makes evaluating the susceptibility of a given protocol to the attack a hard problem. It is especially difficult to prove that a protocol is positively secure, since this requires proof of absence of a successful attack path in a highly complex system. Proving that a protocol is not secure is simple: one only has to provide an attack scenario as a witness. However, it is not necessarily easy, since finding and documenting such a scenario requires a solid understanding of the mechanisms involved and a convenient way to log the events that lead to it.

The treatment in [16] is the only in-depth analysis on the problem that we could find. However, it has limitations that we wanted to expand upon. First, the analysis is limited to a generic, generalized and abstracted protocol representing the class of all TESLA-protected one-way synchronization protocols without regard for any potential specific intricacies of each. Second, the analysis is executed only with model checking via the UPPAAL model checker, so any abstractions made in the creation of the model might influence the applicability of the results. Third, the model and the tool do not allow for even remotely realistic ratios of interval lengths to time units: in the UPPAAL model, an interval can only be in the order of 10 time units long before state space size exceeds memory limitations. Other analysis [2,3] avoids the details of the issue altogether, generally noting that the interdependency of timing and security is a potentially critical problem.

In this paper, we make three key contributions to the subject area of practical vulnerability to the attack of existing and future protocol specifications. We use our own configurable testbed implementation to run simulations of TinySeRSync and ASTS in which they are attacked by an adversary using techniques from [16]. The data from these simulations enables us to make well-founded statements regarding the existing protocols. First, a faithful implementation of TinySeRSync without further mitigation is attackable, albeit with a much easier attack scheme than the one originally outlined. Second, a faithful implementation of ASTS without further mitigation is attackable with exactly the methods outlined in [16]. These statements about the established protocol definition constitute our first key contribution to the subject area. They represent an improvement in the attack analysis, from conjectured vulnerability of concrete protocols after loose study of the describing papers, towards field tests on physically distributed devices running faithful implementations of the protocol descriptions. Our testbed implementation directly represents our second contribution, since it is generic enough that it can be adapted to simulate both existing and future protocols and their behavior, especially with regards to the attack within the scope of this work. Furthermore, we deduce a set of countermeasures to mitigate the attack. These, combined with the analysis and derivation that yields them and puts them into practical context (an improvement over countermeasure suggestions in [16]), constitute our third key contribution. The given countermeasures can be included in future specifications of protocols which involve TESLA-protected one-way time synchronization. We feel that the number of such specifications currently in development gives our latter contributions extra weight.

This paper is structured as follows: Sect. 2 provides an introduction to basic time synchronization techniques, to the TESLA protocol and to the attack vector on which we base our simulation and analysis. In Sect. 3, we present the setup of our experiments and give an overview of our implementation. Section 4 discusses the results of our evaluation. This comprises an overview of our analysis regarding protocol vulnerability as well as a derivation and evaluation of countermeasures. Section 5 concludes this paper.

2   Preliminaries

Before we delve into details about results and interpretation of our simulation runs, we use this section to introduce protocols and techniques that are essential to this work, as well as a rough description of the relevant attack vector.

2.1   One-Way and Two-Way Time Synchronization

Generally, network-based time synchronization is achieved in one of two ways: with one-way or with two-way communication. In two-way mode, the participants exchange time request and response messages, as depicted in Fig. 1 (left). By calculations under the assumption of symmetric network delays (i.e. $\epsilon = 0.5$ in the figure), the client can obtain a value for the clock offset with a maximum error of half the network round-trip [8] (i.e. $\delta/2$ in the figure). In one-way mode, a master periodically sends out messages to many slaves, as depicted in Fig. 1 (right). A given slave then needs a good estimate of the transmission time of the packets in order to calculate the clock offset. Note that there are no guarantees

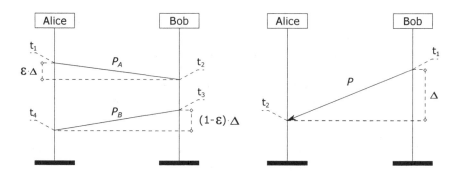

Fig. 1. Two-way (left) and one-way (right) time synchronization (*cf.* [16]).

for the slave regarding the maximum error of these calculations, and specifically any artificial delay on the transmission packet (P in the figure) adds to that error.

2.2   Overview of TESLA

The TESLA protocol [10] was originally designed to authenticate media streams, combining the scalability of asymmetric schemes with the high speed of symmetric cryptography. It applies symmetric-key cryptography, but creates asymmetry by making use of time progression: packets are signed and sent, but the key used to sign them is only disclosed after the so-called *disclosure lag*. A received packet is buffered and can be authenticated only after the key is disclosed. As long as the slave can be certain that the key was not disclosed before the packet was received the authenticity of the signature is guaranteed. In order for TESLA to work, two main concepts are deployed:

The first main concept that is employed is that of using a key chain to be able to commit to a key before using it. To generate a key chain, the master applies a one-way pseudo-random function F to a secret K_n to compute a key value $K_{n-1} = F(K_n)$. It repeats this to obtain $K_{n-i} = F^i(K_n)$ up to K_{-1}, which is called the *key chain commit*, while the next key K_0 is the first one to be used. This creates a chain of keys, with each key being verifiable by only its predecessors. The master applies F', another pseudo-random function, to a *key value* K_i in the chain to generate a *key* K_i'. This key K_i' is used to create the MAC for a packet. Before sending any packets, the master commits to the entire chain by publishing K_{-1}, as well as F and F'.

The second main concept is that of using time intervals. The master defines the starting time T_0 and the length T_Δ of a time interval I_i, $i = 0, \ldots, n$. Each interval I_i is associated with the key K_i. Every packet sent in interval I_i is signed with the key K_i'. In interval I_{i+d}, the key value K_i is then disclosed. A depiction of this concept is presented in Fig. 2.

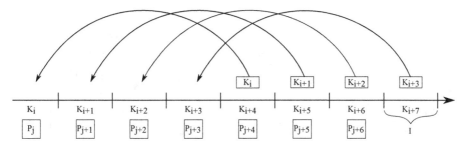

Fig. 2. TESLA authenticates packets with keys disclosed in subsequent packets, in this example after a disclosure delay of $d = 4$ intervals.

2.3   Attacking TESLA-Secured Time Synchronisation Protocols

The attack described in this section was first formulated in [16]. It forms the basis for the behavior of the attacker in our implementation, and is essential throughout this paper. The attack is enabled when the TESLA protocol (or any variant of a scheduled delayed key disclosure) is used to authenticate time distribution in a one-way synchronization setting. Since the protocol itself is time-dependent but, in this application, also directly influences the degree of clock synchronization, the packet authenticity provided can be compromised.

The attacker is assumed to operate under the Dolev-Yao attack model [4]. It is therefore capable of impersonating any member of the network, as long as there is no extra authentication mechanism in place. Notably, it is also capable of delaying any packet. This has a special significance in the context of time synchronization protocols and in the attack explained below.

Attack Synopsis. The attack has two phases. *Phase One* has multiple steps:

1. The attacker consistently delays any packets from the master by δ_1.
2. As soon as the slave uses the time data in the first delayed packet to adjust its clock (usually when it verifies the packet after its disclosure lag), the introduced delay δ_1 starts to take effect.
3. This desynchronization increases the time by which the slave will accept a packet as timely. The attacker is thus able to delay packets by $\delta_1 + \delta_2$.
4. The attacker continues to increase the delay according to the step above.

Eventually, the *desynchroization condition* will be fulfilled, meaning that the clocks will have desynchronized by more than $(d-1)T_\Delta$, where d is the disclosure lag. Phase One of the attack is then complete and the attacker can perform *Phase Two* of the attack. It is now possible to intercept any packet from the master, wait until its respective key has been disclosed and replace it with a bogus packet, for which the attacker can generate a correct MAC. The slave's clock is so far behind that it accepts the packet as timely. By this point, the attacker can fully impersonate the master (including the ability to create valid MACs for forged packets), thus breaking the security of the protocol.

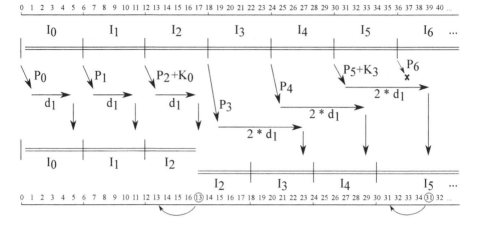

Fig. 3. Illustration of the attack on an example network. Alice adjusts her clock after receiving P_2 and P_5, intervals I_2 and I_5 are prolonged accordingly.

Example Attack. To further illustrate particularly Phase One of the attack, consider the schematically depiction in Fig. 3, where it is demonstrated with specific values $d = 2$ and $T_\Delta = 6$ s and a delay increment of 4 s (numbers chosen for comprehensibility and brevity of the scheme).

- *Step 1:* The attacker delays P_0 by $\delta_1 = 4$ s. The slave checks the timeliness of P_0 and accepts it as timely.
- *Step 2:* Packets P_1 and P_2 are delayed in the same way as P_0. The slave receives P_2 and the key value K_0. The slave authenticates P_0, concludes that its clock is fast by 4 s, and adjusts it accordingly.
- *Step 3:* The attacker delays P_3 and subsequent packets, by $\delta_1 + \delta_2 = 8$ s.
- *Step 4:* In our example, this increase is sufficient, since 8 s $> (d - 1)T_\Delta$.

The slave's clock synchronization error is already large enough after it receives P_5, which enables it to process P_3, after which it adjusts its clock as though it were fast by another 4 s. The slave's clock now reads 31 s, while the master's clock at the same time reads 39 s. The offset between the two clocks has surpassed the value $(d - 1)T_\Delta$; hence, the desynchronization condition is satisfied and Phase One is therefore complete and *Phase Two* can now start. The attacker prevents P_6 and the following packets from ever reaching the slave. It waits until the master discloses K_6 in interval I_8 and derives K_6'. It can now forge a packet Q_6 with any bogus time chosen, use K_6' to create a valid MAC and forward it to the slave. In another forged packet Q_8, it includes the original and correct key value K_6. The slave will use this key to (successfully) authenticate the bogus packet Q_6, since K_6 belongs to the key chain. The slave now uses the bogus time data in Q_6 to adjust its clock, and *Phase Two* is therefore successful.

3 Experiment Setup

The overarching goal for this work was to answer the question to what extent the idea for the attack from [16] would work in practice, on implementations of time synchronization protocols running on distributed devices over physical networks.

3.1 Objectives and Approach

In particular, the analysis was desired to be of a nature that would be helpful in the standardization of future protocols securing one-way time synchronization with mechanisms similar to TESLA. This requirement combined with the overall goal yielded a number of specific objectives:

- **Primary objective:** to provide either of the following:
  - Proof that at least one faithful implementation of an existing protocol specification was successfully attacked,
  - Statement that no implementation of the candidate protocols could be successfully attacked, with a detailed explanation of why the attack failed.
- **Secondary objective** (in case at least one implementation was successfully attacked): to investigate what role any configurable protocol parameters would play. Specifically, to provide both of the following:
  - A set of parameters under which the attack was successful,
  - A different set of parameters under which the attack was not successful.

Therefore, the two existing finished protocol specifications (TinySeRSync and ASTS) mentioned explicitly in that paper were investigated.

The shortest path to a definitive answer would have been to get an original implementation of either of them running in the lab and perform a successful attack on it. It turned out, however, that we would be unable to go that route. For ASTS, there is to the best of our knowledge simply no publically available implementation. Moreover, while there is code available for TinySeRSync, getting it to run proved too difficult, due to the fact that it was developed for the now unavailable TinyOS 1, and is incompatible with TinyOS 2. We therefore decided to create a new implementation [7] of a highly configurable TESLA-protected one-way synchronization protocol and run our experiments on that. This does represent a caveat with regard to the proof of attackablity of the specific protocols. However, we would like to note that the higher access to what-if scenarios was beneficial, and that any analysis of future specifications is likely to benefit more from our testbed implementation than it would have from successful attacks on original implementations. Additionally, we did have the TinySeRSync code available when developing and testing, and can at least attest that we did not find anything in it that suggested different behaviour than what we ultimately tested.

3.2   Testbed Implementation

We limit ourselves to an overview of the most important features of our implementation. More detail can be found in [6] and [7]. The implementation was created using the C++11 programming language. The *Boost* and *Boost.Asio* libraries were used to create efficient, easily readable and extendible code.

Participants. The three participants are modeled as standalone programs interacting with each other. The first is the time *master*. On request, it provides all parameters needed for TESLA (time schedule and the key chain commitment). After initialization, it starts up two periodic timers; one sends out time packets, the other sends out keys according to the disclosure schedule. The second participant is a time *slave* that attempts to synchronize its clock. It is initialized by a request-response scheme to receive the necessary parameters. In the second step, the *loose synchronization* required by the TESLA protocol is established by performing multiple rounds of two-way time exchanges, which also quantify $\delta_{\max}$. Afterwards, the slave goes to a constant listening mode, waiting for incoming packets. From then on, the clock is only adjusted through time messages received via broadcast. The third participant, who serves as the network simulator, is a Man-In-The-Middle (MITM) attacker. It is capable of all behavior necessary to carry out the attack, such as withholding and forging packets.

The Clock. We decided to run different participants on physically separate systems. This implies that different participants also have completely separate system clocks. One downside to this is the lack of a precise way of measuring the exact time difference between two clocks on separate devices. However, in our evaluation, the benefits outweighed the shortcomings: in this way, we were able to model real-world synchronization conditions as closely as possible and eliminate the concern of side effects influencing synchronization.

Clock Adjustment Algorithms. We considered two different ways to adjust a clock. The first way was simply to increase the current clock value by a measured offset. The alternative was to slow down or speed up the clock for a gradual adjustment. In the context of the TESLA protocol (particularly the aspect of delayed authentication), we needed to consider a few pitfalls with respect to performing gradual adjustments. The effect of an adjustment is not yet reflected when the next packet arrives, but rather for packets a few intervals later (after the disclosure lag). Because of the disclosure lag, there is a time lag between the detection and the correction of a measured offset. Offsets will therefore be measured repeatedly. Additionally, there is the question of exactly how much the clock should be sped up or slowed down by to compensate for a detected offset. Using simple constant values can have undesirable effects, namely overcompensation (due to the correction delay mentioned above) or unnecessarily long compensation times. Our solution to this problem was to speed up or slow down the clock in such a way that it was expected to be adjusted to the given offset after $d + 1$ intervals.

3.3   Distributed Setup

For the tests, we deployed the master, slave, and MITM on two separate servers with a large distance between them. The master and the MITM were hosted on a server in the Amazon Web Services Elastic Compute Cloud in Oregon, USA. The slave was hosted on a cloud server run by the local technical university.

4   Experiment Results and Evaluation

Conforming to TinySeRSync and ASTS to the greatest extent possible, we evaluated protocol configurations regarding their susceptibility to the described attack. First, we analyzed in general which parts of the TESLA protocol are generally most relevant to the attack and formulated the core questions for our evaluation. The attack does not target the authenticity of the key packets, nor the authenticity of the time synchronization – at least not directly. Thus, we notice first that the most critical operation, and the core of the entire TESLA protocol, is the timeliness validation. Moving forward, we need to take a closer look at how the packet's timeliness is validated and what the consequences are for the security of the protocol, by the following core questions:

1. To what extent does the clock adjustment influence the timeliness validation?[1]
2. How much of a delay can be introduced so that a packet will still be timely?
3. How fast does the clock adjust, or when is the adjustment process complete?

4.1   Vulnerability of Existing Protocols to the Attack

We examined TinySeRSync and ASTS with the questions above in mind to determine whether they were vulnerable, and if so, how long it would take for an attack to succeed. Both protocols make use of a variant of TESLA. To be more precise, they make use of the μTESLA protocol, a TESLA variation specifically designed to be lightweight enough to work in wireless sensor networks. The difference between traditional TESLA and μTESLA pertains only to the way the initial parameters are distributed and secured: traditional TESLA distributes them via broadcast and secures them with asymmetric signatures, while μTESLA distributes them individually via unicast, secured by symmetric cryptography using pre-shared keys. Since none of this has any impact on the part of TESLA we wish to examine, we forego the distinction between the traditional protocol and its lightweight variant in the following analysis.

---

[1] Since we have occasionally run into misunderstandings about this point, we would like to point out explicitly that none of our results in any way concerns the security of TESLA in a vacuum, nor that of any protocol that uses a TESLA-like mechanism to protect a generic data stream. The results apply only to protocols which use a TESLA-like mechanism to protect exactly a one-way time synchronization protocol.

TinySeRSync. The TinySeRSync protocol [15] was designed for time synchronization in wireless sensor networks and addressed the problems of security for such protocols by employing (μ)TESLA. The first step in the protocol is a secure single-hop pairwise time synchronization technique, which in this publication is called *phase I*. The second step is the actual global secure and resilient synchronization, which employs the TESLA broadcast authentication mechanism to establish a globally synchronized time throughout the entire network. This is called *phase II* in this publication. The two phases run periodically and asynchronously. The only restriction is that phase I has to be completed by a node at least once before it can participate in phase II. The second phase is controlled by a source node (usually a base station), which acts as the real-time reference (master) clock in TESLA environments. The source node broadcasts the reference time periodically, with each time packet being authenticated with the TESLA protocol mechanism by the sensor nodes (slaves). Messages are rebroadcast to reach nodes that cannot directly contact the base station.

A common problem inherent to the TESLA protocol is that its use requires that loose synchronization of the clocks be established. The authors have conveniently solved this problem with the pair-wise synchronization completed in phase I. Each node knows the clock offset to each of its neighbor nodes and the maximum transmission delay for a packet, enabling timeliness validation. Even though TinySeRSync states that it utilizes (μ)TESLA, it makes some significant changes to the protocol ideas. For example, it changes the concept of the intervals and disclosure delay. Broadcast messages are still signed at one point in time and authenticated later when the key is disclosed, but the context differs slightly. Instead of using equally sized, numbered intervals, TinySeRSync uses long intervals R and short intervals r (compare Fig. 4). To be able to check the timeliness, time synchronization messages are sent exclusively in the short intervals, while key messages are sent only in long intervals. A message passes the security condition if the slave is certain that, at the receive time of the message, the key has not yet been disclosed. To ensure this, the slave simply estimates whether the sending time is within a short interval. It is important to note that, even when receiving a message carrying the global time broadcast, the timeliness is checked against the pairwise synchronized clocks. A global time broadcast is therefore merely a payload propagated throughout the network.

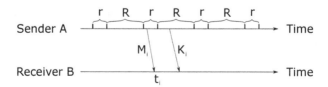

Fig. 4. Illustration of long (R) and short (r) intervals in timeliness validation context

In order to answer Analysis Question 1 (as posed in the beginning of this section), recall that nodes running TinySeRSync have two separate clock values; one describes the clock offset between each two neighbors, while the other describes the clock difference between a node and the base station. The first clock, the offset between two neighbours, is constantly updated via unicast, which is, in the context of our attack vector, immune against attacker-induced delays.

In TinySeRSync, packets are considered timely if the slave estimates that they were sent before the end of the short interval (see Fig. 4 for an illustration). The most decisive feature of TinySeRSync in our context is that the pairwise synchronized clock is used to check timeliness, whereas the global time is not needed and therefore ignored in this part of the validation. The authors describe this technique as *local use* of the (μ)TESLA protocol. Since the pairwise synchronized clock is immune to attacks based on delaying packets from the base station, we expected that TinySeRSync would not be vulnerable to our attack whatsoever. Nonetheless, we set up the experiment with the master and the slave configured as described above, in order to support this expectation in practice. As expected, our attack never worked, since the delays introduced have no cumulative effect.

In conclusion, the significantly altered version of TESLA employed by TinySeRSync does not suffer from vulnerability to the attack proposed. However, it is vulnerable to a related, much simpler attack technique.

Further Security Analysis on TinySeRSync. The TinySeRSync protocol has implemented the idea of reducing the maximum attack delay. It also allows a packet to arrive only in a short part of the interval. However, an oversimplification introduces a conceptional flaw and creates a vulnerability. TinySeRSync changes the notion of TESLA intervals by deploying different (short and long) intervals, but does so without any numbering of the intervals. TinySeRSync's timeliness condition is $t_i - T_0 + \Delta_{A,B} + \delta_{\max} < i(R + r) + r$, where $\Delta_{A,B}$ is the pairwise offset and $\delta_{\max}$ the maximum synchronization uncertainty. This condition ensures that a received message has been sent in a short interval, checking it against the pairwise synchronized clock. The corresponding key of the received message has to be sent and received in the following long interval.

Surveying the timeliness condition, we noticed the lack of any numeration of the intervals. Because of this, the slave can only calculate whether the packet was sent in *a* short interval, but cannot distinguish between different short intervals.

Consider the following attack, for which Fig. 5 provides an illustration. If a packet arrives in a short interval different from the one it was sent in, it will still be accepted as timely. If an attacker delays a packet in such a way that it is late by exactly $r + R$, the timeliness condition will be satisfied, even though the key for that packet has already been disclosed. The security of the protocol is therefore compromised.

We included TinySeRSync's security condition (which is referred to as *pass_secure_time_check* in the TinySeRSync code base) in our implementation and had the MITM successfully insert bogus packets. Hence, attackers with delay capabilities can control a slave's clock almost from the very start of the protocol.

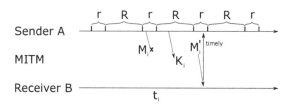

Fig. 5. TinySeRSync's simplified security condition does not differentiate between different intervals other than whether they are short or long. This can be abused.

ASTS. The authors of the ASTS Protocol considered the TinySeRSync protocol to be unnecessarily complex, as it deploys two separate time synchronization mechanisms. Consequently, they introduced a protocol for time synchronization in wireless sensor networks, which is considerably more lightweight and stated to be more accurate [17]. Like the TinySeRSync protocol, it makes use of the (μ)TESLA protocol, but forgoes the secure pair-wise synchronization to achieve its agility. A very simple initial global broadcast is used instead to satisfy the requirement of loose synchronization and to distribute the TESLA parameters. This initial step is executed only once and secured by a single pre-shared key known throughout the network, which is valid only for this first step. Afterwards, the TESLA mechanism as described in [12] is carried out to achieve global time synchronization.

In contrast to TinySeRSync, the ASTS protocol is based on the regular (μ)TESLA protocol with no significant variations. This implies it is likely that the results on ASTS can be generalized to include more generic protocols that employ TESLA-secured one-way synchronization. Most importantly, ASTS has no extra pairwise synchronization with a separate clock mechanism. Only one global clock is adjusted with packets that are broadcasted by the base station. A broadcasted time packet is propagated throughout the network, with each node adding its processing delay to the packet and then rebroadcasting the modified packet to the neighbor nodes. A receiving node calculates the offset to the base station by comparing the arrival time with the packet timestamp under consideration of the processing delay. The local clock is then adjusted by the resulting offset. Therefore, in answer to Question 1, we conclude that the regular clock adjustment process does influence the timeliness validation.

In order to answer Question 2, we examine the timeliness validation of ASTS, which is described in [17] as follows: Assume a node receives a packet at time t_{arrive} in interval i. The latest possible sending time t_{send} of this packet is $t_{\text{arrive}} + \Theta_{\text{max}}$, where Θ_{max} is the difference of the maximum clock difference between the two participants and the maximum network delay of the packet. The protocol suggests using a $\Theta_{\max}$ large enough to be an upper bound of any usual network delay. This value of $\Theta_{\max}$ should still be negligible compared to T_Δ, thus not influencing the following equation. The sending interval can always be calculated as $i_{\text{send}} = \lceil (t_{\text{send}} - T_0)/T_\Delta \rceil$, where T_0 is the interval starting time and T_Δ is the interval length. The timeliness condition is thus: $x < i + d$. A difference of exactly one interval exists between the timeliness of ASTS and original TESLA equations, due to the changed rounding function. This makes ASTS stricter when it comes to validating the timeliness of packets; the time a packet can be delayed by is smaller by one interval length. Given an endpoint delay δ_e, the maximum attack delay δ_{atk} that the MITM can introduce is therefore given by $\delta_{\text{atk}} = T_\Delta(d-1) - (\delta_e + \delta_{\max})$, as shown in Fig. 6. With this knowledge, we can state three dependencies:

Fig. 6. Illustration of the difference between the original TESLA (right) security condition, and the slightly changed version of ASTS (left).

- The maximum delay that can be added is proportional to the interval length.
- The maximum delay that can be added is proportional to the disclosure lag.
- There is a correlation between the maximum clock error $\delta_{\max}$ and the maximum attack delay since increasing $\delta_{\max}$ shortens the time to the next interval.

The authors of ASTS do not specify the way in which the clock is adjusted. We therefore assume, in response to Question 3, that the clock adjustment process is instantaneous, equivalent to *stepping* the clock.

Having answered all of the above questions, we deduce that ASTS is indeed vulnerable to our attack in theory. We conducted a set of experimental attack runs on our implementation in simulation of ASTS to prove this in practice and to evaluate the dependencies stated above. The overall result of the experimental attack runs confirmed that ASTS, as simulated with our implementation, is vulnerable to the attack as specified in [16]. In fact, we concluded that an intelligent attacker carrying out an attack on ASTS would eventually always be successful, regardless of ASTS' exact parameters. Nevertheless, the implications of tuning the different parameters were of great relevance and allowed us valuable insight into potential countermeasures.

4.2 Observations from Test Attack Runs on ASTS

As mentioned earlier, ASTS employs (µ)TESLA protection of one-way time synchronization in such a straightforward way that it is suitable as an example of more generic assessments regarding the security of the scheme. Therefore, many conclusions can be generalized from the data of our attack runs on ASTS, which may thus have implications for ongoing or future specification work.

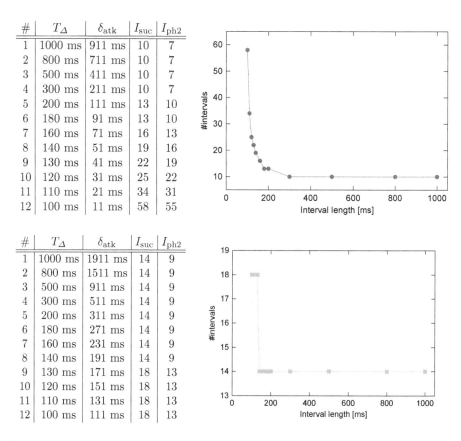

#	T_Δ	δ_{atk}	I_{suc}	I_{ph2}
1	1000 ms	911 ms	10	7
2	800 ms	711 ms	10	7
3	500 ms	411 ms	10	7
4	300 ms	211 ms	10	7
5	200 ms	111 ms	13	10
6	180 ms	91 ms	13	10
7	160 ms	71 ms	16	13
8	140 ms	51 ms	19	16
9	130 ms	41 ms	22	19
10	120 ms	31 ms	25	22
11	110 ms	21 ms	34	31
12	100 ms	11 ms	58	55

#	T_Δ	δ_{atk}	I_{suc}	I_{ph2}
1	1000 ms	1911 ms	14	9
2	800 ms	1511 ms	14	9
3	500 ms	911 ms	14	9
4	300 ms	511 ms	14	9
5	200 ms	311 ms	14	9
6	180 ms	271 ms	14	9
7	160 ms	231 ms	14	9
8	140 ms	191 ms	14	9
9	130 ms	171 ms	18	13
10	120 ms	151 ms	18	13
11	110 ms	131 ms	18	13
12	100 ms	111 ms	18	13

Fig. 7. Data and graphs of attack runs on ASTS with $d = 2$ (top) and $d = 3$ (bottom). Here, T_Δ denotes interval length, δ_{atk} denotes maximum introducable delay per increment, I_{suc} denotes the interval number of the earliest successful attack, and I_{ph2} denotes the interval number of the earliest successful Phase One.

The results of carrying out the experiments with a disclosure delay of $d = 2$ and with $d = 3$ are shown in Fig. 7. In the tables, T_Δ denotes the length of the intervals, δ_{atk} denotes the maximum amount of delay the attacker can introduce with each increment, I_{suc} denotes the number of the earliest interval in which the attack was fully successful, and I_{ph2} denotes the number of the earliest interval after which Phase One of the attack was completed. Note that each of the rows in the tables represents large numbers of successful attacks, from which I_{suc} and I_{ph2} were deduced empirically.

Observations Regarding Duration of the Attack. We have made a few observations regarding the duration of successful attack runs and their implications. These observations have been very helpful in reasoning about countermeasures (see below).

Number of Intervals for Success has Lower Bound. Our first observation was that, given a disclosure delay d, there seemed to be a fixed minimum number of intervals required for the attack to succeed. Investigating further, we have found this to be caused by a combination of the protocol environment and self-inflicted limits of the attacker due to its behavioral model: it takes the next step only when it is sure (from conservative calculations) that the previous step was successful. We also refined an equation to calculate the minimum amount of intervals necessary to successfully carry out the attack (see below).

More than Just Desynchronization. Our second observation is that the desynchronization condition alone is not sufficient. There also needs to be a sufficient amount of time f for the bogus packet to be considered timely. In [16], the need for f was already mentioned, but not quantified. We supply this quantification by demanding that f satisfy the following condition: $f > \delta_{\max} + \delta_e$.

The Role of Endpoint Delay and Uncertainty. The third observation is that the smaller the difference $(\delta_{\max} + \delta_e) - T_{\Delta}$, the more iterations of step 3 are needed. In Fig. 8, we illustrate how the attacker comes closer to the goal with each iteration. If it tried to deliver a bogus packet after three iterations, it would be discarded as being untimely, even though the desynchronization condition is satisfied. Thus, another iteration is needed.

Quantification of Minimum Required Intervals. The experiments with attack runs on ASTS have enabled us to deduce an equation for the earliest interval I_{suc} by which the attack's first phase can have succeeded:

$$I_{\mathrm{suc}} = \left\lceil \frac{T_{\Delta}(d-1) + \delta_{\max} + \delta_e}{\delta_{\mathrm{atk}}} \right\rceil (d+1) + 2d. \tag{1}$$

This represents a refinement over the quantification in [16] due to the ability of our experiments to account for real-world parameters such as $\delta_{\max}$, δ_e, and f.

4.3   Countermeasures and Best Practice

With a few changes to the security condition and the protocol flow, we can successfully mitigate the attack described above. Note that the changes required are significant: complete mitigation comes at the expense of introducing an extra

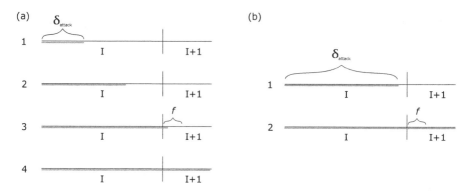

Fig. 8. Visualization of introducing delays during the attack, where f is the amount of time required to forge a bogus packet from intercepted data. In part (a), the delay introduced is small relative to T_Δ; in (b), it is relatively large.

step in the protocol, and this step must involve two-way communication. However, the countermeasures were designed to not negatively affect the quality of the achieved time synchronization, and our experiments have supported our belief that this goal was fulfilled.

Individual Measures. There are two overall building blocks that we examined for their capability to prevent the attack. It turns out that it is only in combination of the two that the attack is fully defended against.

Make the Attack Take Longer. The first general measure is to increase the amount of time required for successful execution of the attack. This can be achieved by combining the following tactics:

- The maximum introducable delay δ_{atk}, should be minimized. For example, one can simply set a limit to the amount of measured offset that is accepted.
- The interval length should be maximized, under the conditions that the synchronization should still work, and that the maximum δ_{atk} should not be increased. One option is to introduce dead space into the intervals where no communication can take place. This would not make sense for most application areas of the TESLA protocol, but does make sense for time synchronization.

Note that such measures alone can only delay the success of Phase One of the attack, not fully prevent it. This brings us to the second general measure.

Introduce a Periodical Synchronization Reset. The second general measure is to introduce a reset to the time synchronization. The protocol must resynchronize via an alternate technique before the time by which the attack can have succeeded. This could be tied to the end of the key chain, for the sake of convenience.

Note that, to provide sufficient guarantees, a reset must entail synchronization via alternative (two-way) communication. Only then can an upper bound be determined for the possible synchronization error. Note that doing this without a good understanding of how long the attack takes to be successful (or with too low an amount in that regard), this measure is wasteful. Any system that largely relies on broadcast probably has good reasons for doing so, and requiring additional two-way communication too often likely defeats the purpose.

Combined Approach. To achieve the goal of completely preventing the attack, the measures described above work only in combination. The first measure gives a guarantee that the protocol is secure up to a given point in time. The second measure ensures that the protocol (including the security guarantee above) is reset before that point in time is reached. From another perspective, the second measure makes the attacker start over with its scheme. The first measure ensures that there is a reasonable point in time to do so. This can neither be too late (which would leave security compromised) nor too early (which would be wasteful of communication resources). Our experiments have suggested that if one of the measures is not taken, or not taken correctly, the attack can always succeed eventually. The converse is also true: in our experiments, if both measures are taken correctly, the attack can never be executed successfully.

4.4   Recommendations for Fixing TinySeRSync and ASTS

From the above, we deduce that in order to fix ASTS' security, one would have to re-introduce a form of pairwise synchronization. Note that this might render stated advantages of ASTS over TinySeRSync invalid.

For TinySeRSync, it seems that the first fix would be to re-introduce the actual numbering of intervals that (μ)TESLA originally prescribes. Given this modification, it seems to us that there would be a reasonable way to combine the two protocol phases (one of which employs two-way time synchronization anyway) to a successful variant of TESLA-protected synchronization.

5   Conclusions

5.1   Summary

We have investigated security issues with the deployment of the TESLA protocol in one-way time synchronization protocols. To this end, we have built an implementation that reflects the security-relevant characteristics of the class of protocols that apply delayed disclosure authentication (e. g. TESLA) to one-way time synchronization. This has enabled us to draw a number of conclusions (presented in Sect. 4), some of which are specific to certain protocols, while others hold generally for the whole class of protocols.

We have conducted a range of tests proving that the attack described in [16] can be executed in a real-world environment with physically distributed devices on a protocol that represents a faithful recreation of ASTS. Furthermore, we have conducted tests proving that TinySeRSync's security measures can be broken, albeit by an attack different from our original concept. Regarding the more general class of protocols, we have supported the theory that, without extra security features beyond those that TESLA provides, the attack can always succeed eventually. In particular, we have reaffirmed our conjecture that the attack cannot be prevented with only one-way communication.

We have also collected a set of countermeasures, some of which can be used to reduce the amount of delay the attacker can introduce, making the attack take longer. In Eq. 1, we quantify the minimum amount of time/intervals the attack will take to execute until packets can be forged at will. With this amount known beforehand, additional countermeasures can be taken early enough that the attack can be completely defeated. However, this still comes with the strict caveat that these additional measures need to involve two-way communication. All of these implementation-based results represent improvements on the work in [16], where the attack was only investigated via model checking.

5.2   Future Work

All relevant in-development or future time synchronization protocol specifications should be analyzed regarding their vulnerability to the attack. It is our hope that the implementation created for this work can support such analyses.

Additionally, further research regarding potential countermeasures would be interesting. Even though we are skeptical of the existence of efficient countermeasures that do not require two-way communication, the value of such a design would be tremendous, especially in environments such as global navigation satellite systems, where communication is designed to be one-way only.

Overall, it should be stated that even with the highlighted issues, we still believe that TESLA is a worthwhile candidate for a protection mechanism for one-way synchronization. Therefore, the next research project we are focusing on are formal proofs of positive statements about the security of TESLA-protected one-way synchronization protocols. Such statements might include that, other than the attack vector described in [16], TESLA-protection of one-way synchronization protocols is secure and/or that TESLA-protection with a given set of added countermeasures overall makes one-way synchronization secure.

Acknowledgment. We would like to express our thanks to Dieter Sibold, for supervising large parts of the work and for valuable input in the creation of this paper.

References

1. Standard for a precision clock synchronization protocol for networked measurement and control systems. https://standards.ieee.org/develop/project/1588.html
2. Annessi, R., Fabini, J., Zseby, T.: It's about time: securing broadcast time synchronization with data origin authentication. In: 2017 26th International Conference on Computer Communication and Networks (ICCCN), pp. 1–11, July 2017. https://doi.org/10.1109/ICCCN.2017.8038418

3. Annessi, R., Fabini, J., Zseby, T.: SecureTime: secure multicast time synchronization. ArXiv e-prints, May 2017
4. Dolev, D., Yao, A.: On the security of public key protocols. IEEE Trans. Inf. Theory **29**(2), 198–208 (1983)
5. Fernandez-Hernandez, I., Rijmen, V., Seco-Granados, G., Sim'on, J., Rodríguez, I., David Calle, J.: A navigation message authentication proposal for the Galileo open service. Navig. J. Inst. Navig. **63**, 85–102 (2016)
6. Hildermeier, G.: Attacking tesla-secured time synchronisation protocols. Master's thesis, September 2017
7. Hildermeier, G.: Testbed implementation for simunlating attacks on tesla-secured time synchronisation protocols, September 2017. https://gitlab1.ptb.de/teiche04/Hildermeier-TESLA-Protected-One-Way-Synchronization.git
8. Levine, J.: A review of time and frequency transfer methods. Metrologia **45**(6), S162–S174 (2008). https://doi.org/10.1088/0026-1394/45/6/S22. <GotoISI>://WOS:000262502900023. http://iopscience.iop.org/0026-1394/45/6/S22/pdf/0026-1394456S22.pdf
9. Mills, D.L.: Internet time synchronization: the network time protocol. IEEE Trans. Commun. **39**(10), 1482–1493 (1991)
10. Perrig, A., Canetti, R., Tygar, J.D., Song, D.: Efficient authentication and signing of multicast streams over lossy channels. In: Proceedings of the 2000 IEEE Symposium on Security and Privacy, S&P 2000, pp. 56–73. IEEE (2000)
11. Perrig, A., Canetti, R., Tygar, J.D., Song, D.: The TESLA broadcast authentication protocol. In: RSA Cryptobytes, vol. 5 (2005)
12. Perrig, A., Szewczyk, R., Tygar, J.D., Wen, V., Culler, D.E.: SPINS: security protocols for sensor networks. Wirel. Netw. **8**(5), 521–534 (2002)
13. Sibold, D., Roettger, S., Teichel, K.: Network Time Security. Internet Draft draft-ietf-ntp-network-time-security-15. Internet Engineering Task Force, September 2016, work in progress. https://datatracker.ietf.org/doc/html/draft-ietf-ntp-network-time-security-15
14. Sibold, D., Roettger, S., Teichel, K.: Using the Network Time Security Specification to Secure the Network Time Protocol. Internet Draft draft-ietf-ntp-using-nts-for-ntp-06. Internet Engineering Task Force, September 2016, work in Progress. https://datatracker.ietf.org/doc/html/draft-ietf-ntp-using-nts-for-ntp-06
15. Sun, K., Ning, P., Wang, C.: TinySeRSync: secure and resilient time synchronization in wireless sensor networks. In: Proceedings of the 13th ACM Conference on Computer and Communications Security, pp. 264–277. ACM (2006)
16. Teichel, K., Sibold, D., Milius, S.: An attack possibility on time synchronization protocols secured with TESLA-like mechanisms. In: Ray, I., Gaur, M.S., Conti, M., Sanghi, D., Kamakoti, V. (eds.) ICISS 2016. LNCS, vol. 10063, pp. 3–22. Springer, Cham (2016). https://doi.org/10.1007/978-3-319-49806-5_1
17. Yin, X., Qi, W., Fu, F.: ASTS: an agile secure time synchronization protocol for wireless sensor networks. In: 2007 International Conference on Wireless Communications, Networking and Mobile Computing, WiCom 2007, pp. 2808–2811. IEEE (2007)

Co-ordinating Developers and High-Risk Users of Privacy-Enhanced Secure Messaging Protocols

Harry Halpin[1]([⊠]), Ksenia Ermoshina[2], and Francesca Musiani[2]

[1] Inria, 2 rue Simone Iff, 75012 Paris, France
`harry.halpin@inria.fr`
[2] Institute for Communication Sciences, CNRS, 20 rue Berbier-du-Mets,
75013 Paris, France

Abstract. Due to the increased deployment of secure messaging protocols, differences between what developers "believe" are the needs of their users and their actual needs can have real consequences. Based on 90 interviews with both high and low-risk users, as well as the developers of popular secure messaging applications, we mapped the design choices of the protocols made by developers to the relevance of these features to threat models of both high-risk and low-risk users. Client device seizures are considered more dangerous than compromised servers by high-risk users. Key verification was important to high-risk users, but they often did not engage in cryptographic key verification, instead using other "out of band" means for key verification. High-risk users, unlike low-risk users, needed pseudonyms and were heavily concerned over metadata collection. Developers tended to value open standards, open-source, and decentralization, but high-risk users found these aspects less urgent given their more pressing concerns.

1 Introduction

The last few years have seen the spread of wide variety of secure messaging applications, and increased interest in these applications due to generalized concerns around privacy and security, caused in part due to the 2013 Snowden revelations. As put by previous work [2], currently developers imagine what properties users likely need, and these properties may or may not actually satisfy the needs of end-users. The first large-scale user study of secure messaging has shown that users are fundamentally confused around secure messaging in particular and how encryption works in general [1]. However, one trenchant criticism of this study is that it does not deal with *high-risk* users who are motivated to learn about encryption. High-risk users may care about very different properties than low-risk users in terms of their threat models. For example, most secure messaging properties do not hide the user identity, with applications like Signal exposing valuable information via associating users with their phone number despite concerns from high-risk users. If developers themselves are relatively low-risk

© Springer Nature Switzerland AG 2018
C. Cremers and A. Lehmann (Eds.): SSR 2018, LNCS 11322, pp. 56–75, 2018.
https://doi.org/10.1007/978-3-030-04762-7_4

users and building tools aimed at high-risk users, then the tools may or may not match the needs of these high-risk users. Furthermore, standards may be biased against high-risk users, as many high-risk users cannot easily participate in standardization discussions, and their interests tend to be represented by developers who may or may not have an accurate understanding of their threat model. Although the vast majority of applications are converging to the "de-facto" Signal Protocol, developers still are still in a state of flux over what the security and privacy properties of secure messaging *should* be due to the lack of a single widespread standard (in contrast to the TLS link layer protocol for client-server encryption) [8]. Also, the newly started IETF Messaging Layer Security (MLS) effort provides an opportunity to finally produce a coherent security standard for secure messaging.[1] We hypothesize that there can be a disconnect when existing applications are developed primarily with the threat models of the developers themselves in mind rather than those of high-risk users, which is understandable given how difficult it is for developers to contact high-risk users. Also, there are also many properties outside of security and privacy that are important to users, such as decentralization, standardization, and licensing. In this study, the properties we investigate are classified into six broad categories: (1) Security Properties, (2) Group Support, (3) Privacy Properties, (4) Decentralization, (5) Standardization, and (6) Licensing.

Although many usable security studies call for end-users to be helped by developers [9], it should not be forgotten that developers can be helped in building new tools by input from user studies [3]. If the lesson from usable security research on secure messaging is that users are fundamentally confused and do not even believe that encryption can defend the confidentiality of their messages, the entire endeavor of creating secure messaging applications may seem futile [1]. Yet one problem with the results of this previous work and other usable security studies is their sample: Low-risk users will likely not have a clear threat model and invest time into understanding how their threat model maps to the properties of applications. Our research contribution is that we demonstrate high-risk users actually do care about the properties of secure messaging applications. By detailing what properties concern these users, we provide valuable feedback to the developer community. This work is the first to do such a study that balances high-risk users, low-risk users, and developers themselves. Our previous qualitative study focused on less than 50 users [2]. The results presented here extend and deepen those results, and they directly contrast and even contradict the results given in the largest quantitative study of 80 low-risk users [1]. We first state our theses, generated after our first study [2] but before the additional interviews given in this study, in Sect. 2. Our qualitative methodology is explained in Sect. 3, with the interviews being delved into in Sect. 4. Finally, we explore the results and future work in Sect. 5.

---

[1] https://datatracker.ietf.org/wg/mls/about/.

2   Problem Statement

Our first thesis is the ***Developer-User Disconnect:*** We hypothesize that *the properties desired by developers are not necessarily desired, or even understood, by users.* The core of the problem is the methodology currently used in the developer community to design protocols, where developers of secure messaging applications hypothesize what properties a protocol should have based on their beliefs about users. These properties may or may not line up with the expectations of users, and therefore the goal of our project is to determine the properties developers believe are important and see if these properties match the properties wanted by users. Though some attempts are made to gather and analyze user experience via online feedback forms and rare offline workshops (observed at international events such as CCC, IFF or RightsCon), contact between high-risk users and developers seems minimal. Such feedback can be produced by tech-savvy high-risk users willing to contribute in co-developing free and open-source projects, although high-risk users are of course often engaged in more pressing issues at hand than dealing with bug reports. Users and developers need to converge in order to harmonize the needs of users with the concrete design decisions made by protocol designers.

Our second thesis is the ***High-Risk User Problem:*** We hypothesize that *high-risk users have different needs and behavior than low-risk users.* Although seemingly obvious, in most studies of end-to-end encrypted messaging, the features and problems users encounter may not be representative of actual end-users as the user base that is often studied in usability experiments in the United States and Western Europe are usually a rather homogeneous selection of students from a low-risk background [1]. Although it can be claimed that all users are to some extent "high-risk" potentially, we would argue that it is sensible to divide users between those *high-risk users* who can in the short-term suffer concrete physical harms such as long-term imprisonment and torture as a result of information security, and those *low-risk users* who do not have immediate consequences due to failures in information security. As put by one user, "We did not have any concerns about security, but then people started disappearing" (H13). High-risk users tend to be located in geopolitical areas where information security is important due to political instability, although well-known activists and persecuted minorities in "stable" countries would count as high-risk users. We hypothesize that high-risk users have different threat models and so different requirements for privacy and secure messaging. Note that this thesis dovetails with the *Developer-User Disconnect Problem*: as most developers are not high-risk users themselves, they imagine the threat model of high-risk users as well as the feature set they may desire and what trade-offs are reasonable, but these projections of the needs of high-risk users could easily be inaccurate.

3   Methodology

Our study combines quantitative methods from usability studies with a qualitative approach based on Science and Technology Studies (STS), trying to follow how developers create a technical artifact based on their motivations and how those – with varying degree of success – attempt to map to the needs of real users [5]. Ethnographic work consists of interviews, typically done in the organic environment of those interviewed, which test particular scientific hypotheses and assumptions. These questions should attempt to elucidate a phenomenon so that a model with some explanatory power can be built of the mental model of those interviewed. Interviews should ideally be cross-cultural and large enough so that the results generalize to some extent.

Note that due to the vast differences in context between developers and users, achieving "representativeness" in the present study is extremely problematic and therefore not a goal. In this regard, while previous studies looked at either a selection of primarily students in London [1] or (our own previous) work on a small subset of "radical" developers (Briar) in contrast to high-risk users in Russia [2], we have expanded the user studies to deal with interviews with corporate developers at corporations as well as high-risk users in places such as Syria (in detail, the Kurdish area of Rojava). This leads to a much more diverse spread of what we term "risk" than previous works. Thus, we continue to distinguish users as either *high-risk* or *low-risk*, based on whether or not the failure to encrypt their messages or other metadata leakage by a secure messaging tools could realistically endanger the user or the person they were communicating with (for example, a situation where the misuse of secure messaging would likely lead to death due to conditions of war or high prison sentences due to participation in a protest). In this regard, we would take a user "at their word" in their subjective reporting if they described the repercussions of their failing to send messages securely.

3.1 Interview Selection Process

Interview subjects were either developers or users. Developers were selected due to pre-existing social relationships with the larger academic community. Although this does create bias, this can be normalized to some extent by doing a large number of interviews as well as taking into account the relatively small size of the global developer community of secure messaging applications. For developers of applications where there was no social relationship, we reached these developers via their GitHub pages. Some developers were selected due to their attendance at conferences such as Real World Crypto in Zurich in January 2018. Interviewed users were selected individuals based on either their attendance at training events in their local environments (both high-risk, in the case of Tunisia and Ukraine, and low-risk in the case of the United States and France) or at conference venues that were likely to attract high-risk users living in regions that, due to the level of repression, made it difficult if not impossible to interview them in their native environment, or would make it such that they could not speak openly in their native environment due to repression. This was the case for users from Egypt, Turkey, Kenya, Iran, where the interviews took place in March 2017 at the Internet Freedom Festival and at RightsCon 2017, as well as in person if possible. All interviews were made between Fall 2016 and Spring

2018, for a total of 90 interviews. We interviewed (30) developers, including developers from LEAP, Pixelated, and Mailpile (PGP), ChatSecure and Ricochet (OTR), Signal, Wire and Conversations (OMEMO) as well as developers from Briar that use their own custom protocol and developers from Microsoft, Facebook, and Google working on security.

As noted earlier, we distinguish between high-risk users (30) and users (including researchers and students) from low-risk countries (30). Note that low-risk users were not randomly selected and so were far from ordinary users, and so were biased towards possessing high knowledge of secure messaging they attended training events or worked in the corporate information security sector. All low-risk users were from the USA/Western Europe. High-risk users included users from Ukraine, Russia, Syria, Lebanon, Egypt, and Iran but also users from countries in Europe (4) that are or were under considerable legal pressure and surveillance due to ongoing court cases. Some high-risk users, due to the conditions in their country, had left (4) or maintained dual residency (2) between their high-risk environment and a low-risk environment. Again, we do not claim that these high-risk users are a "representative" sample, but that the sample should be large enough to demonstrate considerable differences between at-risk users and those that do not think of themselves as particularly at risk. Some of those interviewed (18%) considered themselves "trainers," i.e. people that train others in using secure messaging tools.

3.2 Interview Procedure

Our interviews were conduct using a protocol designed approved by an external Ethics Advisor to be compliant with the European General Data Protection Framework. The forms and full set of precise questions are available online.[2] Given the risk of many users, we took whatever steps the interviewees deemed necessary to protect their privacy. High-risk users did read and consent, but copies of the form were not kept if they wished to remain anonymized without a record. Interviews were done in person or online. If the interview was done online, we allowed the users to use a tool of communication of their choice, and so some interviews were done via secure messaging tools such as PGP and Signal as well as insecure means such as Skype and e-mail. If the interview was done in person, the interview was recorded with an audio recorder with no Internet connection if the interviewee approved, otherwise written notes were taken by hand. Interviews were typically done in English, although they were done in the native language of the speaker if the interviewer could speak the language fluently. We use a dedicated encrypted hard-drive to store the interviews. Before the interview we asked our respondents to carefully read the Information Sheet and the related Informed Consent form and ask any questions regarding the privacy of their interview, their rights over their data, and our methodology. The name of the interviewee was not mentioned during the recording and withdrew any context (such as the country or the city, the precise social movement a user

---

[2] http://www.ibiblio.org/hhalpin/homepage/forms.zip.

was involved in, and so on) if the interviewee asked for this. Interviewees did not have to answer any specific question that they felt uncomfortable answering.

We interviewed 90 people in total, composed of 30 low-risk users as in France, Belgium, the United Kingdom, and the United States; 30 high-risk activists and journalists in Syria, Tunisia, Iran, Egypt, Russia, and Ukraine; and finally 30 developers of applications such as Wire, Briar, Signal, ChatSecure, OTR, and developers at large companies including Google, Microsoft, Facebook, and Paypal. The age of those interviewed varied widely between late teens to over fifty, with the majority of users being in their mid-twenties to early thirties. Developers considered developing secure messaging applications as their main job. Low-risk users and high-risk users had a wide variety of jobs, but were all explicitly interested in secure messaging. The researcher who did the interviews attempted to summarize each of them using a manual coding scheme. The questions used allowed large amounts of free form discussion, and coding often ignores much of these nuances; thus, in the results, actual quotes are often used. When referring to high-risk users, we use the letter "H" and a number, for low-risk users we use the letter "L" and a number, and for developers we use the letter "D" and a number.

4   Interviews

The results of the interviews are presented in this section. For each category of questions, representative quotes have been chosen. The results of the interviews are summarized on a high-level in Table 1. Note that the categories 'high' and 'low' were classified with a strict equal or greater than 50% threshold in terms of importance. If a user did not mention or did not know about a certain property, it was considered to be not important (except in the case of "main threat"). Note that our statistics should not be taken without some variance, and are meant to be used as a general summary. In particular, we do not claim that interview sample size is necessarily representative of a larger homogeneous population, likely due to geographical and cultural variance (for example, there were no interviews with Chinese high-risk users). Nonetheless, the regularities that appear in our interviews should be useful to developers of privacy-enhancing technologies and security standards. The developers of secure messaging applications often put themselves "in the shoes" of high-risk users but naturally have difficulty of arranging interviews with high-risk users themselves.

4.1   Developer Motivation

Developer motivation was quite wide-ranging, but largely could be divided between those who wanted to start privacy-enhanced businesses that would serve both low and high-risk users, to those who were primarily motivated by protecting high-risk users due to human rights concerns that are more traditionally dealt with by the NGO sector. In the case of Wire, the developers felt that they were addressing issues that they had neglected in the original design of Skype,

Table 1. Importance of properties in secure messaging interviews

Interview	Developers	Low-risk users	High-risk users
Main threat	Server (60%)	Server (73%)	Client (60%)
Security (Key verification)	High (53%)	Low (20%)	High (53%)
Security (Ephemeral messaging)	High (83%)	High (83%)	High (90%)
Privacy (Metadata collection)	High (73%)	High (60%)	High (93%)
Privacy (Pseudonymity)	High (53%)	Low (43%)	High (93%)
Group support	High (86%)	High (96%)	High (96%)
Decentralization	High (86%)	High (70%)	Low (43%)
Standardization	High (70%)	High (50%)	Low (40%)
Open licensing	High (70%)	High (60%)	Low (46%)

as "after Skype was sold to Microsoft [they] had an idea of how to build a new Skype...or what Skype should look like 15 years after. One of the biggest gaps that was missing on the market was related to privacy and security." Nonetheless, they had very limited contact with high-risk activists and stated that the application was developed "mainly for private usage" by individuals, leading to some technical limitations such as group chat only supporting up to 128 users that made it unusable for large-scale social movement organizational purposes. However, the goal of Wire was ultimately not to serve high-risk activists, despite its popularity with high-risk activists due to not requiring a phone number like Signal, but to provide secure business communications (D7).

On the other hand, although Briar has very little use from high-risk activists (no users, although two developer users), the entire concept was inspired by inquiries from high-risk activists asking "if LimeWire would be suitable for communication" and that although the developer of Briar (who worked at LimeWire at the time) felt "that it may be suitable ... we can build something suitable on a more social basis," which in turn led to the development of Briar (Michael Rogers, D6). Likewise, the developers of Signal aimed first at high-risk activists, and unlike, Briar have managed to capture a large cross-section of high-risk activists (88%). In fact, the primary group that did not use Signal was developers who were building competing projects and low-risk users who disagreed with its centralization.

From our survey, it appears that more developers in projects are motivated by serving the security and privacy needs of high-risk activists than forming a successful business, although Wire, Matrix, Apple, Microsoft, and Telegram are motivated by business use-cases. Yet strangely, developers from systems aimed at high-risk users (Signal, ChatSecure, Briar) have little actual contact with high-risk users in their systems and were, at least in the case of ChatSecure, surprised by how many high-risk users actually started using their software.

4.2   High-Risk vs. Low-Risk Users

Developers tended to distinguish between low-risk users who are "privacy-aware" and high-risk users such as human rights activists in war-zones. High-risk users, unlike low-risk users as interviewed in earlier studies [1], have a well-defined threat model typically focused on active attacks and client device seizures (60% were more concerned by the latter), but were not certain of the extent to which they were protected by secure messaging applications. However, low-risk users had an implicit threat-model with a focus on passive traffic monitoring and server seizure (73% were more concerned with the server being attacked or monitored than client device seizure, and the rest could not decide). Almost all users had tried PGP (93%) but its average use was weekly or rarely (with a substantial group of users giving up on its usage after attempting to use it), while all users except one[3] found themselves using secure messaging daily.

As has been observed among our interviews, in more high-risk geolocations, the choice of secure messaging application can be due to the politics of its country of origin. For example, in Ukraine, high-risk activists exclude applications and online services that have servers on the territory of Russian Federation or Ukraine and prefer American-based services, with even trainers advocating usages of Gmail and Facebook. Similar dynamics were observed in Iran (with no adoption of PGP and strong preference for Gmail with two-factor authentication), and Egypt, where WhatsApp is popular as the United States is considered as not being part of the threat model. For example, "Iranians use Google and Gmail a lot, they do not care about NSA spying on them, they care about Iranian government not having access to the data. We use Google Drive to upload our personal photos for example. For us the entire motto of 'Use Signal, Use Tor' does not make sense. As soon as the servers are inaccessible for the [Iranian] government, it can be used" (H14).

Indeed, high-risk users noted that their threat model changed over time, as most Tunisian high-risk users we interviewed became less frequent users of PGP and other secure messaging tools after their 2011 revolution, even though some of them were concerned that "surveillance powers were going to be used again soon against us" (H18). As opposed to key verification where their technical grasp of the cryptographic mechanics was often shaky, interviewed high-risk users had well-conceived and often thoughtful threat models based on geopolitics, but varied in a country-specific manner in terms of application preference. Unlike low-risk users who were primarily concerned about corporate or NSA surveillance, high-risk users were more concerned by surveillance from their own nation state, and could accurately assess the geopolitical origin of messaging systems. For example, apparently, Viber had been very popular in the Middle East, until it was discovered it was created by a company based in Israel, and then its usage "declined quickly" among high-risk users (H17).

---

[3] A developer that used only PGP and IRC.

4.3   Security Properties

The main advantage of OTR and Signal-style protocols is that key management is no longer a barrier to entry, and this appeals even to high-risk users. Trainers often found it too difficult to teach even high-risk users the precise security properties of key management, noting that "some trainers think there should be no key discovery at all, it is better to have opportunistic or automatic key discovery as it is happening with Signal. Different encrypted messaging apps have popped up that made it a lot easier to have just an app that will pass on your communication, and the encryption part will be transparent to the user. Having encryption as a default mode is the key part in making encryption popular" (L14). The vast majority of users preferred not having to do key management. The situation got worse as the risk of the situation became worse. Although the YPG in Syria still use PGP, H1 noted that "Every single person needed walking through the steps, when you have a bunch of soldiers who don't even know how to use a computer, they have to install an email client, generate entropy. People would right the wrong email address. People would encrypt the email for their [own] PGP key. They would send me their private key. It was an absolute nightmare" (H1). Yet many high-risk users wanted some form of key verification and out-of-band authentication, even if it was hard to use in practice and they did not use it regularly. Both high-risk and low-risk users insisted on the importance that they could "see encryption happening" in the interface.

Due to their concern with active attacks, high-risk users often try to verify keys (53%) after they receive a notification that the key has been changed in Signal, WhatsApp, Wire or other applications while only (20%) of low-risk users do. High-risk users are afraid that the devices of their friends have been physically accessed, stolen or otherwise taken away by powerful adversaries willing to use physical force and subterfuge to access contacts lists. Yet high-risk users tend to confound device seizure with key material being changed, and do not realize that if a device was seized an adversary could continue communicating using the seized key material. Some do realize this possibility but then try to ascertain the identity of their contacts using out-of-band channels: "If I get a message from Signal for example, saying that my contact's device has changed or his fingerprints changed ... I normally try to get in touch with the person ... I need to hear the voice" (H11). A subset of high-risk users do verify keys on first communication, and check the authenticity of a person if the key material changes informally using context: "I verify keys in PGP, but...I verify the person by other means... we speak about same things. In Jabber also I often just do it manually, without shared secret. But I always check if I receive something warnings about the person's device" (H4). Developers do tend to verify keys, and it seems to be related to habits gained in software development. As shown by previous work, key verification is hard to both understand and use [6].

The most noticeable difference between low-risk users and high-risk users was the targeted and device-centric nature of the threat model of most high-risk users. As device seizure was a primary concern, ephemeral messages were viewed as a required feature for almost all high-risk users (93%). It was also viewed as important by most low-risk users (83%) due to privacy concerns, and some developers were against this feature (17%) as it was felt users may be "tricked" into thinking a message has been deleted from a server when it has not. Furthermore, while developers and low-risk users preferred key material to be stored on a local client device, high-risk users almost always preferred their key material to be stored in an (extra-jurisdictional) server and for them to have the ability to delete their existing device or reinstall quickly on a new device. As noted by H16, "When I cross the airport, I delete all my messages and I export my contacts, then I put them on my laptop, and I delete my contacts from my phone. I use plausible encryption to hide them [the contacts on the laptop]. I use Veracrypt." Plausible deniability became very important to high-risk users in case of device seizure, where it was important to be able to give police authorities access to a clean device or have a second encrypted volume on their device. The fear of Google and the NSA storing large amounts of data for later decryption or data analysis in the long-term is viewed as more of a problem by low-risk users, as this problem does not have immediate consequences for many high-risk users. Instead, their "real risks are house searches, seizing of devices" (H13).

4.4   Privacy Properties

Many developers found increasing privacy through minimizing metadata collection to be the second most important feature (73%) after end-to-end encryption: "End-to-end encryption is a first step. But besides there is a whole new dynamics that needs to happen that's related to all of the metadata and what is it used for" (D14). Yet many developers confused the possibility of a third-party adversary monitoring their communication and so collecting metadata with whether they as developers personally collected data, as exemplified by one developer that stated simply "I do not have anything in my code that would let me know how many people are watching the app right now" (D4). However, many developers also believed they would have to collect some metadata in order to interoperate with features such as push notifications of arriving messages, but they try to limit the harm: "With introducing the push messaging it's the first time we're exposed to possible metadata. But we don't log anything, we don't know who is talking to who, we don't log any information" (D7). Most developers who were aware of third-party data collection and surveillance in general were supportive of using Tor and on disabling the collection of phone numbers in particular, but lacked a comprehensive plan to minimize the collection of data.

All users wanted better privacy in terms of anonymity (defined in terms of unlinkability to their identity due to lack of metadata collection) in secure messaging, and high-risk users found it exceptionally urgent (93%) compared to low-risk users (60%). The same high-risk user (H1) that wanted to get rid of the attachment of identity to phone numbers noted that removing phone number identifiers "introduces a whole new set of problems such as spam and fake addresses." High-risk and low-risk users generally supported reducing data collection and increasing privacy, although often users assumed the encryption of data to hide metadata. A user that had been active in Syria noted that "Turkey is definitely spying on communication, it's really bad I can't use Signal over Tor ... I was always using Tor on my phone, but then I had to switch it off as it would randomly stop working ... I wish I could buy a tablet, and then my device wouldn't be tracked, and I could make Signal calls with normal internet" over Tor (H16). Ukrainian users mentioned social networks such as Vkontakte and Facebook as the main source for de-anonymizing users and insisted on a need of changing privacy settings to allow their friend lists to be more privacy-enhanced and not reveal phone numbers or other personal data in the case of device seizure.

Developers and information security trainers underlined the urgency to find a reliable solution to protecting personal data such as phone numbers in secure messaging applications, as nothing in the field of end-to-end encrypted instant messaging apps offers excellent privacy properties: "Metadata connects you weirdly with other people, and there's more sense in the metadata than in the data itself for technological reasons [...] No one from the messaging apps is trying to solve that. Instead they suggest to sync your address books so they know exactly who you're talking to even though you trust them to somehow make it into hashes or whatever. That's the issue we are not solving with the apps, we make it worse. We now have centralized servers that become honeypots, and it's not about the data, it's about the metadata" as put by Peter Sunde of Heml.is (D9). Developers and trainers associated the leaking of metadata with centralization, although it should be noted that decentralization can just as easily and perhaps more easily leak metadata [7].

4.5 Pseudonyms

The most controversial of security properties is repudiation. Some developers (OTR, Signal, Wire, Briar) believed that a protocol with repudiation (plausible deniability) should be required in secure messaging applications so that a transcript of a chat could not be provably linked cryptographically to the key material of a user in a manner the user could not deny. Post-PGP protocols such as Signal and OTR are defined not to include authentication using traditional non-repudiable cryptographic signatures, but accomplish authentication via other means. In some versions of Signal and OTR, in order to obtain both non-repudiation and 'future secrecy,' Diffie-Hellman key exchanges are combined with key ratchets, but this leads to impersonation attacks due to lack of authentication [4]. Indeed, some form of verification of the user-level authentication was in general viewed as an important feature by high-risk users, as explored earlier in Sect. 4.2.

The social and cryptographic uses of plausible deniability should be separated, as many high-risk activists had clear use-cases for temporary identities and concerns over transcripts being seized. Repudiation is when it can not be proven that any given message *cryptographically* came from a particular user or from an unknown third-party. OTR even went as far as to use malleable encryption to enforce this property. Yet it is unclear if such a cryptographic technical construction would ever lead to plea of plausible deniability being accepted in a legal court (including the infamous use of OTR by Chelsea Manning to communicate with Adrian Lamo, where the logs of the chat were used to convict Manning regardless of repudiation). No high-risk users were aware of any examples where cryptographic deniability was used in actual court cases, as usually the social context and other circumstantial evidence was enough to determine if a user was involved in a conversation.

However, there are many cases where high-risk users wanted plausible deniability on the application level via pseudonyms that could not be linked easily via social context. Their use cases were all related to creating a new identifier and so chat transcripts would be attached to a new and possibly temporary identifier with its own cryptographic keys. Most (93%) high-risk users wanted some ability to set up temporary pseudonymous accounts, and were disappointed with the lack of such accounts on secure messaging applications, which in turn forced them to use shared e-mail inboxes on servers like *riseup.net*, temporary accounts on corporate email servers using GPG, or temporary XMPP+OTR accounts. In contrast, low-risk users did not in general need multiple short-term pseudonymous identities (only 43%). One Russian high-risk user used so-called "one-time secrets" to share information via accessing specific websites via Tor Hidden Services as this offered a possibility to send and receive unique self-destroying messages (H9).

4.6   Group Support

Most (96%) users (regardless of their risk level) wanted support for group messaging, although a substantial minority of developers (14%) were against it due to the problems group messaging would cause for security. Developers of secure messaging apps perceive group support as one of the main challenges, and both high-risk and low-risk users we interviewed wanted some form of group chat. Group size varied dramatically from 2 to 600, but in general the groups wanted by both high-risk and low-risk users tended to have around 25 members. Developing group chats in peer-to-peer systems "is both an important usability feature and a scientific problem" (D11). Yet who has the right to invite and ban participants of a group chat? While Signal, Wire, and Telegram offer the possibility that any member can invite new participants, while Briar puts forward a design "where only the creator of the group has a right to invite and ban participants" as it leads to better "anonymity," although "it leads to a certain centralization within a distributed system" (D6). Group management ends up being important: Russian users had a group chat compromised when members were arrested and their phones seized, but there was no ability to remove the compromised accounts and many users did not realize that the police could be reading their secure group messages until it was too late. Overall, high-risk users and low-risk users were evenly split on whether or not a system should have an administrator deciding who was in the group, while low-risk users wanted archives (65%) and high-risk tended to be against archiving old messages of a group (78%), primarily due to legal concerns.

Another open research and practical challenge is hiding the social graph of participants of the group chat. Developers we interviewed proposed different solutions to this problem. In Briar, every new member of a group chat is only connected with the creator of the group, who is by default the administrator. In contrast, Wire opted for a solution to analyze contact networks of users and to suggest new contacts to users based on this analysis. This data-mining of contacts was criticized heavily by both trainers and the security community as revealing metadata, which would be dangerous to high-risk users, and led one high-risk user to say "I'd rather not use Wire due to that feature, as I'm sure there's at least one [undercover] agent in my contact list and no way can he get the user names of my friends" (H16). Both high-risk and low-risk users also used different applications for different group purposes, with both high and low-risk users tending to use group chat on Facebook Messenger for their work or public life, while preferring WhatsApp or Signal group chat for communications that they considered private. Hiding the metadata of group connections often to strange choices of applications, such as the usage of Crypto.cat in Ukraine despite its security flaws. Many European low-risk activists are under the impression that Telegram has better security and privacy in their group chats than WhatsApp due to mistrust of Facebook, despite this not being the case [4].

4.7   Decentralization

While centralized projects such as Telegram, Signal, or Wire prevail on the market and have large user-bases, developers (86%) and low-risk users (70%) were more enthusiastic about decentralization than high-risk users (43%). Even though they agree on the fact that decentralized systems are harder to design, their motivation to work on decentralized systems was grounded in both the political and technical aspects of decentralization. Politically, decentralization offers 'empowerment' to the user, as it gives users a means to 'control' their own data and developers believe it enables better metadata protection: "You're still not owning your data, all the metadata is controlled by a centralized system, they know all your contacts, who you're messaging at what time. I want people to run their own infrastructure" (L3). Some developers believed the choice of decentralization is inherently connected to not collecting metadata, and felt that models existed which were usable and decentralized: "With Signal it's impossible to create a decentralized system because phone numbers aren't decentralized. With XMPP it's like an email address. Even users who aren't technologically savvy can understand this is my user ID, and this is my server" (D3). Developers involved into production of decentralized protocols noticed that the market reality of secure messaging makes both federated and distributed projects less privileged in terms of financial investments than centralized projects: "It is more challenging to build federated systems because you have to coordinate with other implementers, but also the real problem is the funding! People work on XMPP clients in their free time, so it is not as perfect as a centralized system with proper funding" (D13).

Unlike developers and low-risk users, many high-risk users did not bring up the need for decentralization explicitly and were more interested in getting better software immediately. However, high-risk users did bring it up implicitly in how they formed trust relationships. Decentralization is seen both as technical challenge and social experiment, as it provides infrastructure for specific communities to organize with less dependency on intermediaries. In this sense, developers, high-risk users, and trainers tend to build associations between political organization and technical infrastructure. For example, some developers and trainers justified decentralization as mirroring the organization of anti-authoritarian social movements. In terms of choice, there was a preference for systems that were considered trustworthy politically by high-risk users. These high-risk users expressed concerns about centralized systems collecting their metadata and delivering that metadata to their local adversary, although few realized this would be possible in most decentralized systems as well, albeit in a distributed form [7].

4.8   Standardization

High-risk users tend ed not prioritize the use of open standards (only 40% supported), although low-risk – and almost all corporate users – were concerned (50%). In stark contrast, most developers (70%) care deeply about standards, as they felt standards were "something they would eventually be working on" (D11). Yet there was widespread discontent with existing standards bodies, as the "XMPP community is very conservative" (D13) and "the IETF is not the same beast it was in the early days" (D8). Instead, most developers shared the philosophy that they would build the application first, and then focus on standardization and decentralization via the use of open standards at a later date. In the case of secure messaging, it was still felt that more development was needed on the code and standardization would only slow down existing development efforts. Developers adopted the Signal Protocol because they felt it was the best design available, even if it was not fully standardized and they had to re-code it.

Tensions between centralization and decentralization go hand-in-hand with debates over standards in online debates within developer community. A well-known argument in favor of centralization and against standards was published by Moxie Marlinspike (Signal core developer) in his blog.[4] This blog-post, called "The eco-system is moving," has attracted considerable attention and is widely quoted by developers as a reason not to use standards, as centralization offers better control while federation can be "dangerous" in terms of security (D11), as it is hard to audit all the different implementations of the protocol and ensure correct updates. Developers from PGP, XMPP, and other protocols (Briar, Ricochet, etc.) strongly oppose this critique from Signal in their own blog-posts.[5] For example, one XMPP developer working on encryption states that the "extensibility of XMPP is not a danger in itself. A good extension will spread naturally.

---

[4] https://whispersystems.org/blog/the-ecosystem-is-moving/.
[5] https://gultsch.de/objection.html.

Moreover, there's a permanent incentive to innovate in XMPP" (D13). This has led developers in certain communities to try to standardize a version of the Signal Protocol, the OMEMO standard, in the XMPP Foundation. Signal developers are concerned about the technical competence of having third-party developers standardize their protocol. Corporate developers shared this concern, and have started their own Messaging Layer Security Working Group at the IETF in order to avoid licensing issues around the Signal Protocol and create better support for secure group messaging (see footnote 1).

In terms of PGP, developers from encrypted e-mail providers such as *riseup.net* and community efforts by PGP client developers such as "Autocrypt"[6] are working on running code first so that, in the future, PGP standards can be extended to have properties such as authentication and easier key management, but they see fixing the standards as a far-off long-term goal that is "way off in the distance future" (D8). In contrast, corporate users and developers uniformly feel standards are of utmost importance for deployment. As noted by Brian LaMacchia, Microsoft "actively participates in many standardization organizations such as IETF and W3C. We also have to play in certain national standards bodies" and that standards were necessary as "early standards in crypto were set by private companies that had fundamental patents...that hindered development."

4.9   Licensing

Viewpoints on licensing varied, although most developers (70%) preferred open-source licensing due to the ability to alter and copy code. Developers found the GPL frustrating in terms of the Signal Protocol and its lack of a standard, as it prevented the integration of their application with platforms like the Apple App-Store or in their corporate eco-system, and hoped to use the same basic protocol but under a more permissive license. As stated by a Wire developer, "The Signal Protocol is open source under the GPL that means you can't integrate it into a commercial product and that's why Whisper Systems were getting large licensing agreements from Facebook and Google and WhatsApp to integrate without opening up all of their source code" (D13). Developers, even for companies that support closed-source software, tended to support open source as a necessary compliment to open standards, noting that "Open standards people get together and agree on specifications and the specification is freely available and there's no blocking intellectual properties" but "open source provide a couple of benefits: easy to test and debug interoperability, and if you make reference then anyone can download and start to use it....In crypto, it's really important you make open implementations because it's the way people audit the code to make sure people don't have backdoors or privacy-violations." GPL usage was viewed as an often vital lifestyle choice by low-risk users (60%): "If I don't like mainstream in media, if I don't like mainstream in music – why would I like mainstream on my computer?" (L2). High-risk users were concerned over metadata leaking by

---

[6] https://autocrypt.org/.

having to pay for applications and many did not have funds to purchase proprietary applications, and a few low-risk users preferred closed-source commercial platforms with a commitment to privacy, like Threema, and were happy to have to pay for services.

Unlike low-risk users studied in previous work [1], some high-risk users understood that open-source was necessary for trust even if they mostly did not view it as important (46%) as a working program: "All security experts whom I trust all use Signal, and we must use something that is secure and easy-going and that we can use all together so we decided to use that and we just hope it is safe. I think they looked at the source code, I did not but I have to trust them" (H15). Low-risk users tended to be more strict about licensing. High-risk users who are trainers recognized that an easy-to-use interface with cutting-edge features (including new emojis) mattered: "You can say OK we verified this application, it's legit, it does what it says. But the user interface part is key in reaching the audience. Features, looking nice, easy to use. This is what you need to have success with users" (H14). Rather than look at code themselves, high-risk relied on 'word-of-mouth' from other high-risk users in terms of code quality. No low-risk or high-risk user mentioned formal verification or academic peer review as a criteria for adopting protocols.

5   Results

In order to design protocols appropriately, the intentions and needs of users need to be brought into greater co-ordination with those of developers. However, this is not as trivial as there are distinct classes of users, ranging from high-risk and low-risk users. In addition, a subset of both high-risk and low-risk users end up being trainers that train other users. Although we did not have time to thoroughly explore the entire space of possible levels of risks and levels, it does appear high-risk and low-risk users have very different threat models, with high-risk users generally being concerned over physical device compromise and targeted active attacks on their person with low-risk users being more concerned over passive attacks and server-seizures. High-risk users defined their threat model against a local active adversary, often the police or secret agencies of their government or a nearby hostile government, rather than a global passive adversary such as the NSA. In contrast, developers usually view their threat model as the NSA, a global powerful adversary, despite the lack of attention to privacy properties like metadata collection in secure messaging protocols. While developers created their applications for high-risk users, they were in general concerned mostly with the particulars of messaging protocols, and not threats such as device seizures, although the move to ephemeral messaging in Signal shows growing awareness of this threat model.

Our first initial thesis (*Developer-User Disconnect*) is in essence correct, but needs to be nuanced. Users do want confidentiality and group messaging, as do developers. Yet in other properties there is a disconnect, as many users also want privacy protection, do not need cryptographic repudiation, and do not care as much as developers about decentralization, open standards, and open source licensing. While key management is important to keep simple, key verification ended up being important to high-risk users, even though it was widely misunderstood as a way to prevent client device seizure. Both low-risk and high-risk users are also actively interested in privacy and even anonymization to resist metadata collection. Still, the problems are subtle in points where the application does not line up with user expectations. For example, users often believe Signal protects metadata and keeps their conversations anonymous. For example, even though Signal does not log metadata (outside the last time a user installed the application and the time of last connection), a NSA-level powerful adversary could simply watch the encrypted messages going in and out of the Signal server in order to capture the social graph of users. More easily, a captured device would reveal the phone numbers of all other Signal contacts. Although some applications such as Tox and Ricochet do achieve a degree of protection against the social network mapping attacks that some high-risk users worry about, high-risk users are in general much more aware of Signal and find it easy to use, while the anonymized Tox and Ricochet applications were unknown amongst the high-risk users we interviewed. Some issues that are important for developers, such as standards or decentralization, are not in general as important to either low or high users, but viewed positively. Licensing (and having code open-source) is equally important to developers. Interestingly, high-risk users do prefer open-source code, although they usually do not inspect it themselves. More studies of how high-risk users trust code could be very enlightening.

In terms of our second initial thesis (*High-Risk User Problem*), high-risk users have vastly different behavior and therefore properties than low-risk users. High-risk users have well-defined (if implicit) threat models, prefer open-source, are more concerned over device seizure than server seizure, and are concerned over privacy, including not just metadata collection in general but having phone numbers from secure messaging applications such as Signal being leaked or captured. Therefore, we are left with the curious situation of high-risk users in Ukraine preferring Cryptocat, which suffered from serious security vulnerabilities in early versions but did not require phone numbers like Signal. High-risk users also notice privacy-invasive behavior, such as the mining of contact information by Wire. However, high-risk users are not homogeneous, as the social and geopolitical differences between high-risk users lead to vastly different eco-systems of applications. Therefore, for future work we need to explore the differences between different high-risk groups of users across a wider variety of countries to see what generalizable patterns emerge. Note that the same likely holds for low-risk users, as low-risk technological enthusiasts are likely very different than typical corporate business users, and further work needs to be done studying the variety of low-risk users as well.

A story may be illustrative of how serious the problems faced by high-risk users are, and the issues with adoption that are faced by even the most at risk users of secure messaging. When the YPG was first adopting PGP, H1 noted that "I spent several days teaching the guy who smuggles people for the YPG to use PGP and email. In the end, he got frustrated and said'Why do I have to learn all this ...? We're not the mafia.' He smuggles people across the border across to ISIS territory, and each foreigner worth 100,000 USD. He uses Facebook on Android." However, H1 said that recently more and more of the YPG have been moving to Signal, with the majority of his own communication being through Signal and only"occasionally" unencrypted email and PGP, although "you'd be surprised how many people still use Facebook Messenger and normal phone calls." The reason he stated that secure messaging was that the YPG media site"was bombed a few months ago, tons of people have died, buildings collapsed. Just that one thing happened, suddenly raised the awareness of electronic cyber-defense, it gave power to the voices pushing that narrative, that we need to improve our cybersecurity. Before it wasn't seen as so important. They believe that bombing was caused by electronic surveillance. Because they targeted .... due to observation of where the signals are coming from, what they are doing and what they are saying." Although it is no doubt true that people who consider themselves low-risk users may not care or understand about issues around encryption and metadata [1], a single catastrophic event can cause users to reassess their own risk levels and adopt new tools. For high-risk users, the properties of secure messaging systems may very well be a matter of life or death, and developers of security standards should actively engage with at-risk users by any means necessary.

6   Conclusion

In the case of security properties, key management was universally regarded as a problem, even by high-risk users, but high-risk users did want to have some ability to verify contacts, although they believed current interfaces were clumsy. Due to issues with key management and usability, there was a move by high-risk users away from PGP and towards applications such as Signal and Telegram. More obscure security features, such as deniability, built on top of the cryptographic primitives themselves were not viewed as high-priority, while privacy features such as ephemeral messaging, pseudonyms, metadata protection (such as hiding phone numbers), and even unobservability in using the application, were considered of utmost importance. In general, with a few exceptions such as Briar, developers were not working actively on privacy properties, although it was considered a worthy goal. All users needed group support, but groups are defined differently across different applications, and matching user expectations around the different types of secure group messaging, which will likely require different trust assumptions and protocol choices, has not been systematically done. Decentralization is taken quite seriously by developers as a design goal, although a few of the more popular applications such as Signal have given up on it, and it is less important to high-risk users except in terms of privacy. Standards are also considered important by most developers, although most developers also believe running code is more important and standards are not a concern of end-users. Standpoints on licensing varied among both low-risk and high-risk users, although developers show a clear preference for open-source licensing due to the ability to alter and copy code.

In conclusion, protocols for secure messaging needs to be aligned with real high-risk user needs and with real-world threat models. Addressing this disconnect will require more communication between developers and users, as well as a more nuanced understanding of the contexts in which different groups of users operate and their relational graphs (which may put users that are normally, in theory, low-risk in the high-risk category). Ideally, future work will address how knowledge flows create the formation of differing priorities between developers and both low-risk and high-risk users. A more accurate mental model is needed of the differences between high-risk and low-risk users are needed: For example, it could be possible that there is a "hierarchy of threat models" so that high-risk users have more pressing local adversaries that aim to access their devices and map their social networks, while in the absence of these adversaries, concern even for high-risk users would shift to issues of pervasive surveillance and server seizures. More detailed studies are needed to fully elucidate the differences and commonalities between the threat models of users in order to build more effective secure communications tools.

Appendix: Questionnaire

The complete set of questions is available online (see footnote 2). A subset of relevant questions analyzed in this paper are:

- **Main Threat:** Can you define "who is your enemy"? What would happen to you if your enemy got your messages? What do you worry about more, your device being seized or the server?
- **Security (Key Verification):** How do you usually get someone's public key? In person or searching on a server? How do you usually get someone's public key? Does it seem to be some third party does it for you, and if so, who exactly finds the other users for you? Do you verify keys? What do you do when your software tells you something is wrong with a key? What is, according to you, the most secure and trusted way to exchange and update keys?
- **Security (Ephemeral Messaging):** Are you more concerned over your old messages being read or new messages being read? Do you want to search through or archive your old messages? Do you need repudiation? [Explain a transcript example]
- **Privacy (Metadata Collection):** Do you worry about any data these tools store, and what data? Do you know if these tools store your list of contacts on their servers? Do you worry these servers could be monitored, or seized?
- **Privacy (Pseudonymity):** Do you think you have more than one online identity? How would you describe it/them? And how encryption changes it/them ? Do you think it's a problem to have several online identities? Do you need to be fully anonymous? Do you need multiple identities? Do you feel that different parts of your online identity are linked to cryptographic keys? If you have to, how do you manage these keys?

– **Group Support:** Do you use group chat? How many people in average are there in your group chats? Does the group have an administrator? How are people let in the group? Do new members of groups need to read old messages, like in a mailing list?

– **Decentralization:** Do you know if [application they use] is centralized or decentralized? Does being centralized change something for you? Do you trust the centralized server? Do you trust the people behind it? What is the worse thing that could happen to them? What is decentralization? How can you explain it?

– **Standard:** Do you know what a standards is (like HTML and email)? Is the use of open standards in messaging and email important? Is the protocol you use standardized, working towards a standardization or do you prefer not to standardize the protocol?

– **Open Licensing:** Do you know what a software license is? What's your choice of licensing? Is being able to look at source code important?

References

1. Abu-Salma, R., Sasse, M.A., Bonneau, J., Danilova, A., Naiakshina, A., Smith, M.: Obstacles to the adoption of secure communication tools. In: 2017 IEEE Symposium on Security and Privacy (SP) (SP 2017). IEEE Computer Society (2017)
2. Ermoshina, K., Halpin, H., Musiani, F.: Can Johnny build a protocol? Co-ordinating developer and user intentions for privacy-enhanced secure messaging protocols. In: European Workshop on Usable Security (2017)
3. Green, M., Smith, M.: Developers are not the enemy!: the need for usable Security APIs. IEEE Secur. Priv. **14**(5), 40–46 (2016)
4. Kobeissi, N., Bhargavan, K., Blanchet, B.: Automated verification for secure messaging protocols and their implementations: a symbolic and computational approach. In: IEEE European Symposium on Security and Privacy (EuroS&P) (2017)
5. Oudshoorn, N., Pinch, T.: How Users Matter: The Co-construction of Users and Technology. MIT Press, Cambridge (2005)
6. Schröder, S., Huber, M., Wind, D., Rottermanner, C.: When signal hits the fan: on the usability and security of state-of-the-art secure mobile messaging. In: European Workshop on Usable Security. IEEE (2016)
7. Troncoso, C., Isaakidis, M., Danezis, G., Halpin, H.: Systematizing decentralization and privacy: lessons from 15 years of research and deployments. Proc. Priv. Enhancing Technol. **2017**(4), 404–426 (2017)
8. Unger, N., et al.: SoK: secure messaging. In: IEEE Symposium on Security and Privacy (SP), pp. 232–249. IEEE (2015)
9. Zurko, M.E., Simon, R.: User-centered security. In: Proceedings of the Workshop on New Security Paradigms, pp. 27–33. ACM (1996)

Building Blocks in Standards: Improving Consistency in Standardization with Ontology and Reasoning

Marcello Balduccini[1(✉)] and Claire Vishik[2]

[1] Saint Joseph's University, Philadelphia, PA, USA
marcello.balduccini@sju.edu
[2] Intel Corporation, Austin, TX, USA
claire.vishik@intel.com

Abstract. International standardization in ICT has grown in importance due to the rapid technology development, the increasing need for interoperability, and the global nature of the digital infrastructure. However, technical resources available to international standards bodies have become more limited. With its focus on international collaboration and consensus, the standardization community has not invested significantly in the automation of the process of developing standards. In this paper, we describe potential gains in efficiency with an ontology-based approach and automated reasoning. As part of the exploratory phase of the project, we built a prototype ontology and evaluated the benefits of automated reasoning to improve the process of developing and harmonizing broadly understood ICT assessment standards. The exploratory phase confirmed feasibility and clarified the benefits of the ontology-based approach to standardization, but also highlighted difficulties and unsolved problems in this area.

Keywords: Assessment standards · Ontology · Knowledge engineering
Automated reasoning

1 Introduction

In the past two decades, the importance of open international standards in ICT (Information and computer technologies) increased significantly, while the resources available to develop new standards became scarce (see, e.g., (Boje 2015)). The dynamic cycle of technology development, the massive need for integration, where previously-independent technology domains have to be connected, and the global nature of the digital infrastructure combined to elevate the need for international standards. At the same time, the availability of industry experts decreased as companies shifted their focus to core technologies and products. While governments, universities, and consultants stepped in, the standardization community felt the strain as the need to develop and ratify new standards became more acute.

As a result, it often takes a long time to develop new standards and update the existing ones, and the pace of standardization has been out of step with the technology needs for some time. Additionally, as the body of available standards continued to

© Springer Nature Switzerland AG 2018
C. Cremers and A. Lehmann (Eds.): SSR 2018, LNCS 11322, pp. 76–94, 2018.
https://doi.org/10.1007/978-3-030-04762-7_5

grow and the diversification of the ICT space intensified, it has become more difficult to ensure consistency of approaches used in similar standards. Standards bodies, such as ISO, have taken a number of steps to improve the level of harmonization, enforcing unified formats, rules for references, and consistent terminology (see, e.g., ISO 704 "Terminology: Principles and Methods"). But creating a formal process to re-use building blocks used in standards beyond terminology and some other components has proved challenging.

In this paper, we propose an automated approach based on ontologies and reasoning that could pave the way for the re-use of standard building blocks in standards. In order to test our methodology, we have defined a set of building blocks in a sample of broadly understood assessment standards and created a prototype that demonstrates the feasibility of this approach.

While we don't advocate anything approaching automated standard generation, we consider mechanisms to improve consistency of the body of standards and speed up standards development necessary for the standardization community to keep pace with the needs of the technology and society. The open consensus driven process for developing international standards is one of the greatest achievement that made possible the development and deployment of the global digital infrastructure. The efficiency of this process will be enhanced by the ability to automate repetitive tasks and to achieve greater harmonization among diverse requirements described in standards.

The nature of standardization, a process based on collaboration and consensus, will always require a significant amount of time, we believe that the efficiency and consistency can be increased by employing knowledge engineering techniques. In addition to speeding up the development of consistent standards with non-conflicting requirements, the proposed approach can also lead to the development of more focused and context driven requirements, especially in the area of ICT assessment that is the purpose of the study described in this paper.

2 ICT Security and Privacy Assessment Standards

Over the past decades, a number of standards related to various types of assessments were developed in various standards bodies. For the purpose of this work, we describe assessment standards and those that can facilitate the evaluation of products, technologies and ecosystems. The assessment standards comprise a variety of approaches, including governance, secure development lifecycles, risk management, deterministic product testing, and many other. Examples of complementary approaches include the following:

1. ISO/IEC 15408. Evaluation criteria for IT security
2. ISO/IEC 17825Testing methods for the mitigation of non-invasive attack classes against cryptographic modules
3. ISO/IEC 18045. Methodology for IT security evaluation
4. ISO/IEC TS 19249:2017 Catalogue of architectural and design principles for secure products, systems and application
5. ISO/IEC 19790:2012. Security requirements for cryptographic modules

6. ISO/IEC 19792:2009. Security evaluation of biometrics
7. Most standards from the 27000 series, e, g., ISO/IEC 27034
8. ISO/IEC 29134:2017. Guidelines for privacy impact assessment
9. ISO/IEC 29190:2015. Privacy capability assessment model

These standards are represented by highly structured documents that comprise similar building blocks, such as principles, requirements, or components of processes. Some of these building blocks are similar, but not identical in these standards, and others are very specific to the context that is the subject of a standard. In the course of the first stage of our project, we evaluated several standards documents, with the objective to:

1. Determine the extent of structural and semantic similarities in different assessment related standards.
2. Develop a prototype ontology to capture relationships among these building blocks.
3. Obtain the insights from this experiment.
4. Define the advantages of the approach with regards to the efficiency and flexibility of the standardization process that an ontology could provide.

For this project, we focused on structural building blocks, e.g., principles or processes. In other research projects focusing on defining ontologies for security related standards (see, e.g., de Franco Rosa 2018 1/2), building blocks were defined based on semantics, e.g., risk or vulnerability. Ideally, both structural and semantic building blocks need to be defined, but semantics could also be presented differently in the model, as demonstrated in this work.

3   Ontologies and Their Use in Standardization and Related Areas

In order to evaluate the feasibility of structural and semantic analysis of ICT assessment standards based on ontology and other knowledge engineering methods, we need to start with the definitions.

An *ontology* is a formal, logic-based representation of knowledge typically aimed at supporting reasoning by means of logical inference. Broadly speaking, an ontology is a collection of statements in a logical language representing a given domain in terms of classes (i.e., sets) and subclasses of objects, individuals (i.e., objects of a specific class), and relationships between objects and/or classes. For instance, an ontology of standards produced by ISO/IEC JTC1 SC27 (IT Security Techniques)[1] might contain a *Document* class capturing the set of all standard documents, and a subclass 27000_*series*. *ISO_IEC_27032* would then be an individual of class 27000_*series*. To describe the title of a standard document, one might introduce a relationship *hasTitle*(*doc*, *str*) where *doc* is a document and *str* is a string, e.g. *hasTitle*(*ISO_IEC_*27032, "*Guidelines for cybersecurity*"). Additionally, one could specify that *ISO_IEC_*27034_*part_*1 and

---

[1] https://www.iso.org/committee/45306.html, ISO/IEC JTC 1/SC 27 IT Security techniques.

ISO_IEC_27034_part_2 are part of *ISO_IEC_27034* by means of a suitable relationship, e.g.:

$$partOf(ISO\_IEC\_27034\_part\_1, ISO\_IEC\_27034),$$
$$partOf(ISO\_IEC\_27034\_part\_2, ISO\_IEC\_27034).$$

Ontologies are utilized in a wide range of areas, from media to robotics, and from engineering to medicine. Researchers working in the areas of standardization have applied ontologies for a variety of purposes, but typically to create a semantic meta model of a complex space. Huang and Li (2010) used ontologies to link standards tags relating properties of the IoT space to the descriptions of the functions they denote. In the medical field, Cai et al. (2014) used an ontology to standardize and classify adverse drug reactions based on Adverse Drug Reaction Classification System. Ramanauskaitė et al. (2013) described how ontologies could be used to map existing security standards, and Fenz and Ekelhart (2009) developed ontologies to formalize security knowledge and make it more amenable to various analyses. Gonzalez-Perez et al. (2016) developed an ontology for ISO software engineering standards, complete with a prototype demonstrating their approach.

Outside of the research literature, several standardization efforts have explored or used ontologies to make sense of complex subject areas, such as IoT (Internet of Things) or Smart Cities. Ontology-based standards exist, mostly to provide a model for complex interactions, such as ISO/TS 19150 ("Geographic Information—Ontology"[2]). However, the use of ontologies for harmonization and process efficiency that is common in, e.g., requirements engineering, has not been adapted to standardization, with the exception of some experimental studies. In the paper, we hope to demonstrate that some level of automation is feasible in the field of standardization as well and that it is compatible with the currently used standards development processes.

4   Ontology-Based Representation of Standard Documents

The analysis of various standard documents from the ISO/IEC 19000 series and 27000 series showed that documents can be viewed as consisting of a hierarchically-organized collection of *building blocks*, each describing a key component of the document. A relatively small number of structural building blocks is shared by all documents analyzed:

- Concepts – concepts used throughout the document.
- Definitions – definitions of notions.
- Guidelines –guidelines pertaining to the standard.
- Principles – guiding principles used in the document.
- Process – a process (or task) being standardized.
- Purpose – purpose of the document or of a part of the document.

---

[2] https://www.iso.org/standard/57465.html.

- Test – one or more tests being standardized, possibly used as part of a process.
- Misc – general-purpose block

The types of building blocks are formalized in the prototype ontology as subclasses of class "Building Block", as shown in Fig. 1.

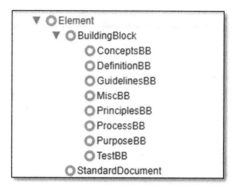

Fig. 1. Ontology fragment: classes for building blocks and standard document

Note that the specific selection of types of building blocks listed above is intended only for demonstration of the proposed formalization and not as a definitive list and that it is limited to structural building blocks. Analysis of further documents may well result in additional types of building blocks or in a reorganization of their hierarchy. Although the prototype ontology was built manually, the structured nature of standards provides an option to build it semi-automatically, by harvesting certain types of structures, clustering terms by frequency, and other methods developed by the text processing and knowledge engineering communities.

An occurrence of a building block in a document is captured by an individual of a suitable class. When available, a string representing the title is associated with a building block by means of relation *hasTitle*. Similarly, relation *hasBody* specifies the main narrative of the building block. The concepts (see below) identified in the title are associated with the building block by relation *mainTopic*.

The hierarchy of building blocks that make up a document is captured by relation *partOf*, so that *xpartOfy* holds if building block y is a component of x, where x is an individual of class Element, i.e. a building block or a standard document (see Fig. 1).

For instance, a clause defining guidelines related to communicating roles and responsibilities might be captured in the ontology by an individual of class GuildelinesBB, which is linked to its parent clause by relation *partOf*. Figure 2 provides an illustration of such an individual.

Next, we identified reoccurring relevant terms, such as "assurance," "authority," and "framework." We noted that these terms are often used to form combinations, which appear to have importance in defining the content of a building block. The terms typically have specific functions within a combination, and we have identified three main categories of these: "Activity," "Concern," and "Context". To formalize these combinations, we introduced the Concept class with associated relations *includesActivity*, *includesConcern*, and *includesContext*. Each relation informally states that a given Concept individual includes a term with the indicated function. The occurrence of multiple terms with the same function is formalized by multiple occurrences of a suitable relation.

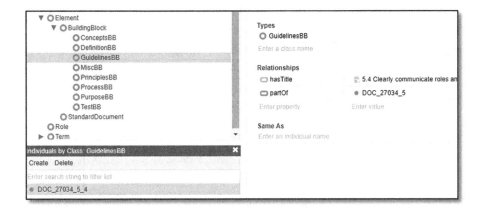

Fig. 2. Individual for clause 5.4 of ISO/IEC 27034

The terms are currently organized hierarchically along three categories matching the categories of functions identified in the combinations.[3] For the sake of illustration, we created a notional set of frequent terms. The three branches of the term hierarchy are shown in Fig. 3.

Figure 4 illustrates the definition of a sample individual for the concept "application-security verification framework".

In order to indicate that the narrative of a certain building block contains a concept, we introduce relation *containsConcept*, where *xcontainsConcepty* means that building block *x* contains an occurrence of concept *y*. For instance, a clause might contain occurrences of concepts "Application-Security Verification" and "Application-Security Verification Scheme". Hence, the definition of the corresponding building block would include the items shown in Fig. 5.

In a similar way, concepts that occur in the title of a building block are captured by relation *hasMainTopic*.

The formalization of building blocks in assessment-related standards offers a foundation for several efficiency-related opportunities that will be the subjects of future work. Some of them are listed below:

---

[3] While this approach is convenient for illustration purposes, preliminary examination of a broader set of documents seems to suggest that the same term may be used for multiple functions. In that case, it may be more appropriate to organize the term hierarchy along other dimensions than the functions themselves.

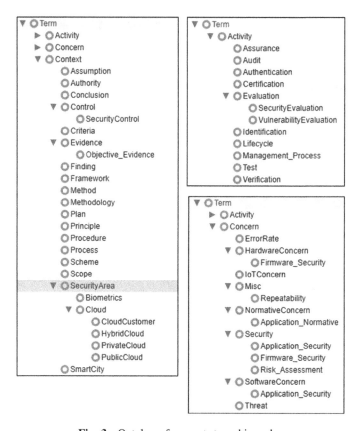

Fig. 3. Ontology fragment: term hierarchy

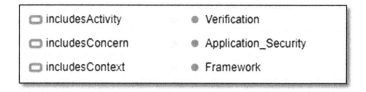

Fig. 4. Concept individual for "application-security verification framework"

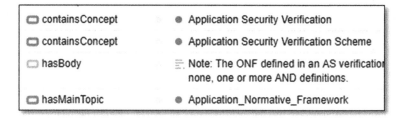

Fig. 5. Concepts occurring in clause 10.3.19 of ISO/IEC 27034

1. Harmonize building blocks from different standards that are meant to denote the same context.
2. Pre-populate new or updated standards with typical building blocks that already exist.
3. Update building blocks across several standards when an error or an inconsistency are found or when the technology environment changes.
4. Build context-driven and focused assessments that combined components of several areas, such as privacy, SDL (Secure development lifecycle), safety, and governance.
5. Ensure greater harmonization across diverse standards and detect potential conflicts between assessment requirements.

Having built a prototype ontology in order to extract the recurring components in assessment standards, we can now evaluate the advantages provided by automated reasoning capabilities.

5 Inference and Reasoning Capabilities

An ontology can be used to achieve sophisticated inference and querying capabilities, and this is useful for the document analysis, such as the analysis of standards.[4] The SPARQL query language (Harris, Seaborne and Prud'hommeaux 2013) allows for efficient extraction from an ontology of data satisfying certain criteria. The basic syntax of a SPARQL query is:

$$SELECT ? var_1 ? var_2 ? var_3 \ldots$$
$$WHERE$$
$$\{ ? var_x \, rel_A ? var_y \, .$$
$$? var_y \, rel_B ? var_z \, .$$
$$\ldots$$
$$\}$$

where each variable $?var\_i$ is a placeholder for an ontology item of interest and every rel_i is the name of a relationship. Note the syntax used for relations in the *WHERE* block, where $?var_x rel_A ?var_y$ stands for the more traditional mathematical logic atom $rel_A(?var_x, ?var_y)$. Typically, the variables from the *SELECT* line also occur in the *WHERE* block, but additional variables may appear in the block. When a tuple of items is found such that the *WHERE* block is satisfied, the tuple of items corresponding to the variables from the *SELECT* line is considered to be an answer to the query. For instance, consider the query:

---

[4] In fact, a whole hierarchy of ontology-based languages exist, with varying degrees of expressivity and computational complexity. A thorough discussion is beyond the scope of this paper.

$$SELECT\,?part\,?doc\_class$$
$$WHERE$$
$$\{\,?part\,partOf\,?doc\,.$$
$$?doc\,type\,?doc\_class$$
$$\}$$

where *type* is a built-in relationship stating that the left-hand side is an individual of the class mentioned on the right-hand side. Intuitively, the query identifies all documents that are part of another document (*?partpartOf?doc*), finds the class of the containing document (*?doctype?doc_class*) and yields all pairs consisting of a document part and of the class of the containing document. When evaluated against the sample ontology given earlier, the query will yield the answers:

$$(ISO\_IEC\_27034\_part\_1, 27000\_series)$$
$$(ISO\_IEC\_27034\_part\_2, 27000\_series)$$

For increased flexibility of representation, we make also use of an extension of propositional logic called *Answer Set Programming (ASP)* (Gelfond and Lifschitz 1991) (Marek and Truszczynski 1999). ASP is a rule-based language, where a rule is a logical formula of the form:

$$l_0 \leftarrow l_1, l_2, \ldots, l_m, not\ l_{m+1}, \ldots, not\ l_n.$$

Every l_i is a *literal*, i.e. an atom of the form $rel(c_1, c_2, \ldots, c_l)$ – where each c_i is a numerical or string constant – or an expression $\neg a$ for some atom a. Intuitively, the above rule states that, if all of $l_1, \ldots, l_m$ hold and *there is no reason to believe* (conveyed by the *not* keyword) that any of $l_{m+1}, \ldots, l_n$ hold, then l_0 must hold.

A *program* is a set of rules. When a literal l can be derived from a program Π, we write:

$$\Pi \models l$$

A formal description of the semantics of ASP can be found in (Gelfond and Lifschitz 1991). For use in this paper, we will somewhat simplistically define an *answer set* of a program Π as one of the sets of literals that can be derived from Π.[5]

Following common representational practices, we allow for logical variables to be used as arguments of literals. A logical variable is a string denoted by an uppercase initial (unless enclosed by double-quotes). For instance, $partOf(Part, 27000\_series)$ is a literal whose first argument is the logical variable *Part* and whose second argument is the string constant 27000_series. A rule containing variables is viewed as an abbreviation for all rules that can be obtained by replacing all variables by all possible

---

[5] Certain programs have multiple answer sets. For example, $\{p \leftarrow notq. q \leftarrow notp.\}$ has two answer sets, $\{p\}$ and $\{q\}$, corresponding to two alternative, equally possible views of the world captured by Π..

constant symbols. For example, suppose one would like to identify all documents that are not subdivided further in document parts. This can be accomplished by the rules:

$$hasParts(Doc) \leftarrow partOf(Part, Doc).$$
$$monolithic(Doc) \leftarrow not\, hasParts(Doc).$$

Assuming that one is given information about document parts in the form of *partOf* atoms, then the first rule will yield the atom *hasParts*(d) for every document d that is subdivided. The second rule will yield an atom *monolithic*(d) for every document d for which there is no reason to believe that *hasParts*(d) holds. So, given information about *ISO_IEC_27034* and *ISO_IEC_27032* as in the prototype ontology, the rules will yield *hasParts*("ISO_IEC_27034") and *monolithic*("*ISO_IEC_27036*").

5.1   Towards Automation of Information Extraction

A number of approaches have been developed to simplify the automated generation of ontologies or to support the semi-automatic generation of an ontology and a related knowledge base. They are typically based on the frequency of occurring terms, their positioning or proximity to other terms. Even with the automated generation, the maintenance of automated ontological models presents a problem in areas where ontologies are commonly used, such as Geographic Information Systems (GIS) or biomedical databases. Fortunately, advances have been made helping automate the creation or maintain the maintenance of single or linked ontologies. Innovative approaches are described in Alobaidi et al. (2018) for biomedical databases or in Fraga and Vegetti (2017) for manufacturing and product data. In pursuing the automation of the ontology creation process, we are helped by the fact that standards-related documents are highly structured, due to the requirements of standards bodies and traditions of standards development. As a result, the automation process is considerably simplified, although it requires a rigorous high-level model to make it meaningful.

At this stage of our work, we do not commit to a specific way of obtaining the information captured by the ontology. At some point, tools may be built for standard document creation that automatically create the ontology as a by-product. On the other hand, one might develop dedicated information extraction techniques for processing existing documents. For our study, we have developed a basic but effective technique that enables extraction of information from existing documents. We describe it as it may lay the foundations of more sophisticated approaches.

The algorithm we devised takes in input an *input ontology* representing concepts and building block types (see Sect. 4), and a set of files containing clauses of a standards document. The algorithm produces an *output ontology* that can be used for the reasoning processes described in this paper. The output ontologies for multiple standards documents can be easily merged by applying traditional ontology-manipulation tools. To facilitate the task of the algorithm, each concept in the input ontology is augmented with a list of synonyms. For instance, concept "Application Security Verification Framework" has synonym "AS Verification Framework."

Each *clause file* lists the clause number (e.g., 10.3.19) followed by its title. The rest of the file contains the narrative of the clause. A special *document file* contains the number of the document (e.g., 27034) and its title.

The algorithm begins by creating an individual of class Standard Document with the title and number provided by the document file. Next, each clause file is processed and a building block individual is created. The class of the individual is determined from the title of the clause, by identifying occurrences of the names of building blocks found in the ontology (augmented with plurals and other syntactic variations). If the building block cannot be identified, the algorithm defaults to type Misc. The clause number is used to identify the parent clause, if it exists. The association is made by means of relation *partOf*. The text of the title and of the text of the clause are linked with the individual by means of relations *hasTitle* and *hasBody*.

Next, the clause title is inspected for occurrences of the concepts and their synonyms, which are then associated with the building block individual by means of relation *mainTopic*. Note that, in some cases, the title of a clause should be interpreted within the context set forth by higher-level clauses. For instance, in ISO/IEC 19792 ("Security evaluation of biometrics"), the title of clause 6, "Security evaluation", should be interpreted within the context of the document, i.e. "Security evaluation for biometrics." For this reason, the algorithm allows for the manual specification of additional text to be considered in the determination of the main topic of a clause.

Finally, the text of the clause is matched against the known concepts in a similar way. Matching concepts are associated with the building block individual by means of relation *containsConcept*.

For an example application of the algorithm, consider clause 3 of ISO/IEC 27034, with title "Terms and definitions." The input ontology from Sect. 4 does not contain a building block matching the title, and thus the algorithm creates a building block individual of class Misc and suitable attributes (title, etc.). When the text of the clause is inspected for occurrences of known concepts, the algorithm finds various matches, including:

- Application Security Authority
- Application Security Verification
- Application Security Verification Scheme
- Application Normative Framework
- Application Security Audit.

6   Automated Reasoning in Support of Standardization

We have identified two broad classes of reasoning tasks that appear to be relevant to the process of document creation and querying, the ***drill-down*** type of query and the ***harvest*** type of query.

For each type of the query, we formalized the type of reasoning involved by means a set of axioms that make it possible to carry it out through the general-purpose logical inference mechanisms introduced earlier. The reasoning process is broken down into two parts: ontology-based querying and non-monotonic reasoning. The former applies relatively light-weight inference mechanisms to efficiently extract a broad set of relevant pieces of information from the ontology. The latter applies more sophisticated inference mechanisms to the restricted set of pieces of information identified in order to obtained the desired answer.

The process of answering a query Q can thus be reduced to checking whether Q follows from ontology Ω and axioms Λ, i.e.:

$$\tau(\Omega) \cup \Lambda \vDash Q$$

where $\tau(\Omega)$ denotes the set of tuples extracted from Ω through ontology-based querying. At the current stage, ontology-based querying is implemented by SPARQL queries and checking for entailment ($\vDash$ in the above equation) is reduced to finding answer sets of suitable ASP programs. Next, we discuss in more details the types of reasoning tasks considered and the axioms that formalize them.

In the **drill-down task**, the user looks for clauses relevant to a certain concept and may progressively refine the query to focus on particular types of documents or sets of clauses. For example, a user might want to investigate all the building blocks, technical, procedural, or descriptive, that apply to deployment of IoT edge devices while developing a standard document describing a new IoT framework. An example query is:

"What are the typical components of the existing frameworks?"

In response to this query, the reasoning mechanism will identify all building blocks pertaining to the description of frameworks and return the list of building blocks contained in them and whose types reoccur in all frameworks. This is accomplished as follows:

- $\tau(\Omega)$ identifies (*) every building block whose main topic (given by relation *hasMainTopic*) is a concept whose context (relation *includesContext*) is term Framework, and (*) all building blocks that are part of it. The query yields a set of triples $(root, bblock, type)$ where *root* is the identifier of the building block with suitable main topic, *bblock* is one of its constituents, and *type* is the type of *bblock* (see Fig. 1).
- Λ identifies the building block types that occur in all triples of $\tau(\Omega)$. The two key axioms are:

$$\neg common(T) \leftarrow$$
$$root(R1), root(R2),$$
$$contains\_bb\_type(R_1, T),$$
$$not\ contains\_bb\_type(R_2, T).$$

$$common(T) \leftarrow$$
$$contains\_bb\_type(R, T),$$
$$not\ \neg common(T).$$

The first axiom finds every building block type that occurs in the description of one framework, but not in some other. Relations *root* and *contains_bb_type* are obtained from the triples of $\tau(\Omega)$ (axioms omitted). The second axiom states that a type T is common to all framework descriptions if it occurs in at least one of them and was not flagged by the first axiom.

- Q is the atom *common*(T), i.e. one is interested in every building block type T for which *common*(T) holds.

For illustration purposes, let us suppose that an ontology contains building blocks for two frameworks, an application security verification framework (clause 1), a hardware security verification framework (clause 3.5) and a process-related framework (clause 7.2). Specifically, for the former the ontology contains the following components:

- A purpose building block (clause 1.1)
- A concepts building block (clause 1.2)
- A test building block (clause 1.3)
- A guidelines building block (clause 1.4)
  For the hardware security verification framework, the ontology contains:
- A concepts building block (clause 3.5.1)
- A purpose building block (clause 3.5.2)
- A misc building block (clause 3.5.3)
  For the process-related framework, the ontology contains:
- A process building block (clauses 7.2.1)
- A concepts building block (clause 7.2.2)

One can check that, for this example, $\tau(\Omega)$ will contain the triples

$(1,1.1, PurposeBB), (1,1.2, ConceptsBB), (1,1.3, TestBB), (1,1.4, GuidelinesBB),$
$(3.5,3.5.1, ConceptsBB), (3.5,3.5.2, PurposeBB), (3.5,3.5.3, MiscBB),$
$(7.2,7.2.1, ProcessBB), (7.2,7.2.2, ConceptsBB)$

One can also check that the only atom of the form *common*(T) entailed by $\tau(\Omega) \cup \Lambda$ is *common*("*conceptsBB*"). The reasoning mechanism has thus determined that the only type of building block the (known) frameworks share is *ConceptsBB*. Note that, while this is a simple example, it can be easily extended by adding suitable axioms, e.g. to find building blocks that are most frequently occurring or occurring at least with a certain frequency.

Let us now turn our attention to ***harvest*** queries that can assist in, e.g., the creation of new standards by identifying and harvesting relevant components of existing documents. A sample harvest query might ask:

"What are the relevant building blocks for a Security development lifecycle (SDL) framework for IoT?"

Let us assume that background knowledge related to SDL is available to the reasoning mechanism through the ontology or encoded by axioms such as:

$$decomposed\_in(sdl, "Audit").$$
$$decomposed\_in(sdl, "Verification").$$
$$decomposed\_in(sdl, "Assurance").$$

Additional background knowledge might state that, in the case of frameworks for auditing, verification, and assurance, one should consider IoT-related concerns, hardware-related concerns and software-related concerns. For illustration purposes, we show the axioms that determine if two concepts are similar based on the above statements about concerns and activities:

$is\_audit\_verification\_assurance("Audit").$
$is\_audit\_verification\_assurance("Verification").$
$is\_audit\_verification\_assurance("Assurance").$

$is\_hw\_sw\_iot\_concern(CRN) \leftarrow tc\_subclassof(CRN, "HardwareConcern").$
$is\_hw\_sw\_iot\_concern(CRN) \leftarrow tc\_subclassof(CRN, "SoftwareConcern").$
$is\_hw\_sw\_iot\_concern(CRN) \leftarrow tc\_subclassof(CRN, "IoTConcern").$

$tc\_subclassof(X, X) \leftarrow class(X).$
$tc\_subclassof(X, Y) \leftarrow subclassof(X, Z), tc\_subclassof(Z, Y).$

$similar\_to(C_1, C_2) \leftarrow$
$\qquad includesActivity(C_1, ACT),$
$\qquad includesActivity(C_2, ACT),$
$\qquad is\_audit\_verification\_assurance(ACT),$
$\qquad includesContext(C_1, "Framework"),$
$\qquad includesContext(C_2, "Framework"),$
$\qquad includesConcern(C_1, CRN_1),$
$\qquad includesConcern(C_2, CRN_2),$
$\qquad is\_hw\_sw\_iot\_concern(CRN_1),$
$\qquad is\_hw\_sw\_iot\_concern(CRN_2).$

The first three axioms describe the set of activities of interest. The next three axioms capture the set of (possibly indirect) subclasses of *HardwareConcern*, *SoftwareConcern* and *IoTConcern* (see Fig. 3). To identify possibly indirect sub-classes, the axioms leverage relation *tc_subclassof* (abbreviation of transitive closure of *subclassof*), which is defined in a standard way by the following two axioms. The last axiom states that two concepts C_1 and C_2 are similar if they include the same audit, verification or assurance activity, have context *Framework*, and include concerns that are (possibly indirect) subclasses of *HardwareConcern*, *SoftwareConcern* or *IoTConcern*.

The query can thus be reduced to finding building blocks for frameworks whose main topic is an SDL framework for IoT or a framework similar to it, as defined by the above axioms. That is, given an axiom:[6]

$$relevant(ROOT\_BB) \leftarrow$$
$$concept(C_2),$$
$$includesContext(C_2, "Framework"),$$
$$includesConcern(C_2, "IoTConcern"),$$
$$decomposed\_in(sdl, ACT),$$
$$includesActivity(C_2, ACT),$$
$$hasMainTopic(ROOT\_BB, C_1),$$
$$similar\_to(C_1, C_2).$$

query Q is captured by atom $relevant(ROOT\_BB)$.

Given the prototype ontology, since SDL includes verification activities, the application-security verification framework discussed earlier is potentially relevant to the query – were it not for the fact that it is related to application security, rather than IoT. A similar argument holds for the hardware verification framework. This gap is bridged by the background knowledge.

Thus, one can check that, while no building block exists for an SDL framework for IoT, $\tau(\Omega) \cup \Lambda$ entails two atoms of the form $relevant(ROOT\_BB)$: $relevant(1)$, indicating the application-security verification framework (clause 1) is a match for the query, and $relevant(3.5)$, indicating that the hardware security verification framework (clause 3.5) is another match for the query. In fact, both have context *Framework*, describe an activity of interest (*Verification*), and have a concern that is a subclass of *HardwareConcern*, *SoftwareConcern* or *IoTConcern*. Specifically for clause 1, while the application-security verification framework does not mention concern *SoftwareConcern*, it is related to application security, which, based on the knowledge from Fig. 3, is a software-related concern.

7   Benefits and Obstacles

The area of standardization, and specifically a sample of security assessment related standards that we have evaluated, demonstrate excellent premises for knowledge engineering and automated reasoning. The creation of standards is a structured collaborative process that results in highly structured documents. Thus, extracting building blocks from standards, organizing them within an ontology, developing reasoning tools, and incorporating the use of ontology and reasoning at certain stages of the development of standards is feasible, as was confirmed by our experiment.

Moreover, some level of automation and harmonization in the development of standards would speed up the development process. With limited resources, increasing specialization of experts, diverse ICT infrastructures, and shortening technology lifecycles, expanded use of technology will be vastly beneficial.

---

[6] We omit the axiom for matching of SDL framework for IoT, which is straightforward.

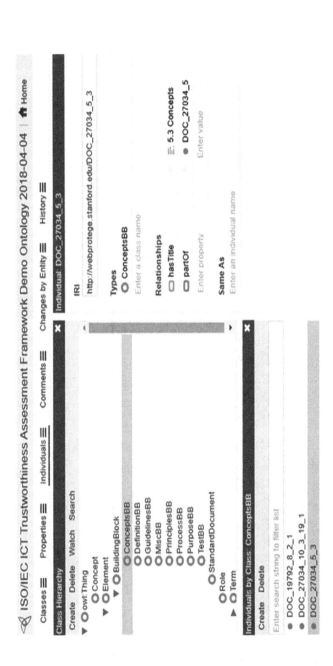

Fig. 6. Prototype system: ontology creation page

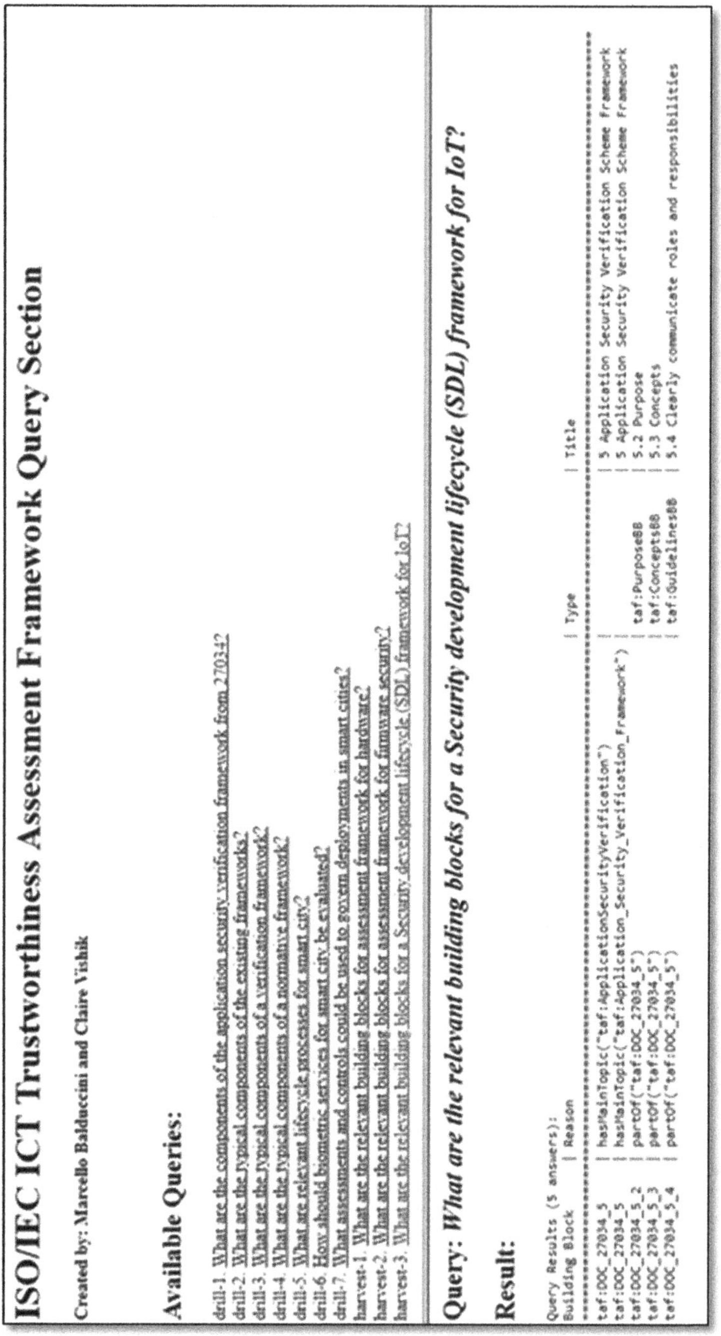

ISO/IEC ICT Trustworthiness Assessment Framework Query Section

Created by: Marcello Balduccini and Claire Vishik

Available Queries:

drill-1. What are the components of the application security verification framework from 27034?
drill-2. What are the typical components of the existing frameworks?
drill-3. What are the typical components of a verification framework?
drill-4. What are the typical components of a normative framework?
drill-5. What are relevant lifecycle processes for smart city?
drill-6. How should biometric services for smart city be evaluated?
drill-7. What assessments and controls could be used to govern deployments in smart cities?
harvest-1. What are the relevant building blocks for assessment framework for hardware?
harvest-2. What are the relevant building blocks for assessment framework for firmware security?
harvest-3. What are the relevant building blocks for a Security development lifecycle (SDL) framework for IoT?

Query: *What are the relevant building blocks for a Security development lifecycle (SDL) framework for IoT?*

Result:

```
Query Results (5 answers):
Building Block      | Reason                                                      | Type              | Title
========================================================================================================================================
taf:DOC_27034_5     | hasMainTopic("taf:ApplicationSecurityVerification")         |                   | 5 Application Security Verification Scheme Framework
taf:DOC_27034_5     | hasMainTopic("taf:Application_Security_Verification_Framework") |                | 5 Application Security Verification Scheme Framework
taf:DOC_27034_5_2   | partOf("taf:DOC_27034_5")                                   | taf:Purpose88     | 5.2 Purpose
taf:DOC_27034_5_3   | partOf("taf:DOC_27034_5")                                   | taf:Concepts88    | 5.3 Concepts
taf:DOC_27034_5_4   | partOf("taf:DOC_27034_5")                                   | taf:Guidelines88  | 5.4 Clearly communicate roles and responsibilities
```

Fig. 7. Prototype system: query demonstration interface

Although the knowledge engineering community developed a wide range of tools to support the ontology-based management of some standard building blocks, the nature of the standardization process makes the initial investment in the technology and process difficult for standards bodies. Most standards experts are volunteers, spending a fraction of their working time on the development of standards and specifications. Even with the highly structure nature of standards, the planning and creation of the initial ontology is a daunting task, but it may become necessary as the need for standards continues to expand.

Another obstacle is connected to the positioning of the ontology within a standardization field. In order to be effective, the ontology itself and/or the building blocks it organizes need to be standardized. Although many areas of technology development have become automated and now rely on tools and processes these tools enforce, this change has not yet happened in standardization. The development of assessment-related standards has decade long traditions that served the field well. Creating an ontology to formalize building blocks and relationships among them may require reassessment of some practices.

However, we believe that the circumstances have aligned to make automation of some parts of the standardization process more important. The lack of cross-domain expertise among experts, the sheer number of existing standards, and the needs of the global digital infrastructure make some levels of formalization of building blocks in standards inevitable. And greater formalization is likely to lead to increase in automation.

8   Conclusions and Future Work

The first stage of our work was exploratory, but it confirmed the feasibility of the ontology-based management of standards, while also highlighting many difficulties along the way. We have built a prototype ontology based on a sample of ISO/IEC standards and determined that there are easily detectable building blocks that can help technologists working in the areas of security or "trustworthiness" assessment to build and update standards faster, to detect conflicts, and to promote harmonization within the field. Screenshots of the prototype system can be found in Figs. 6 and 7.

We have also taken stock of the obstacles to introducing ontologies into standardization. Overcoming these obstacles will be an important area of the future work. Defining the structure of the most common building blocks as well as methodologies to promote harmonization in standards will be another important direction. The improvement of the techniques for automated reasoning in the context of ICT assessment-related standards will continue to be important. Finally, applications of this work to adjacent areas, such as automated classification of standards, will be explored.

References

Alobaidi, M., Malik, K.M., Hussain, M.: Automated ontology generation framework powered by linked biomedical ontologies for disease-drug domain. Comput. Methods Programs Biomed. **165**, 117–128 (2018)

Boje, D.M. (ed.): Organizational Change and Global Standardization Solutions to Standards and Norms Overwhelming Organizations. Routledge, New York (2015)

Cai, M.C., et al.: ADReCS: an ontology database for aiding standardization and hierarchical classification of adverse drug reaction terms. Nucleic Acids Res. **43**(D1), D907–D913 (2014)

de Franco Rosa, F., Jino, M., Bonacin, R.: Towards an ontology of security assessment: a core model proposal. In: Latifi, S. (ed.) Information Technology - New Generations. AISC, vol. 738, pp. 75–80. Springer, Cham (2018). https://doi.org/10.1007/978-3-319-77028-4_12

de Franco Rosa, F., Jino, M., Bueno, P.M.S., Bonacin, R.: Coverage- based heuristics for selecting assessment items from security standards: a core set proposal. In: 2018 Workshop on Metrology for Industry 4.0 and IoT, pp. 192–197. IEEE, April 2018

Fenz, S., Ekelhart, A.: Formalizing information security knowledge. In: Proceedings of the 4th International Symposium on Information, Computer, and Communications Security, pp. 183–194. ACM (2009)

Fraga, A.L., Vegetti, M.: Semi-automated ontology generation process from industrial product data standards. In: III Simposio Argentino de Ontologías y sus Aplicaciones (SAOA)-JAIIO 46 (Córdoba 2017) (2017)

Gelfond, M., Lifschitz, V.: Classical negation in logic programs and disjunctive databases. New Gen. Comput. **9**, 365–385 (1991)

Gonzalez-Perez, C., Henderson-Sellers, B., McBride, T., Low, G.C., Larrucea, X.: An ontology for ISO software engineering standards: 2) proof of concept and application. Comput. Standards Interfaces **48**, 112–123 (2016)

Harris, S., Seaborne, A., Prud'hommeaux, E.: SPARQL 1.1 query language. W3C Recommendation **21**(10), 778 (2013)

Huang, Y., Li, G.: A semantic analysis for internet of things. In: 2010 International Conference on Intelligent Computation Technology and Automation (ICICTA), vol. 1, pp. 336–339. IEEE (2010)

Marek, V.W., Truszczynski, M.: Stable models and an alternative logic programming. In: Apt, K. R., Marek, V.W., Truszczynski, M., Warren, D.S. (eds.) The Logic Programming Paradigm: a 25-Year Perspective, pp. 375–398. Springer, Heidelberg (1999). https://doi.org/10.1007/978-3-642-60085-2_17

Ramanauskaitė, S., Olifer, D., Goranin, N., Čenys, A.: Security ontology for adaptive mapping of security standards. Int. J. Comput. Commun. Control (IJCCC) **8**(6), 813–825 (2013)

Defeating the Downgrade Attack on Identity Privacy in 5G

Mohsin Khan[1,2(✉)], Philip Ginzboorg[3,4], Kimmo Järvinen[1,2],
and Valtteri Niemi[1,2]

[1] University of Helsinki, Helsinki, Finland
{mohsin.khan,kimmo.u.jarvinen,valtteri.niemi}@helsinki.fi
[2] Helsinki Institute for Information Technology, Helsinki, Finland
[3] Huawei Technologies, Helsinki, Finland
philip.ginzboorg@huawei.com
[4] Aalto University, Espoo, Finland

Abstract. 3GPP Release 15, the first 5G standard, includes protection
of user identity privacy against IMSI catchers. These protection mechanisms are based on public key encryption. Despite this protection, IMSI
catching is still possible in LTE networks which opens the possibility of a
downgrade attack on user identity privacy, where a fake LTE base station
obtains the identity of a 5G user equipment. We propose (i) to use an
existing pseudonym-based solution to protect user identity privacy of 5G
user equipment against IMSI catchers in LTE and (ii) to include a mechanism for updating LTE pseudonyms in the public key encryption based
5G identity privacy procedure. The latter helps to recover from a loss of
synchronization of LTE pseudonyms. Using this mechanism, pseudonyms
in the user equipment and home network are automatically synchronized
when the user equipment connects to 5G. Our mechanisms utilize existing LTE and 3GPP Release 15 messages and require modifications only
in the user equipment and home network in order to provide identity
privacy. Additionally, lawful interception requires minor patching in the
serving network.

Keywords: 3GPP · IMSI catchers · Pseudonym · Identity privacy
5G

1 Introduction

A generic mobile network has three main parts: (i) user equipment (UE); (ii)
home network (HN), i.e. the mobile network where the user has a subscription;
and (iii) serving network (SN), i.e. a mobile network that the UE connects to in
order to avail services.[1] The UE includes mobile equipment (ME) and a universal
integrated circuit card (UICC). The UE is said to be roaming when the SN and
HN are different. When both the UE and HN are made to 5G specifications,

---

[1] The notation used in this paper is summarized in Appendix A.

© Springer Nature Switzerland AG 2018
C. Cremers and A. Lehmann (Eds.): SSR 2018, LNCS 11322, pp. 95–119, 2018.
https://doi.org/10.1007/978-3-030-04762-7_6

it is possible that the 5G UE connects to a legacy serving network, e.g., the LTE (long term evolution, or 4G) serving network. It is important to allow such a "downgraded" connection, because – especially in the early phases of 5G adoption – 5G coverage will be spotty compared to LTE.

International mobile subscriber identity (IMSI) is a globally unique identity of a mobile user. Identity privacy means that long-term user identities remain unknown to everyone else besides UE, SN, and HN. IMSI catchers, i.e. malicious devices that steal IMSIs in order to track and monitor the mobile users, are a threat to users' identity privacy [1–4]. Passive IMSI catchers attack by eavesdropping; active IMSI catchers attack by impersonating an SN. Mobile networks had protection against passive IMSI catchers since GSM, but until 5G they did not protect users against active IMSI catchers.

Third generation partnership project (3GPP) Release 15, the first 5G standard, includes protection against active IMSI catchers [5]. This protection is implemented so that the UE encrypts its identity using public key encryption with the public key of the HN [6]. The concealed identity is called subscription concealed identifier (SUCI). This protection works only when the SN is also a 5G entity because an SN from LTE, 3G or GSM networks would not know how to process the SUCI. This implies that an active IMSI catcher can mount a downgrade attack against a 5G UE so that it impersonates an LTE SN and exploits LTE's weakness in order to steal the IMSI of the 5G UE. In this paper, we propose mechanisms to prevent this downgrade attack.

Our solution uses pseudonyms that have the same format as IMSI for LTE communication to defeat the downgrade attack. The idea of using pseudonyms in IMSI format to confound IMSI catchers in mobile networks has been studied in several works during the recent years [7–12]. We take a similar approach as proposed in these papers. A pseudonym looks like a normal IMSI, but its last nine to ten digits are randomized and frequently changing.[2] The UE is provisioned with two pseudonyms in the beginning and it gets fresh pseudonyms during AKA runs. It uses these pseudonyms instead of IMSI to identify itself when connecting to an LTE SN. The UE uses the SUCI instead of IMSI to connect to a 5G SN. Our solution piggybacks on existing messages involved in the LTE and 5G authentication and key agreement (AKA) protocols to deliver new pseudonyms to the UE and does not require additional messages.

Since the space of pseudonym having IMSI format is limited, pseudonyms need to be reused, i.e., disassociated from one user and reallocated to another. On the other hand, a 5G UE may connect to multiple SNs simultaneously [6]; causing the UE to use different pseudonyms to connect to different SNs. Hence, it is a challenge for the HN to know when it can disassociate a pseudonym from a current user and reallocate it to a new user. In our solution the UE embeds

---

[2] The first five to six digits of the IMSI identify the country and the home network of the mobile user. Even though these digits allow linkability in certain cases, (e.g., if in a visited network there is only one roaming UE from a specific country), these digits are not randomized, because they are needed to route initial requests for authentication data for roaming UE to the correct home network.

information about its LTE pseudonyms into the SUCI. This enables efficient reuse of pseudonyms in the HN and accurate billing. The UE does not need a pseudonym to connect to a 5G SN. Hence, even in the unlikely event, where the UE and HN lose synchronization of pseudonyms, the synchronization can be restored because the UE obtains a new LTE pseudonym from the HN simply by connecting to a 5G SN.

This paper advances protocol design, beyond what is described in papers [7–12], as follows:

(i) The HN can reuse pseudonyms even when a UE has simultaneous connections to multiple SNs.
(ii) The states of pseudonyms in UE and HN will remain synchronized, given that the HN and the UE function correctly.
(iii) For the case where UE and HN get desynchronized due to some unlikely errors, we have detailed a re-synchronization mechanism for pseudonyms' state in UE and HN. The mechanism is based on running a 5G AKA with a 5G SN.

Any enhancement of user identity privacy must support Lawful Interception (LI), i.e. selective interception of individual subscribers by legally authorized agencies. In Sect. 5.2 we describe how LI is supported in the Release 15 enhancement to user identity privacy (where UE encrypts its identity) and propose to supplement pseudonym-based solution with similar features. Adding support for LI into our pseudonym-based solution requires software update (patching) in the core network elements of the LTE SN; it does not require patching in the radio access network elements (base stations).

In this paper we consider the LTE SN in detail. Same solution can be adapted for 3G SNs in a straightforward manner. Its adaptation to GSM would require additional measures because GSM lacks means to authenticate any message received by a mobile device. An example of such a measure has been described in [7].

2 Preliminaries

An IMSI is a globally unique number, usually of 15 decimal digits, identifying a subscriber in GSM, UMTS and LTE systems. The first 3 digits of an IMSI represent the mobile country code (MCC); the second 2 or 3 digits represent the mobile network code (MNC); and the last 10 or 9 digits represent the mobile subscription identification number (MSIN) [13]. The long-term subscriber identifier in 5G system is called Subscription Permanent Identifier (SUPI) [14]. It may contain an IMSI, or a network-specific identifier for private networks.

Figure 1 illustrates a high-level architecture of mobile networks. The UE of a user, which has a subscription with the HN (home network), connects with the SN (serving network) to get services. If the SN and the HN are different networks, we say that the UE is roaming. In that case, the SN and the HN connect with each other over the IP Exchange (IPX) network. The link between the UE and the SN is initially unprotected in LTE, 3G and GSM networks. In 5G, some information sent over this initial link may be confidentiality protected using the public key pk of the HN. Information needed for routing in IPX cannot be confidentiality protected (otherwise, routing would not work) [15].

The HN stores the $(IMSI, K)$ pairs of all its subscribers in the subscription database. The 5G HN also has a public/private key pair pk, sk. The UE includes an ME and a UICC. The UICC is tamper resistant: a malicious entity can not read its content without sophisticated instruments. The universal subscriber identity module (USIM) is an application that runs in the UICC.

In LTE, the USIM stores the IMSI and the subscriber-specific master key K of the user. Please note that if a UE conceals the IMSI using K, the HN would not know which K to use to decrypt the message. Moreover, the UE is not provisioned with any SN-specific keys. Thus, the IMSI is initially sent unprotected over the link between the UE and the SN in LTE. Also in 3G and 2G the IMSI is initially sent unprotected over the link between the UE and the SN. But in 5G the USIM may also store the public key pk of the HN; and then the UE, before identifying itself, can send encrypted (by the key pk) message to the HN.

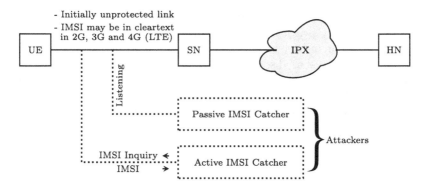

Fig. 1. Schematic illustration of mobile network.

When a UE wants to connect to a SN, the SN wants to know the identity of the user so that the user can be billed. The SN sends an IMSI inquiry to the UE. Since the link between the UE and the LTE (also 3G and 2G) SN is initially unprotected, the UE has to respond with its IMSI in cleartext. A passive IMSI catcher listens to the radio channel and waits for IMSIs sent in cleartext. An active IMSI catcher impersonates a legitimate SN and makes an IMSI inquiry. The UE has no way to distinguish an active IMSI catcher from a legitimate SN before authenticating the SN. Hence, the UE invariably sends the IMSI to the attacker in cleartext.

The identification is followed by mutual authentication based on challenge and response. We will now outline the basic principle of the authentication protocol. The SN provides the identity of the user to the HN. The HN (i) prepares a random challenge; (ii) computes the expected response to the challenge, an authentication token, and an anchor key; (iii) may compute some other required information. The response, authentication token and anchor key are computed using the master key K. An authentication token includes information that protects the integrity of the challenge and defeats replay attack. The challenge, response, authentication token, anchor key and also some other relevant information are collectively known as an authentication vector (AV). The HN sends the AV to the SN.

The SN sends the challenge and the authentication token to the UE. The UE verifies the integrity and freshness of the challenge using the master key K. If the verification result is positive, the UE computes the expected response to the challenge using the master key K and sends the response to the SN. If the expected response that the SN received from the HN matches with the response that the UE sent, the authentication is successful.

The authentication and key agreement protocols of LTE and 5G networks – known as LTE AKA [16] and 5G AKA [6] – are based on the above principle. In LTE AKA, if the authentication is successful, and if the UE that participated in the AKA is attaching with the SN for the first time, then the SN sends a location update (LU) message to the HN [12,17]. Once a UE is authenticated, the SN gives it a temporary identity – known as globally unique temporary UE identity (GUTI) – with confidentiality and integrity protection over a secure channel that has been established based on the authentication. Since then, the UE uses GUTI to identify itself to the SN. The use of GUTI defeats the passive IMSI catchers. However, the use of GUTI does not defeat active IMSI catchers. This is because the UE or the SN may have lost the GUTI, or the UE may visit a new SN. In either case, the SN would make an IMSI inquiry towards the UE. The UE would have to respond with IMSI in cleartext, otherwise it would be locked out of the network.

Once a UE is attached to an SN, the UE may go to idle mode. When there is downlink data available for an idle UE, the SN would page the UE to wake it up, using the IMSI or the GUTI (of that UE) in the paging message. It is worth mentioning that a new authentication may be in initiated by the SN after UE responds to a paging message.

3   Related Work

The attack on user identity privacy by active IMSI catchers has been known since GSM, and numerous defence mechanisms against this attack have been proposed in the literature. We identified two major trends in these mechanisms: the first is based on pseudonyms and the second on public key cryptography. Below, we list works that we consider to be the most relevant to this paper.

In Herzberg et al. [18], one-time pseudonyms are created by probabilistic encryption of the user's identity using a key that is known only by the HN. The HN sends a set of pseudonyms to the UE when the UE and the HN have a secure communication channel.

Publications proposing cellular network pseudonyms in the same format as IMSI, but with randomized, frequently changing MSIN, include [7–10]. In Broek et al. [7] and Khan and Mitchell [8] the pseudonym's update is embedded in a random challenge, RAND, of AKA. Khan and Mitchell [11] identified a weakness in solutions proposing cellular network pseudonyms in the same format as IMSI, which could be exploited to desynchronize pseudonyms in the UE and the HN. They also proposed a fix. Khan et al. [12] found a weakness in [11] and proposed a solution. We will refer to the solution in [12] as the KJGN scheme.

Asokan [19] described how public key encryption can be used to achieve identity privacy in mobile environments. In this solution, only the HN has a public/private key pair and the UE is provisioned with the public key of the HN. The UE encrypts identity information using public key before sending it to the HN. Køien [20] suggests using identity based encryption (IBE) to defeat IMSI catchers in LTE. Khan and Niemi [21] propose the use of IBE to defeat IMSI catchers in 5G networks.

5G is the first generation of mobile networks that includes protection against active IMSI-catchers. 3GPP has decided that users' identities will be protected in 5G by including public key encryption [6]. The idea is similar to Asokan [19]. In addition, the possibility to include IMSI in the paging message has been removed. We will now outline the working of 5G protection mechanism [6].

The UE conceals the 5G user's long-term identities with Elliptic Curve Integrated Encryption Scheme (ECIES) [22,23] before sending them to the SN. ECIES is a hybrid encryption scheme that combines an elliptic curve based public key cryptography with secret key cryptography; it is a semantically secure probabilistic encryption scheme ensuring that successive encryptions of the same plaintext with the same public key result in different ciphertexts with very high probability. Specifically, [6] includes two ECIES profiles, both for the approximately 128-bit security level. Both profiles use AES-128 [24] in CTR mode [25] for confidentiality and HMAC-SHA-256 [26,27] for authenticity in the secret key cryptography part but use either Curve25519 [28,29] or secp256r1 [23] elliptic curves for the public key cryptography part.

A UE that is provisioned with the HN's public key pk,[3] uses it to construct SUCI by computing $\mathcal{E}_{pk}(\text{MSIN})$—the encryption of MSIN with the HN's public key pk—and concatenating it with certain cleartext information. As defined in [6], this cleartext information includes HNID, the home network identifier enabling successful routing to the HN, SUPIPSI for defining the scheme (i.e., either a null scheme or the ECIES profile), and HNPKI for denoting which public key was used in encryption. ECIES guarantees that MSIN can be decrypted from SUCI only by the HN who holds the private key corresponding to pk. Hence, the users' identities are protected.

Please note that public-key based solutions, where the IMSI is delivered to the network encrypted by the public key of the network, are conceptually

---

[3] The standard [6] does not require the HN to provision pk into every UE. If HN has not provisioned its pk into a UE, then that UE will not conceal its long-term identity with this mechanism.

simpler than pseudonym-based solutions, because the latter need a mechanism for changing pseudonyms while keeping the set of pseudonyms in the UE and the HN synchronized. On the other hand, the impact of pseudonyms in IMSI format on legacy network nodes between UE and HN is smaller than of IMSI encrypted by a public key of the network, because the format of IMSI encrypted by a public key of the network is quite different from plaintext IMSI.

4   Our Solution

The 5G standard protects long-term user identity against active IMSI catchers by using SUCI (generated by the public key of the HN) [6], as outlined in Sect. 3. Despite this protection in 5G, a fake LTE SN can still mount a downgrade attack on the identity privacy of a 5G UE.

We mitigate the downgrade attack as follows: instead of IMSI, a 5G UE in LTE network uses pseudonyms that have the same format as IMSI. In addition, when a 5G UE runs 5G AKA, it also synchronizes its LTE pseudonyms with the HN. In our solution:

1. a 5G UE uses pseudonyms to connect with LTE SNs and Release-15 SUCI to connect with 5G SNs;
2. only the HN allocates and releases pseudonyms of mobile users; initially the HN allocates two pseudonyms per 5G user and provisions them into those users' USIMs;
3. a 5G UE gets new pseudonyms by participating in authentication protocols: LTE AKA or 5G AKA; the two latest pseudonyms received by the UE during successful AKA are denoted by p_1 and p_2;
4. in order to support simultaneous connections with several SNs, our solution:
   (i) uses subscriber-specific counter d of pseudonyms maintained by the HN;
   (ii) keeps track of in-use pseudonyms in 5G UE and HN, using sets P_{UE} and P_{HN}, respectively; the elements of these sets are pairs (p_i, d_i) of pseudonyms and their respective counters (see Fig. 2);
   (iii) piggybacks information about pseudonyms in 5G UE within the Release-15 SUCI.

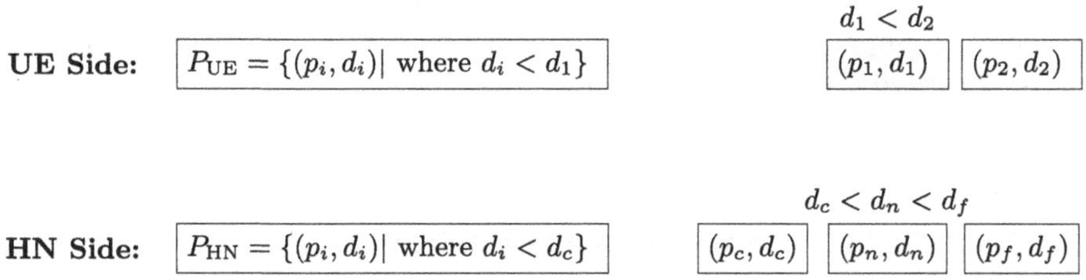

$$d_1 < d_2$$

UE Side: $\boxed{P_{\mathrm{UE}} = \{(p_i, d_i)|\ \text{where } d_i < d_1\}}$ $\boxed{(p_1, d_1)}$ $\boxed{(p_2, d_2)}$

$$d_c < d_n < d_f$$

HN Side: $\boxed{P_{\mathrm{HN}} = \{(p_i, d_i)|\ \text{where } d_i < d_c\}}$ $\boxed{(p_c, d_c)}$ $\boxed{(p_n, d_n)}$ $\boxed{(p_f, d_f)}$

Fig. 2. Pseudonyms in UE and HN

The 5G UE will use only p_1 or p_2 when replying to IMSI inquiry from an LTE SN. The set P_{UE} contains pseudonyms that 5G UE received before p_1 and p_2. The UE deletes pseudonyms from P_{UE} based on policy provided by the HN that could include, e.g., pseudonyms' lifetime or the maximum size of P_{UE}. The P_{HN} contains pseudonyms that the HN thinks are in P_{UE}, and it deletes pseudonyms from P_{HN} according to another policy. One objective of these policies is that the HN should not delete a pseudonym which the UE has not deleted yet. Thus, the pseudonyms in the UE constitute a subset of that UE's pseudonyms in the HN. In short, the UE informs the HN about its oldest pseudonym when it connects with a 5G SN using SUCI, and then the HN is able to reduce the set P_{HN}. Please note that as long as the UE is connecting to LTE SN only, the size of P_{HN} grows. It will be explained later how to avoid that P_{HN} grows too much.

Our solution does not modify the structure and/or length of any existing message. Also, it does not introduce any new messages on top of what 3GPP has standardized; it only introduces changes in the 5G UE and its HN. However, to enable lawful interception in the SN, we would need some changes in the LTE SNs too. This issue is discussed in Sect. 5.2.

As standardized, a 5G USIM comes with an IMSI, a master key K and the HN's public key pk embedded in it. A 5G USIM in our solution also has to include two pseudonyms p_1, p_2 and a key κ, shared with HN, for decrypting the pseudonyms. Similarly, along with the user's IMSI, and master key K, the HN in our solution has to store additional information: the shared key κ for encrypting pseudonyms and three pseudonyms p_c, p_n, and p_f (where the subscripts stand for "current," "next" and "future"). Ideally $p_1 = p_c$ and $p_2 = p_n$.

When a pseudonym p is allocated to a subscriber, it is associated with a subscriber-specific counter d. We require that d is a strictly monotonically increasing integer variable that increases each time the HN allocates a new pseudonym to the subscriber.

4.1   LTE AKA Based Solution

This solution is shown in Fig. 3. It is built on top of the KJGN scheme, which was built on top of LTE AKA. The differences to LTE AKA are indicated by darker font in the figure. The additions on top of KJGN scheme include the use of the counter d_i, which is associated with pseudonym p_i, and the sets P_{UE}, P_{HN}. One major modification is in the condition on which a UE or the HN forget pseudonyms. Supplements for lawful interception are not shown in Fig. 3; they will be discussed separately in Sect. 5.2.

Description.

(1) An LTE SN inquires the UE about the IMSI.
(2) The UE chooses one of the pseudonyms p_1, p_2 and assigns it to q.
(3) The UE sends q to the SN.

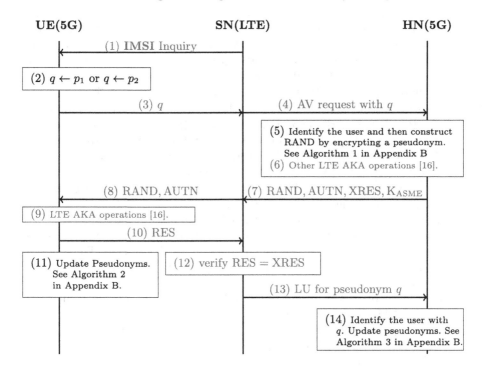

Fig. 3. Solution, when the SN is from an LTE network.

(4) The SN sends an AV request for the pseudonym q to the HN. It is worth mentioning here that in most of the times the user identifies itself with GUTI. Sometimes the user would implicitly identify itself by responding to a paging message. In either case, if the SN wants to perform an LTE AKA, the SN requests an AV to the HN for the pseudonym/IMSI that was associated with the GUTI or was used in the paging message.

(5) The HN checks if the pseudonym q is in use for any subscriber. If yes, the HN starts to prepare the AV. It first constructs the random challenge RAND. A new pseudonym is embedded (encrypted with key κ) in the RAND. Detail of how RAND is constructed is presented in Algorithm 1 in Appendix B. We also describe it in the following.

- The 128-bit long random challenge RAND is created by encrypting (using key κ that can be generated from the master key K) the pseudonym p_f, its counter d_f, an error correction flag (ECF) and a randomly chosen l-bit long $salt$. If the pseudonym p_f is null, a new m-bit long p_f is chosen randomly from the pool of unused pseudonyms. Then d_f is set to the current value of the counter CTR, which is a strictly monotonically increasing counter maintained by the HN. It increases each time the HN generates a new pseudonym. The flag ECF is by default set to 0 but a 5G HN may set it to some other values to notify the UE about an error in the UE's pseudonym state.

- The value of l is equal to $(128 - \text{length}(d_f) - \text{length}(ECF) - m)$. The value of m depends on how many digits of the IMSI are randomized. Since the number of randomized digits can be at most 10, $m \leq 34$. The length of d_f and ECF depends on implementation; $\text{length}(d_f) \leq 24$ and $\text{length}(ECF) \leq 2$ bits should be enough. This implies $l \geq 68$.

(6) The HN computes other parts of authentication vector AV (in addition to the RAND), e.g., the expected response XRES to the challenge RAND, anchoring key K_{ASME}, and authentication token AUTN [12,16].

(7) The HN sends RAND, AUTN, XRES and K_{ASME} to the SN.

(8) The SN forwards RAND and AUTN to the UE.

(9) The UE performs LTE AKA related operations, e.g., verifying MAC in AUTN, computing response RES* [12,16].

(10) If everything is fine in Step (9), the UE sends RES to the SN.

(11) The UE decrypts RAND to extract embedded pseudonym p, and the counter d; and updates the pseudonyms p_1, p_2 if p is new. These operations are presented in Algorithm 2 in Appendix B, and also described in the following.

  - UE decrypts RAND using key κ and gets p, d, ECF and *salt* (Line 1).
  - In an LTE AKA, the ECF bit is always set to 0.
  - If the pseudonym p is a new pseudonym i.e., $d > d_2$, then the UE inserts (p_1, d_1) into P_{UE} and sets $(p_1, d_1), (p_2, d_2) \leftarrow (p_2, d_2), (p, d)$. See lines through 7–10.
  - If $d \leq d_2$, then p is considered as an old pseudonym and the UE does not update pseudonyms.
    - If somehow the value of d_2 (in the UE) gets corrupted and becomes larger than d_f (in the HN), the UE would never be able to accept new pseudonyms anymore just by running LTE AKA. But even then the UE can still obtain a new pseudonym by running a 5G AKA.

(12) The SN compares RES and XRES; the SN stops if RES $\neq$ XRES.

(13) The SN sends an LU message to the HN for the pseudonym q.

(14) The HN searches for a user s.t., $q \in \{p_n, p_f\}$. If found, and p_f is not null, then the HN inserts (p_c, d_c) into P_{HN} and sets $(p_c, d_c), (p_n, d_n), (p_f, d_f) \leftarrow (p_n, d_n), (p_f, d_f), (NULL, NULL)$. See Algorithm 3 in Appendix B.

4.2 5G AKA Based Solution

This solution is used for: (i) delivering a new pseudonym to a 5G UE using 5G AKA; (ii) notifying the HN about pseudonyms that the UE is not using anymore; so that those pseudonyms can be reused in HN; and (iii) re-synchronization of pseudonym states in the (rather unlikely) erroneous situation where d_2 becomes greater than d_f. It is required to deliver new pseudonyms to a 5G UE even when the UE has not used the existing pseudonyms to connect with a legitimate LTE SN. This is because, the UE may have used those pseudonyms with an active IMSI catcher. If a 5G UE always connects with a 5G SN, and does not get new pseudonyms by participating in 5G AKA, then the 5G UE will have the same pseudonym for long time. So, if an active IMSI catcher makes many IMSI inquiries over this long time, then the UE would respond to each of those IMSI inquiries with the same pseudonym. Thus, an active IMSI catcher would be able to track and monitor the user with this long-lived pseudonym.

This solution is built on the 5G AKA protocol of Release 15 [6]; with changes only in the 5G UE and the HN. Thus, the solution is transparent to the 5G SNs of release 15. The solution requires the HN and the USIM to contain all the information the LTE AKA based solution (see Sect. 4.1) requires. Moreover, it requires the HN to have a public/private key pair pk, sk and the USIM to be provisioned with the HN's public key pk. The solution is presented in Fig. 4. The changes in 5G AKA are marked by darker texts.

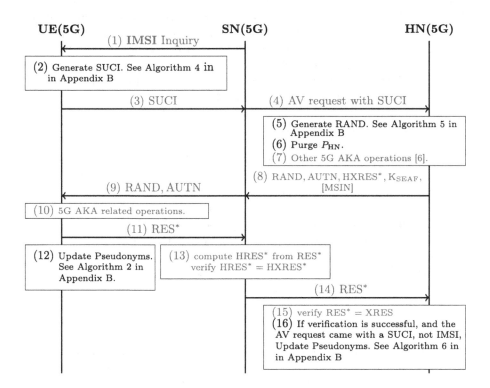

Fig. 4. Solution when the SN is from a 5G network.

Description.

(1) A 5G SN inquires the UE about the IMSI.
(2) The UE generates a SUCI. Construction of SUCI by encrypting MSIN using the HN's public key pk is discussed in Sect. 3 and in [6]. We bring changes in the plaintext that is encrypted into SUCI. Along with MSIN, we also encrypt two counters: δ_{min} and δ_{max}. Here, δ_{min} is the smallest counter of all the pseudonyms in the UE. Thus, the HN can know, which pseudonyms

the UE is not using anymore; consequently they can be allocated to other UEs. The value of the counter $\delta_{\max}$ is always set to d_2. Our construction of SUCI is presented in Appendix B, Algorithm 4, and also described in the following.

- UE computes MAC T of message $MSIN||\delta_{\min}||\delta_{\max}$ with master key K (Line 1).
- UE encrypts $MSIN||\delta_{\min}||\delta_{\max}||T$ with HN's public key pk.
- The ciphertext is concatenated with other information that are in plaintext: HN identifier, the public key identifier of the HN, and the SUPI protection scheme identifier (Line 2). The outcome is returned as SUCI.

(3) The UE sends SUCI.

(4) The SN forwards the SUCI to the HN, requesting an AV. Note that, in most of the times the user identifies itself with GUTI. Sometimes the user would implicitly identify itself by responding to a paging message. In either case, if the SN wants to perform a 5G AKA, the SN requests an AV to the HN with the IMSI that was associated with the GUTI or in the paging.

(5) The HN constructs the RAND by embedding a pseudonym in it. The detail is presented in Algorithm 5 as described in the following.

- The HN extracts MSIN, $\delta_{\min}, \delta_{\max}$ and T from the encrypted part of the SUCI using the private key sk of the HN (Line 1).
- Verifies the MAC T using master key K (Line 2). If the verification is unsuccessful, the algorithm stops. If the verification is successful, the algorithm continues as following.
- Checks if p_f is $NULL$. If yes, an m-bit long p_f is randomly allocated (from the pool of free pseudonyms) and d_f is set to CTR (Lines 4, 5). CTR is a subscriber-specific counter maintained by the HN. It increases every time the HN generates a new pseudonym.
- Sets ECF to 0. Then checks if $\delta_{\max}$ is greater than d_f. If yes, it sets ECF to 1. See Lines from 7 to 10.
- An l-bit long random $salt$ is chosen (Line 11).
- (p_f, d_f) is set into (p, d) i.e., $(p, d) \leftarrow (p_f, d_f)$. See line 12.
- $(p, d, ECF, salt)$ is encrypted with key κ. The ciphertext is RAND. (Line 13). It is worth mentioning that the key κ can be derived from the master key.
- The value of m and l is discussed in Sect. 4.1.

(6) HN removes pseudonyms from P_{HN} which have counter smaller than $\delta_{\min}$.

(7) HN performs other operations of 5G AKA except constructing RAND [6].

(8) HN sends an AV (RAND, AUTN, HXRES*, K_{SEAF}, MSIN) to the SN.

(9) SN forwards the RAND and AUTN to the UE.

(10) UE performs 5G AKA related operations e.g., verifying AUTN and computing the response RES* to the challenge [6].

(11) UE sends the response RES* to he SN.

(12) UE decrypts RAND; extract the embedded pseudonym from the RAND; and updates the pseudonyms in the UE. Algorithm 2 presents the details. This algorithm is partially described in Sect. 4.1. In 5G AKA the ECF might be set to 1 by the HN. In this case the UE would empty the set P_{UE},

set $(p_1, d_1), (p_2, d_2) \leftarrow (p, d - 1), (p, d)$ and terminates the algorithm at this step. This is needed to recover from a very unlikely error situation where d_2 gets corrupted in the UE. We explain the details in the end of Sect. 5.1.

(13) SN computes HRES* as a function of RES*; compares HRES* with HXRES*.

(14) If the comparison in last step matches, SN forwards the RES* to the HN.

(15) The HN compares RES* and XRES.

(16) If the comparison in previous step matches, HN checks whether the AV (associated with the current current 5G AKA run) came with a SUCI or an IMSI. If with a SUCI, HN checks if the pseudonym p that was embedded in the RAND is still p_f. If yes, the HN moves (p_c, d_c) to P_{HN} and sets $(p_c, d_c), (p_n, d_n), (p_f, d_f) \leftarrow (p_n, d_n), (p_f, d_f), (NULL, NULL)$. Consequently, the HN would embed a new pseudonym in the RAND while responding to the next AV request. Details are presented in Algorithm 6 in Appendix B. On the other hand, if the UE identified itself with GUTI or responded to a paging message, then the subsequent AV request sent by the SN would be with an IMSI, not with a SUCI. Consequently the pseudonyms would not be updated in HN. This means, in response to the next AV request, the HN will embed the same pseudonym in the RAND.

Step (16) helps the system to avoid generating unnecessary pseudonyms. If a 5G UE attempts to connect with an LTE SN using a pseudonym, but the subsequent LTE AKA fails or no LTE AKA follows (possibly because the SN is an active IMSI catcher), then the next time the UE tries to connect with a 5G SN, it uses SUCI instead of GUTI. In this way the UE can notify the HN that it needs new pseudonym, and it would receive a new pseudonym in the next AKA. Thus, the solution avoids generating unnecessary pseudonyms.

4.3   Allocation of Pseudonyms

In our solution, the pseudonyms are allocated to users by the HN. A pseudonym must not be allocated to two different users at the same time, because such double allocation would hinder correct call routing and billing; e.g,. a user could receive the bill for services used by another user. As new pseudonyms are generated for a user, the older pseudonyms are stored in the sets P_{HN} and P_{UE}. A pseudonym should not be allocated to a new user as long as it is in P_{HN} and P_{UE} of any other user. If pseudonyms are never removed from P_{HN} and P_{UE}, the system will eventually run out of free pseudonyms. Hence, policies are needed for removing pseudonyms from these sets. One objective of these policies is that, a pseudonym should not be deleted from P_{HN} of a user that is not yet deleted from the set P_{UE} of that user.

The HN randomly allocates a new pseudonym for a user from a pool of free pseudonyms, maintained by the HN. A pseudonym p can be in the pool of free pseudonyms only if it is not in the set P_{HN} (or used as p_c, p_n, or p_f) for any user. To keep the pool of free pseudonyms large enough, the HN needs to remove old pseudonyms that are not anymore used by a UE from P_{HN}. Before removing a pseudonym p from P_{HN}, the HN needs to know that the UE is no longer using it and has removed it from the corresponding P_{UE}.

In our solution, a UE removes pseudonyms from P_{UE} according to the policies provisioned in the UE by the HN. The UE notifies the HN about the pseudonyms that the HN can remove from the P_{HN}. The UE sends (encrypted in the SUCI message) the smallest counter value δ_{min} of all the pseudonyms available in the UE. The HN then removes (from P_{HN}) all pseudonyms that have smaller counter values than δ_{min}. The UE sends δ_{min} with both integrity and confidentiality protection within the encrypted part of SUCI, as discussed in Sect. 4.2.

As mentioned earlier, as long as the UE is connecting to LTE SN only, the size of P_{HN} grows. We will explain next how to avoid that P_{HN} grows too much. The HN needs to have a cap for the size of P_{HN}. If the cap is reached, the HN would not generate any future pseudonym p_f for the user—but will always embed the same pseudonym p_n in the RAND. As a consequence, the user does not enjoy full identity privacy before it connects to a 5G SN using SUCI; the SUCI would include δ_{min} and the HN would be able to reduce P_{HN}. The details of using this cap are left for further study. The cap should be large enough so that it takes a reasonably long time for a UE to reach the cap; on the other hand the cap should be small enough so that a set of legitimate but malicious UE can not exhaust the pseudonym space by connecting to LTE SNs many times. Another topic for future work is how to maximize the chance that the UE would connect with a 5G SN using SUCI. For example, the UE may connect to 5G in order to reduce the size of P_{UE}, even if the user is not paying for 5G services. Another way to recover is to send a message to the user about the situation; suggesting to connect to a 5G SN to enjoy better privacy. Other, more sophisticated techniques than capping the size of P_{HN} can also be in the scope for further study.

It is important to define when the UE can decide that it no longer uses a pseudonym and it can be removed from P_{UE}. The pseudonyms in P_{UE} are stored because the UE should be able to respond to paging messages sent by the SN. Therefore, if a UE has a pseudonym (and the associated GUTI) that has not been used for a reasonably long time (as defined in the policy) and the UE is currently connected to a different SN, the pseudonym can be removed.

The UE may have an old pseudonym in P_{UE} that is associated with a GUTI and a security context but has no other pseudonyms associated with the same SN and the UE is currently connected to this SN. In such a case, the UE would initiate a new registration procedure with the SN using pseudonym p_1 or p_2. If this registration is successful, the UE can remove the old pseudonym from P_{UE}. The UE may also follow a guideline set by the HN to remove pseudonyms from P_{UE}; e.g., remove pseudonyms that are older than one day.

How Large the Sets P_{UE} and P_{HN} Can Be. In the HN, if 50% of MSIN space is used by normal IMSI and pseudonyms, and the allocation of a new pseudonym in HN involves (i) generating a random MSIN, and (ii) checking if that MSIN value has been already allocated, then on the average it would take two tries (each try consisting of (i) and (ii)) for the HN to find a free MSIN.

Because of efficiency reasons, we do not want to exceed this number of tries on the average. It follows that the target number of tries and the current level of MSIN space allocation determine the maximum for the average number of pseudonyms per user. Thus, the policy of handling the size of P_{UE} has to be adjusted so that the average size of P_{UE} would not exceed a certain limit, which in the worst case could be in the order of ten.

We estimate that only a small fraction of MSIN's space, in the order of 1% or less, is in currently in use in the major mobile networks. The biggest fraction, roughly 3%, of the MSIN's space seems to be in use in China Mobile networks, which has three MNC codes [30] and 910 million subscribers [31]. If the average size of P_{HN} is ten, then for each subscriber, around 13 (also p_1, p_2 and IMSI) elements from the MSIN space would be allocated on the average. Therefore, the fraction of in use MSIN's space will grow by a factor of 13, e.g., from 3% to 39%.

Alternative Allocation Mechanisms. In our solution, pseudonyms are allocated to users in the HN. Another approach would be to generate pseudonyms on the UE side. However, in this other approach, the HN has to be able to map a pseudonym with the correct IMSI of the user. Here we briefly present few alternative options and their downsides.

In this option, the UE may perform format preserving encryption (FPE) of the MSIN with a shared symmetric key and use the ciphertext along with MCC and MNC to construct the pseudonym. There may be only one shared key for the whole network, or separate shared keys for each small group of users. Only one key for the whole network is not secure because an attacker can easily know the key. Indeed, the attacker would only need to be a valid subscriber of the HN and the ability to read the UICC. On the other hand, separate shared keys for each small group do not result into good privacy. If the size of the group is k, the subscriber can achieve only k-anonymity. This is because the user would need to identify the user's group in plaintext. In the roaming case, it could be even worse than k-anonymity. For instance, it could be the case that only one member of the group is roaming in a certain country at a certain time point.

Another option is that the UE pseudorandomly generates pseudonyms—e.g., by hashing the IMSI and a salt using the shared master key. The UE uses m bits of the hash digest along with the MCC and MNC a to construct the pseudonym. Similarly, the HN would need to compute the hash digest (of m bits) of all the IMSIs (of all the valids subscribers) with the salt using the respective master keys. If the salt is chosen by the UE based on an agreed scheme (e.g., the salt is the current date), then the HN has to compute hash digest for each subscriber according to that scheme (e.g., once in a day) and store in a hash table. However, since m is only around 34 bits, there would have many collisions—mutiple IMSIs will be hashed to the same pseudonym. The HN would consult with the hash table when it receives a pseudonym. Due to many collisions in the hash table, pseudonyms would be ambiguous.

5   Analysis of Our Solution

In our solution, the pseudonyms are delivered to the UE with confidentiality protection using the key κ. Hence, an IMSI catcher cannot know a pseudonym before the UE uses it. This provides unlinkability across the pseudonyms. Once a UE switches to use a new pseudonym, the UE appears as a new (previously unknown) user in the network. Same pseudonym may be transmitted many times in different RAND. However, the challenge still remains fresh and random because of the randomly chosen l-bit long *salt*; the value of l can be as long as 68 bits. Since a user keeps using the same pseudonym until it obtains a new pseudonym, the UE is exposed to an active IMSI catcher for the time. This exposure mostly coincides with the already existing exposure of the GUTI. In the rest of this section we analyze our solution from important aspects of using IMSI-like pseudonyms in mobile networks: (i) synchronization of pseudonyms, (ii) LI and patching, (iii) billing and charging, and (iv) performance overheads.

5.1   Synchronization

What is Desynchronization? We say that a UE is desynchronized with the HN if the pseudonyms p_1 and p_2 of the user in the UE side are no more associated with the same user in the HN side. In other words, a UE is desynchronized with the HN if the following condition holds.

$$(p_1, d_1), (p_2, d_2) \notin \{(p_c, d_c), (p_n, d_n), (p_f, d_f)\} \cup P_{\text{HN}}$$

The UE is not allowed to use any other pseudonyms than p_1, p_2 in response to an IMSI inquiry from an LTE, 3G or GSM SN. Consequently, when the UE responds to an IMSI inquiry with p_1 or p_2, the HN would fail to retrieve the correct IMSI. As a result, the subsequent AKA would fail and the UE will not be able to join the network.

Can Desynchronization Happen? If both the HN and UE function correctly desynchronization can not happen. We will present our argument in this section. In principle, desynchronization may happen if one of the following cases happen:

1. If UE accepts a pseudonym that is not generated in the HN
2. If HN deletes $(p_1, d_1), (p_2, d_2)$ from $\{(p_c, d_c), (p_n, d_n), (p_f, d_f)\} \cup P_{\text{HN}}$
3. If UE accepts a pseudonym that was generated for the user in the HN but the HN has already deleted the pseudonym

First, we discuss Case 1. Since a pseudonym is embedded in the RAND, the integrity of the pseudonym is protected if the integrity of the RAND is protected. The integrity of the RAND with the help of the MAC that is a part of the AUTN. So, the UE would never accept a pseudonym that was not generated in the HN; consequently, Case 1 can never happen.

Second, we discuss Case 2. The HN never deletes $(p_c, d_c), (p_n, d_n), (p_f, d_f)$. The HN may delete a pseudonym (p_i, d_i) from P_{HN} if the HN has decrypted a

$\delta_{\min}$ from a valid SUCI such that $d_i < \delta_{\min}$; see Step 6 of 5G AKA based solution in Sect. 4.2. Since, the UE would never deletes $(p_1, d_1), (p_2, d_2)$, the value of $\delta_{\min}$ would be at most d_1. This implies $\delta_{\min} \leq d_1 < d_2$. Consequently, the HN would not delete $(p_1, d_1), (p_2, d_2)$ from P_{HN}.

Third, we discuss Case 3. As discussed in Case 2, if pseudonym (p_i, d_i) is deleted from P_{HN}, then d_2 would be greater than d_i, because $d_i < \delta_{\min} \leq d_1 < d_2$. Remember that a UE would accept a pseudonym (p_i, d_i) only if $d_i > d_2$. Thus (p_i, d_i) would never be accepted by the UE.

Resynchronization. However, if due to some unlikely errors in UE and HN, desynchronization happens, our solution can bring back a desynchronized user into a synchronized state automatically just by connecting to a 5G SN. This is because a 5G UE does not need a valid pseudonym to participate in a 5G AKA, and the UE would get a valid pseudonym if it can participate in a valid 5G AKA. This is a major advantage because, as discussed in [12], such a desynchronized user would otherwise have to go to a mobile network operator's shop to change the UICC.

Also, if d_2 in the UE gets corrupted and becomes larger than d_f, then the UE would not be able to accept a new pseudonym; see Algorithms 1, 2 and 5. If d_2 becomes a large enough value, then the UE might not accept new pseudonyms anymore. However, the 5G UE is able to resynchronize with HN even if such a corruption happens; just by connecting to a 5G SN using SUCI and running a 5G AKA.

Since the UE would embed $\delta_{\max}$ (which is equal to d_2) in the SUCI message, the 5G HN would know (Algorithm 4) if such a corruption has happened, see Algorithm 5. To help the UE fixing the corruption, the 5G HN would set the ECF in the RAND, see Algorithm 5. The UE decrypts the RAND and extracts the pseudonym (p, d). If the ECF is set, the UE would accept the pseudonym even though $d < d_2$, see Algorithm 2. Since, acceptance of such a pseudonym may break the consistency with other pseudonyms in the UE, the UE deletes all other pseudonyms it has. Pseudonyms p_1, p_2 holds the same value as p; d_1 gets the value $d - 1$ and d_2 gets d. Thus the UE goes back to a state similar to the beginning.

5.2   Lawful Interception and Patching

Lawful Interception (LI) involves selectively intercepting communications of individual subscribers by legally authorized agencies. The agency typically provides the long-term identifier of the target UE or service to the network operator, which must have the means to intercept communications of the correct target based on long-term or permanent identifiers associated with that target. There is a requirement that a network operator is able to intercept without the need to rely on another network operator or jurisdiction. In particular, an SN does not need to share LI target identities of roaming UE with an HN and vice versa [32, 33].

In order to support LI in Release 15, where the UE encrypts its identity using the public key of the HN, (1) the HN provides long-term identifier of the UE to the SN during authentication and key agreement procedure; and (2) both UE and SN use long-term identifier of the UE as one of the inputs to the derivation of master session key. The visited network gets the long-term identifier of the UE as a result of (1), while (2) ensures that the UE and visited network can communicate only if both use the same long-term identifier of the UE.

In order to support LI in our pseudonym-based solution, we propose to add (1), and possibly also (2), into the existing legacy core network elements (MME and HSS in LTE; MSC, SGSN, and HLR in 3G/GSM) by software upgrade. The scope of this software upgrade appears to be much smaller, compared to adapting Release 15 solution into the existing legacy networks. This is mainly because adapting Release 15 solution to legacy networks is likely to impact also the radio access networks: the format of encrypted identifier in Release 15 is quite different from the cleartext IMSI, while in our solution the pseudonym is in the format of IMSI.

The LI feature (1) can be implemented in our solution as follows: in the AV request, the SN informs the HN that it is patched and when the HN returns the AV, it includes the MSIN as part of the AV.

Adding support for (2) is more complicated, especially in the cases of 3G and GSM. In LTE, the SN extracts the MSIN and uses it as an additional input in deriving the master session key and the UE is also informed that the SN is patched by piggybacking on RAND so that the UE also uses the MSIN in computing the master session key. In 3G and GSM there is no concept of master session key. Therefore, the MSIN has to be used directly in derivation of ciphering and integrity keys.

Please note that this complication appears also in the case where Release 15 public-key based solution would be adapted for legacy networks.

Typically, an organization of mobile network operators, like GSMA (GSM Association), could discuss and agree on a deadline in order to provide enough time for operators to patch their networks.

If some legacy network has not completed the patch by the agreed deadline, it is OK for other operators to ignore that failure and start using the pseudonyms-based protection of identity privacy. The LI in the network that is late in patching would not work fully for roaming 5G UEs.

In the case of a public key-based solution, if some mobile operator is late with a patch, then roaming 5G UEs would not be able to join that network.

5.3   Charging and Billing

Mobile users are charged based on CDRs (call detailed records) that are generated in the serving network. A CDR includes IMSI and records chargeable event (like the service used). The home network then adds charges to the bill of subscriber that is associated with the CDR's IMSI.

After a pseudonym-based solution is adopted, a CDR may contain a pseudonym in place of IMSI. (Indeed, if the UE uses pseudonym in IMSI format when it communicates with SN, and the SN does not get the long-term identifier of that UE – for instance, because it was not patched for LI, then the SN has no other choice but to put the UE's pseudonym into the CDR.) For this reason the home network has to consult a log of pseudonym allocations when it maps from UE identifiers in received CDRs to the actual subscribers' data [8,12]. That log includes the following information: (i) the pseudonym, (ii) the IMSI of the subscriber whom the pseudonym is given to, (iii) the time when HN allocated the pseudonym to the subscriber, (iv) the time when the subscriber started using the pseudonym (i.e., the time of the first successful AKA run of that subscriber with the pseudonym), (v) the time when the UE notified that it is no longer using the pseudonym, and (vi) list of SNs that the user has attached with using this pseudonym. The home network has to maintain the log at least until the billing is settled, and possibly for longer time, to comply with the local authority's guidelines.

In order to keep the billing accurate, a UE that stops using pseudonym p and deletes it, must also stop using the GUTI and the security context associated with p. Let us illustrate what may happen otherwise. A UE1 that is visiting SN1, removes a pseudonym p from its P_{UE} but keeps the GUTI and the security context. The UE1 also informs the HN (via 5G SUCI) that it has removed the pseudonym p. Therefore, the HN sends the pseudonym p to the pool of free pseudonyms; subsequently, p is allocated to another subscriber and delivered to UE2 in SN2.

If UE1 continues to identify itself in SN1 by the GUTI associated with p as it consumes services, then SN1 will generate a CDR that contains the pseudonym p, which is at that time is allocated to UE2. As a result, UE2 will be charged for the service consumed by UE1 in SN1. This may continue until there is a new AKA run between UE1 and SN1, or until the GUTI expires. However, the HN has enough information in the pseudonym allocation log to resolve the correct UE who created the CDR.

5.4   Performance Overheads

In our solution the pseudonyms' delivery protocol between UE and HN is piggy-backed on existing AKA messages. The structure of AKA messages remains the same, but parts of those messages are constructed and interpreted differently. We list here the additional tasks that have to be done by HN and UE.

Most of those tasks have to be done in the HN: First, the HN has to store a set of in-use pseudonyms per subscriber, maintain a pool of free pseudonyms, and be able to allocate pseudonyms from this pool uniformly at random.

Second, as mentioned in Sect. 5.3, the HN needs to log pseudonym assignments for charging purposes. Keeping this log adds to the storage overhead in the HN and computational overhead in the charging system.

Third, the HN has to generate a random l-bit *salt* and encrypt the pseudonym and *salt* using the symmetric key κ. The 5G HN has also to verify the MAC of the message that is encrypted into the SUCI. But the overheads due to these symmetric-key cryptographic operations are negligible.

Fourth, there is one-time, initial provisioning effort into the USIM of: (i) the initial pseudonyms, and (ii) a policy for forgetting pseudonyms.

On the UE side, one extra decryption is needed to extract the pseudonym embedded in RAND. This symmetric-key decryption has negligible overhead. In addition, UE has to maintain a set of pseudonyms based on the policy provisioned by the HN.

6   Conclusion

3GPP Release 15, the first release of 5G system, includes protection of long-term identity of mobile users against active IMSI catching. But in a typical case where 5G UE also supports LTE, it is still vulnerable to LTE IMSI catchers. This threat can be mitigated by adopting pseudonyms in the format of IMSI in LTE.

We propose a solution where the Release 15 mechanism for protecting user identity privacy is used for synchronizing the LTE pseudonyms in the format of IMSI between the UE and HN, thus making the LTE pseudonyms more robust. Our solution can automatically bring a desynchronized user back to synchronized state just by connecting to a 5G network. For LI purpose, the required patching effort in the legacy SNs is reasonable. All in all, pseudonym-based solution is a potential candidate for confounding IMSI catchers in legacy networks.

Questions for future study include the following: (i) Is it a good idea to encrypt the pseudonyms always with the same key? (ii) What data structure can be used to maintain the pool of free pseudonyms? (iii) What part of the solution has to be implemented in the USIM and what part in the ME? Capping the size of the set P_{HN}, when the UE is connecting only with LTE SNs, is also a subject of further study. The resilience of pseudonym-based solution to computational errors in HN, SN, or UE would also be an important area of investigation.

Appendix A   Summary of Notation

AUTN	authentication token used to verify the integrity of the RAND; computed by the HN; sent to the SN as part of the AV; used in both LTE AKA and 5G AKA
AV	authentication vector; a bunch of information that the HN sends to delegate the authentication to the SN
CDR	call detailed record
d_i	the counter value (time stamp) associated with pseudonym p_i by the HN
δ_{min}	the smallest counter of all the pseudonyms available in the UE. The UE embeds it in the SUCI
δ_{max}	it is always set to the current value of d_2. The UE embeds it in the SUCI

ECF	error correction flag, piggybacked on the random challenge RAND. the 5G HN sets this flag to inform the UE that the UE's pseudonym state is corrupted
5G AKA	an authentication protocol used in 5G
GSM	Global System for Mobile Communications
HN	Home network; the UE is subscribed with this network
IMSI	international mobile subscriber identity
κ	a symmetric key shared only between the USIM and the HN
K	the symmetric key, also known as master key, shared only by the USIM of a user and the HN
K_{ASME}	anchoring key – subsequent encryption and integrity protection keys are derive from it; computed by the HN and sent to the SN as part of the AV
l	bit length of the *salt* that is used as a part of the plaintext that is encrypted into RAND
LTE AKA	an authentication protocol used in LTE network
LU	location update; when a user attaches to an LTE SN for the first time, after the authentication succeeds, the SN send an LU message to the HN
m	number of bits used to generate the randomized decimal digits to construct pseudonyms; $m \leq 40$
ME	mobile equipment, usually a mobile phone
p_c, p_n, p_f	the pseudonyms in the HN; p_c for the current pseudonym, p_n for new pseudonym and p_f for the future pseudonym; ideally expectation is $p_1 = p_c, p_2 = p_n$ or $p_1 = p_n, p_2 = p_f$
P_{HN}	the set of pairs (p_i, d_i) maintained by the HN for a specific UE
p_1, p_2	the pseudonyms the UE is currently using
P_{UE}	the set of pairs (p_i, d_i) maintained by the UE
q	the pseudonym that a UE uses to identify itself
RAND	is the 128-bit long random challenge; chosen/constructed by HN; sent to SN as part of the AV; SN forwards it to the UE; used in both LTE AKA and 5G AKA
RES	response sent by the UE to the random challenge RAND in LTE AKA
SN	serving network; the UE connects with this network
SQN	the sequence number used by the USIM and the HN, both in LTE AKA and 5G AKA to defeat replay attack
UE	user equipment (USIM + ME)
UICC	universal integrated circuit card
USIM	universal subscriber identity module
XRES	expected response (to RAND) from the UE; computed by the HN; sent to the SN as part of the AV; used in LTE AKA
XSQN	the sequence number sent by the HN to the UE

Appendix B   Algorithms

Algorithm 1. Construct RAND for LTE AKA in HN

Input: $q, (\text{IMSI}, \kappa, (p_c, d_c), (p_n, d_n), (p_f, d_f)), CTR$; where q is the pseudonym received in the AV request, the vector following q contains the relevant records of the user in the subscription database s.t., $q \in \{\text{IMSI}, p_c, p_n, p_f\}$ or $(q, *) \in P_{\text{HN}}$, and CTR is a non decreasing counter that the HN maintains. CTR increases once in a configured time interval.

Output: RAND

1: **if** $p_f = NULL$ **then**
2:     allocate $p_f \in \{0, 1\}^m$ randomly from the pool of free pseudonyms
3:         $d_f \leftarrow CTR$
4: **end if**
5: choose $salt \in \{0, 1\}^l$ randomly
6: $(p, d) \leftarrow (p_f, d_f)$
7: $ECF \leftarrow 0$ ▷ this flag might be set to 1 by a 5G HN to indicate an error
8: RAND $\leftarrow E_\kappa (p, d, ECF, salt)$
9: **return** RAND

Algorithm 2. Update Pseudonyms in UE

Input: RAND, p_1, p_2

Output: updated pseudonym states in the UE

1: extract $p, d, ECF, salt$ by decrypting RAND using key κ
2: **if** $ECF = 1$ **then**   ▷ it means, the UE has unreasonably large d_2
3:     empty the set P_{UE}
4:     $(p_1, d_1), (p_2, d_2) \leftarrow (p, d - 1), (p, d)$
5:     **return**
6: **end if**
7: **if** $d > d_2$ **then**
8:     $P_{\text{UE}} \leftarrow P_{\text{UE}} \cup \{(p_1, d_1)\}$
9:     $(p_1, d_1), (p_2, d_2) \leftarrow (p_2, d_2), (p, d)$
10: **end if**

Algorithm 3. Update Pseudonyms in HN after LTE AKA

Input: $q, (P_{\text{HN}}, (p_c, d_c), (p_n, d_n), (p_f, d_f))$; where q is the pseudonym received in the AV request, the vector following q contains the records of the user in the subscription database s.t., $q \in \{p_n, p_f\}$

Output: updated pseudonym states in the HN

1: **if** $p_f \neq NULL$ **then**
2:     $P_{\text{HN}} \leftarrow P_{\text{HN}} \cup \{(p_c, d_c)\}$
3:     $(p_c, d_c), (p_n, d_n), (p_f, d_f) \leftarrow (p_n, d_n), (p_f, d_f), (NULL, NULL)$
4: **end if**

Algorithm 4. Generate SUCI

Input: MSIN, K, $\delta_{\min}$, $\delta_{\max}$, HNID, pk, HNPKI, SUPIPSI; where $\delta_{\min}$ is the counter of the earliest pseudonym in P_{UE}; $\delta_{\max}$ is d_2; HNID is the HN ID, usually MCC||MNC; pk is the public key of the HN; HNPKI is the public key identifier of the HN; SUPIPSI is the SUPI protection scheme identifier

Output: SUCI

1: $T \leftarrow \text{MAC}_K (\text{MSIN}||\delta_{\min}||\delta_{\max})$
2: $\text{SUCI} = \text{HNID}||\text{HNPKI}||\text{SUPIPSI}||\mathcal{E}_{pk} (\text{MSIN}||\delta_{\min}||\delta_{\max}||T)$
3: **return** SUCI

Algorithm 5. Construct RAND for 5G AKA

Input: sk, SUCI, κ, (p_f, d_f), CTR; where sk is the private key of the HN, SUCI is received from the SN in the AV request, κ is the subscriber-specific key to encrypt pseudonyms, (p_f, d_f) is the subscriber's pseudonym and its counter that would be embedded in RAND

Output: RAND

1: extract MSIN, $\delta_{\min}$, $\delta_{\max}$, and T by decrypting SUCI using secret key sk
2: **if** $T = \text{MAC}_K (\text{MSIN}||\delta_{\min}||\delta_{\max})$ **then**
3:     **if** $p_f = NULL$ **then**
4:         allocate $p_f \in \{0,1\}^m$ randomly from the pool of free pseudonyms
5:         $d_f \leftarrow CTR$
6:     **end if**
7:     $ECF \leftarrow 0$
8:     **if** $\delta_{\max} > d_f$ **then**   ▷ It means the UE has unreasonably large d_2
9:         $ECF \leftarrow 1$
10:     **end if**
11:     choose $salt \in \{0,1\}^l$ randomly
12:     $(p,d) \leftarrow (p_f, d_f)$
13:     $\text{RAND} \leftarrow E_\kappa (p, d, ECF, salt)$
14:     **return** RAND
15: **end if**

Algorithm 6. Update Pseudonyms in HN after 5G AKA

Input: p, $(P_{HN}, (p_c, d_c), (p_n, d_n), (p_f, d_f))$; where p is the pseudonym that was embedded in the RAND of the 5G AKA in question, the vector following p contains the relevant records of the user participated in the AKA.

1: **Output:** updated pseudonyms in the HN
2: **if** $p_f = p$ **then**
3:     $P_{HN} \leftarrow P_{HN} \cup \{(p_c, d_c)\}$
4:     $(p_c, d_c), (p_n, d_n), (p_f, d_f) \leftarrow (p_n, d_n), (p_f, d_f), (NULL, NULL)$
5: **end if**

References

1. Soltani, A., Timberg, C.: Tech firm tries to pull back curtain on surveillance efforts in Washington, September 2014. https://www.washingtonpost.com/world/national-security/researchers-try-to-pull-back-curtain-on-surveillance-efforts-in-washington/2014/09/17/f8c1f590-3e81-11e4-b03f-de718edeb92f_story.html?utm_term=.96e31aa4440b. Accessed 14 July 2017
2. PKI Electronic Intelligence: 3G UMTS IMSI Catcher. http://www.pki-electronic.com/products/interception-and-monitoring-systems/3g-umts-imsi-catcher/. Accessed 6 July 2018
3. Dabrowski, A., Pianta, N., Klepp, T., Mulazzani, M., Weippl, E.: IMSI-catch me if you can: IMSI-catcher-catchers. In: Proceedings of the 30th Annual Computer Security Applications Conference, ACSAC 2014, pp. 246–255. ACM, New York (2014)
4. Ney, P., Smith, J., Gabriel, C., Tadayoshi, K.: SeaGlass: enabling city-wide IMSI-catcher detection. In: Proceedings on Privacy Enhancing Technologies. PoPETs (2017)
5. 3GPP: TS 22.261 Service requirements for next generation new services and markets (2018). https://portal.3gpp.org/desktopmodules/Specifications/SpecificationDetails.aspx?specificationId=3107
6. 3GPP: TS 33.501 Security architecture and procedures for 5G System, March 2018. https://portal.3gpp.org/desktopmodules/Specifications/SpecificationDetails.aspx?specificationId=3169
7. Van den Broek, F., Verdult, R., de Ruiter, J.: Defeating IMSI catchers. In: Proceedings of the 22nd ACM SIGSAC Conference on Computer and Communications Security, CCS 2015. ACM (2015)
8. Khan, M.S.A., Mitchell, C.J.: Improving air interface user privacy in mobile telephony. In: Chen, L., Matsuo, S. (eds.) SSR 2015. LNCS, vol. 9497, pp. 165–184. Springer, Cham (2015). https://doi.org/10.1007/978-3-319-27152-1_9
9. Norrman, K., Näslund, M., Dubrova, E.: Protecting IMSI and user privacy in 5G networks. In: Proceedings of the 9th EAI International Conference on Mobile Multimedia Communications, MobiMedia 2016. ICST (2016)
10. Ginzboorg, P., Niemi, V.: Privacy of the long-term identities in cellular networks. In: Proceedings of the 9th EAI International Conference on Mobile Multimedia Communications, MobiMedia 2016. ICST (2016)
11. Khan, M., Mitchell, C.: Trashing IMSI catchers in mobile networks. In: Proceedings of the 10th ACM Conference on Security and Privacy in Wireless and Mobile Networks (WiSec 2017), Boston, USA, 18–20 July 2017. Association for Computing Machinery (ACM), United States, May 2017
12. Khan, M., Järvinen, K., Ginzboorg, P., Niemi, V.: On de-synchronization of user pseudonyms in mobile networks. In: Shyamasundar, R.K., Singh, V., Vaidya, J. (eds.) ICISS 2017. LNCS, vol. 10717, pp. 347–366. Springer, Cham (2017). https://doi.org/10.1007/978-3-319-72598-7_22
13. 3GPP: TS 23.003, 15.4.0 Numbering, addressing and identification, June 2018. https://portal.3gpp.org/desktopmodules/Specifications/SpecificationDetails.aspx?specificationId=729
14. 3GPP: TS 23.501 System Architecture for the 5G System (2018). https://portal.3gpp.org/desktopmodules/Specifications/SpecificationDetails.aspx?specificationId=3144

15. Khan, M., Ginzboorg, P., Niemi, V.: IMSI-based routing and identity privacy in 5G. In: Proceedings of the 22nd Conference of Open Innovations Association FRUCT, Jyvaskyla, Finland, May 2018
16. 3GPP: TS 33.401 V15.0.0 Security architecture (Release 15), June 2017. https://portal.3gpp.org/desktopmodules/Specifications/SpecificationDetails. aspx?specificationId=2296
17. 3GPP: TS 23.012 V14.0.0 Location management procedures (Release 14), March 2017. https://portal.3gpp.org/desktopmodules/Specifications/ SpecificationDetails.aspx?specificationId=735
18. Herzberg, A., Krawczyk, H., Tsudik, G.: On travelling incognito. In: 1994 First Workshop on Mobile Computing Systems and Applications. IEEE Xplore (1994)
19. Asokan, N.: Anonymity in a mobile computing environment. In: First Workshop on Mobile Computing Systems and Applications. IEEE, Santa Cruz (1994)
20. Køien, G.M.: Privacy enhanced mutual authentication in LTE. In: 2013 IEEE 9th International Conference on Wireless and Mobile Computing, Networking and Communications (WiMob), pp. 614–621, October 2013
21. Khan, M., Niemi, V.: Concealing IMSI in 5G network using identity based encryption. In: Yan, Z., Molva, R., Mazurczyk, W., Kantola, R. (eds.) NSS 2017. LNCS, vol. 10394, pp. 544–554. Springer, Cham (2017). https://doi.org/10.1007/978-3-319-64701-2_41
22. Certicom Research: SEC 1: Elliptic Curve Cryptography. Standards for Efficient Cryptography, Ver. 2.0, May 2009. http://www.secg.org/sec1-v2.pdf
23. Certicom Research: SEC 2: Recommended Elliptic Curve Domain Parameters. Standards for Efficient Cryptography, Ver. 2.0, January 2010. http://www.secg. org/sec2-v2.pdf
24. NIST: Advanced Encryption Standard (AES). FIPS PUB 197 (2001)
25. NIST: Recommendation for Block Cipher Modes of Operation: Methods and Techniques. SP 800–38A (2001)
26. Krawczyk, H., Bellare, M., Canetti, R.: HMAC: Keyed-Hashing for Message Authentication. RFC 2104, February 1997
27. NIST: Secure hash standard (SHS). FIPS PUB 180-4 (2012)
28. Bernstein, D.J.: Curve25519: new Diffie-Hellman speed records. In: Yung, M., Dodis, Y., Kiayias, A., Malkin, T. (eds.) PKC 2006. LNCS, vol. 3958, pp. 207–228. Springer, Heidelberg (2006). https://doi.org/10.1007/11745853_14
29. Langley, A., Hamburg, M., Turner, S.: Elliptic Curves for Security. RFC 7748, January 2016
30. Interactive digital media GmbH: Mobile Country Codes (MCC) and Mobile Network Codes (MNC). http://www.mcc-mnc.com/
31. Wikipedia: List of mobile network operators. https://en.wikipedia.org/wiki/List_of_mobile_network_operators
32. 3GPP: TS 33.106: 3G security; Lawful interception requirements (2018). https://portal.3gpp.org/desktopmodules/Specifications/SpecificationDetails. aspx?specificationId=2265
33. 3GPP: TS 33.126 V15.0.0 Lawful Interception requirements, June 2018. https://portal.3gpp.org/desktopmodules/Specifications/SpecificationDetails. aspx?specificationId=3181

Identity Confidentiality in 5G Mobile Telephony Systems

Haibat Khan$^{(\boxtimes)}$ (ID), Benjamin Dowling, and Keith M. Martin

Information Security Group, Royal Holloway, University of London, Egham, UK
Haibat.Khan.2016@live.rhul.ac.uk,
{Benjamin.Dowling,Keith.Martin}@rhul.ac.uk

Abstract. The 3rd Generation Partnership Project (3GPP) recently proposed a standard for 5G telecommunications, containing an identity protection scheme meant to address the long-outstanding privacy problem of permanent subscriber-identity disclosure. The proposal is essentially two disjoint phases: an identification phase, followed by an establishment of security context between mobile subscribers and their service providers via symmetric-key based authenticated key agreement. Currently, 3GPP proposes to protect the identification phase with a public-key based solution, and while the current proposal is secure against a classical adversary, the same would not be true of a quantum adversary. 5G specifications target very long-term deployment scenarios (well beyond the year 2030), therefore it is imperative that quantum-secure alternatives be part of the current specification. In this paper, we present such an alternative scheme for the problem of private identification protection. Our solution is compatible with the current 5G specifications, depending mostly on cryptographic primitives already specified in 5G, adding minimal performance overhead and requiring minor changes in existing message structures. Finally, we provide a detailed formal security analysis of our solution in a novel security framework.

Keywords: 5G security · Authentication · Privacy · Mobile networks

1 Introduction

While many mobile users may be comfortable with the fact that their service provider is able to identify them and track their geographical location ubiquitously, fewer are likely to be comfortable with an arbitrary third party having this capability. In hand of a third party, such capability could lead to undesirable breaches of end user privacy, opening the door to a range of potential consequences, such as harassment, stalking, employee monitoring, commercial profiling, etc. For these reasons, the global mobile telephony standardization body, the 3rd Generation Partnership Project (3GPP) has identified the following essential requirements related to user privacy [8]:

© Springer Nature Switzerland AG 2018
C. Cremers and A. Lehmann (Eds.): SSR 2018, LNCS 11322, pp. 120–142, 2018.
https://doi.org/10.1007/978-3-030-04762-7_7

- **User Identity Confidentiality**[1]: The permanent identity of a user to whom a service is delivered cannot be eavesdropped on the radio access link.
- **User Location Confidentiality:** The presence or the arrival of a user in a certain area cannot be determined by eavesdropping on the radio access link.
- **User Untraceability:** An intruder cannot deduce whether different services are delivered to the same user by eavesdropping on the radio access link.

In mobile telephony systems, networks allocate to each SIM card a unique identifier,[2] known up to the Fourth Generation (4G) as an *International Mobile Subscriber Identity* (IMSI) and for the Fifth Generation (5G) as a *Subscription Permanent Identifier* (SUPI). As authentication between a user and its service provider is based on a shared symmetric key, it can only take place after user identification. However, if the IMSI/SUPI values are sent in plaintext over the radio access link, then users can be identified, located and tracked using these permanent identifiers. To avoid this privacy breach, the SIM card is assigned temporary identifiers (called *Temporary Mobile Subscriber Identity* (TMSI) until 3G systems and *Globally Unique Temporary User Equipment Identity* (GUTI) for 4G and 5G systems) by the visited network. These frequently-changing temporary identifiers are then used for identification purposes over the radio access link.

However, there are certain situations where authentication through the use of temporary identifiers is not possible. For instance, when a user registers with a network for the first time and is not yet assigned a temporary identifier. Another case is when the visited network is unable to resolve the IMSI/SUPI from the presented TMSI/GUTI. An active man-in-the-middle adversary can intentionally simulate this scenario to force an unsuspecting user to reveal its long-term identity. These attacks are known as "IMSI-catching" attacks [17] and persist in today's mobile networks including the 4G LTE/LTE+ [20].

Defeating IMSI Catchers in 5G. IMSI-catching attacks have threatened all generations (2G/3G/4G) of mobile telecommunication for decades [5]. As a result of facilitating backwards compatibility for legacy reasons, this privacy problem appears to have persisted [6]. However, the 3GPP has now decided to address this issue, albeit at the cost of backward compatibility. In case of identification failure via a 5G-GUTI, unlike earlier generations, 5G security specifications do not allow plaintext transmissions of the SUPI over the radio interface [11]. Instead, an *Elliptic Curve Integrated Encryption Scheme* (ECIES)-based privacy-preserving identifier containing the concealed SUPI is transmitted [22]. We elaborate upon the details of this scheme further in Sect. 3.1.

---

[1] The official 3GPP documentation uses the term "Identity Confidentiality" to refer to the privacy of user identity. We follow the 3GPP naming convention.

[2] Users can also be identified through other unique identifiers, for instance *International Mobile Equipment Identity* (IMEI) which uniquely identifies the mobile equipment. However, it is only the IMSI/SUPI which is used for initial identification purposes.

Motivation. It is hoped that 5G specifications will be finalized in 2019. The first practical 5G deployments can then be expected a number of years later. However, it will almost certainly take a decade or so before all legacy systems are likely to be upgraded to 5G. It would thus seem that IMSI-catching attacks will remain an issue in the mid-term future, possibly even beyond 2030. By that time practical quantum computers will pose a much more immediate threat than they do today [3,14], particularly with respect to cryptographic schemes such as ECIES, which are known to be vulnerable to quantum algorithms. The impact of quantum computers on mobile networks is already being discussed within the telephony industry [18], with a call to implement quantum-secure cryptography. It is thus imperative that 5G security specifications such as 3GPP TS 33.501 [11] (hereafter referred as TS 33.501) contain options for quantum-resistant schemes. Fortunately, 5G security has mostly relied upon symmetric cryptography for achieving its security objectives. However, the ECIES-based identification mechanism is an exception. In this paper, we propose a symmetric alternative to the ECIES mechanism, so that the "all symmetric" stature of 5G security can continue in a quantum future. Any proposal for an alternative user identification scheme for 5G systems should strive to satisfy the following requirements:

- Provision appropriate privacy guarantees such as anonymity and unlinkability against a quantum adversary.
- The performance overhead should be minimalistic.
- Offer appropriate deterrence against loss of synchronization between the user and its home network.
- Fulfill "Lawful Interception" requirements (details in Sect. 2.3) in mobile telecommunications.
- Ideally should adhere to the existing message structures as specified in current 5G specifications.

Our Contributions. The contributions of this paper are listed as below:

- We detail limitations of the ECIES-based identification scheme of TS 33.501.
- We present an alternate quantum resistant scheme which overcomes the limitations identified in the 3GPP scheme.
- We develop an appropriate model of security and formally prove the privacy guarantees offered by our proposal in this model.

Related Work. To our knowledge, this is the first work on 5G identity confidentiality since the publication of TS 33.501. Before a protection scheme was chosen, a study was conducted by 3GPP to evaluate a number of potential solutions. In total 24 proposals were considered, details of which can be found in the associated report 3GPP TR 33.899 (cf. Clause 5.7.4) [7]. Most (but not all) proposals were based on public-key cryptography, and the ECIES-based mechanism was selected as the final candidate. The few symmetric-key proposals all relied on utilizing pseudonyms for privacy purposes, and thus were susceptible to desynchronization attacks potentially causing permanent DoS attacks on the mobile users.

Various academic works have considered "IMSI-catching" attacks. The major thrust of these papers has been to devise a solution for 3G/4G without modifying the existing message structures out of concern for legacy devices and backwards-compatibility. Broek et al. [2] introduced a proposal based on changing pseudonyms, and required no modifications to the existing infrastructure. As a result of reliance on changing pseudonyms this solution was susceptible to desynchronization attacks. A similar proposal was that by Khan and Mitchell [15] which relied on using a set of IMSIs for a particular *USIM* to offer some degree of pseudonymity, however as in the case of [2], this solution could also get knocked out of the service permanently. Khan and Mitchell, based upon their previous work, subsequently presented an improved solution [16]. This solution relied on using a dynamic pseudo-IMSI for identification purposes, however identity desynchronization attacks still had the potential to cause permanent denial of service. Thus their solution is accompanied with an identity recovery mechanism (in case of desynchronization) which required no changes to the existing message structures. However, this solution fails to satisfy the LI requirements (see Sect. 2.3) without further changes to the existing message structures.

Paper Outline. The rest of the paper is organized as follows: Sect. 2 gives background on the 5G security architecture. Section 3 details the current identity confidentiality mechanism of 5G and its limitations. Section 4 introduces our proposal for 5G identity confidentiality, we define a security framework in Sect. 5 with which to assess our proposal, and in Sect. 6 presents its analysis. Finally, Sect. 7 concludes the article.

2 Essential Background on 5G Telephony

Here we explain the pertinent constituents of the 5G security ecosystem. We use a simpler terminology than that used in TS 33.501 in order to improve clarity.

2.1 Network Architecture

The mobile telephony network architecture consists of three major entities. *User Equipment* (UE), refers to a complete mobile phone and covers both the *Mobile Equipment* (ME) (the phone) and the *Universal Subscriber Identity Module* (USIM) (the SIM card). The USIM represents the relationship between the subscriber (end user) and its issuing *Home Network* (HN). During the USIM registration, the HN stores a unique SUPI, telephone number and other subscriber related data, including a secret key K and sequence number SQN, in the USIM. These subscriber related parameters also get stored by the corresponding HNs in their databases. These stored parameters later form the basis for security between the UEs and their HNs. Usually, a semi-trusted *Serving Network* (SN) provides the subscribers with access to the services of their HN. These services are provisioned after mutual authentication and establishment of a secure channel between the UE and SN with the help of the HN. When roaming, the serving network is referred to as the visited network. The communication medium between the UE and SN is wireless while that between the SN and HN is almost always a wired one.

2.2 Terminologies and Identities

A SUPI as defined in 3GPP TS 23.501 is usually a string of 15 decimal digits [12]. The first three digits represent the *Mobile Country Code* (MCC) while the next two or three form the *Mobile Network Code* (MNC) identifying the network operator. The length of the MNC field is a national affair. The remaining (nine or ten) digits are known as *Mobile Subscriber Identification Number* (MSIN) and represent the individual user of that particular operator. Each decimal digit of the SUPI is represented in binary by using the *Telephony Binary Coded Decimal* (TBCD) encoding [10]. The IMEI which uniquely identifies the ME, is a string of 15 digits. If the IMEI is sent in plaintext over the radio interface it could compromise user privacy; however from 4G onwards, the 3GPP specifications prohibit a UE from transmitting the IMEI until after establishment of a secure channel.

2.3 The 5G AKA

Security of communications between mobile subscribers and their service providers requires mutual authentication and key agreement. The 3GPP standard for 5G security specifies two *Authenticated Key Agreement* (AKA) protocols, *Extensible Authentication Protocol AKA'* (EAP-AKA') and 5G-AKA. EAP-AKA' is specified in RFC 5448 [1] while 5G-AKA is detailed in TS 33.501 (cf. sub-clause 6.1.3.2) [11]. The two protocols are mostly identical, we therefore consider only the 5G-AKA further in this paper. The 5G-AKA is instantiated with a set of seven unrelated symmetric key algorithms, denoted as $f_1, \ldots, f_5$, f_1^* and f_5^*. Algorithms f_1, f_2 and f_1^* act as message authentication functions, while f_3, f_4, f_5 and f_5^* are used as key derivation functions[3]. Detail of how these cryptographic algorithms are used for calculation of various parameters and a pictorial representation of the 5G-AKA can be found in Table 1 and Fig. 1 respectively. As already described in Sect. 2.1, the shared long-term secret key K, sequence number SQN and long-term identity $SUPI$ are stored in both UE and HN during USIM registration. The sequence numbers assure freshness in the 5G-AKA. All key derivation for 5G-AKA is performed using the Key Derivation Function (KDF) specified in 3GPP TS 33.220 [9]. The 5G-AKA protocol works as follows:

0. [4]To initiate authentication, the UE sends the SN either the 5G-GUTI in a "registration request" message or the SUCI as response to an "identifier request" message (See Sect. 3 for further details).

---

[3] The 3GPP documentation uses the term "key generating function" for these algorithms, while these are technically key derivation functions.

[4] This first Step is numbered 0 because its not an exclusive part of the AKA but rather the identification phase.

Table 1. Description of 5G-AKA parameters

Parameter	Content/description
$RAND$	128 bit random challenge
SQN	48 bit sequence number
AMF	16 bit authentication management field
$SNname$	Serving network name
AK	$f_5(K, RAND)$
CK	$f_3(K, RAND)$
IK	$f_4(K, RAND)$
RES	$f_2(K, RAND)$
MAC	$f_1(K, SQN\|RAND\|AMF)$
$AUTN$	$(SQN \oplus AK\|AMF\|MAC)$
$RES^*/XRES^*$	$KDF(CK\|IK, SNname\|RAND\|RES/XRES)$
$HXRES^*/HRES^*$	$SHA256(RAND\|XRES^*/RES^*)$
K_{AUSF}	$KDF(CK\|IK, SNname\|SQN \oplus AK)$
K_{SEAF}	$KDF(K_{AUSF}, SNname)$
AV	$(RAND\|AUTN\|HXRES^*\|K_{SEAF})$

1. In case of a 5G-GUTI, the SN extracts the corresponding SUPI from its database and forwards it along with its serving network name (SN name) to the HN in an "authenticate request" message. Otherwise the SUCI is sent instead of the SUPI.
2. If the SUCI is received in an authenticate request message by HN, it de-conceals (for details see Sect. 3.1) the SUPI from it. It further derives the expected response XRES* and generates the authentication vector AV. The AV consists of a random challenge RAND, an authentication token AUTN, a hash of expected response HXRES* and an anchor key K_{SEAF} which is cryptographically bound to the requesting SN.
3. The HN stores XRES*.
4. The HN forwards the 5G AV (RAND, AUTN, HXRES*, K_{SEAF}) in an "authenticate response" message to the SN.
5. The SN forwards RAND, AUTN to the UE in an Auth-Req message.
6. Upon receiving the RAND and AUTN, the UE verifies the freshness and authenticity as described in [8]. It then computes the response RES* and derives the anchor key K_{SEAF} to be used for establishment of the secure channel with the SN.
7. The UE returns RES* in an Auth-Resp message to the SN.
8. The SN then computes the hash of the response HRES* from the received RES* and compares HRES* with XHRES*. If they are equal, the SN considers the authentication successful.
9. The SN then sends RES*, as received from the UE, to the HN in an "authentication confirmation" message (containing the SUPI or SUCI and the serving network name).

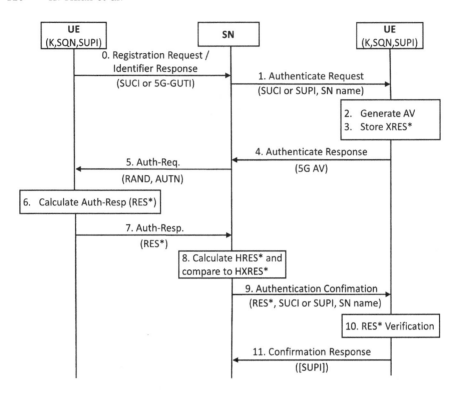

Fig. 1. Overview of the 5G-AKA protocol

10. When the HN receives a confirmation message, it compares RES* with the stored XRES*. If these two are equal, the HN considers the confirmation message as successfully verified.
11. Finally, the HN indicates to the SN in a "confirmation response" message whether the confirmation was successful or not. If the HN received a SUCI from the SN when authentication was initiated, and if the confirmation is successful, then the HN also includes the SUPI in this message.

Lawful Interception. Note that in Step 11 of the 5G-AKA, the HN provides the SUPI of the UE to the SN after successful authentication. This is due to the Lawful Interception (LI) requirements. The law enforcement agencies of almost all countries require that their local service providers should have the capability to locate and track any particular mobile user within the country. The SUPI is later used as an input to the session key derivation function between UE and SN. This ensures that the SUPI value provisioned by the HN is the one claimed by the UE, otherwise the communication breaks down.

3 Identity Confidentiality in 5G

In the 5G system, *Subscription Concealed Identifier* (SUCI) is a privacy preserving identifier containing the concealed SUPI. The UE generates a SUCI using a protection scheme (see Sect. 3.1) with the public key of the HN that was securely provisioned to the USIM during the USIM registration. Only the MSIN part of the SUPI gets concealed by the protection scheme while the home network identifier (MCC/MNC) gets transmitted in plaintext. The data fields constituting the SUCI are:

- **Protection Scheme Identifier.** This field represents the null scheme[5] or any other specified protection scheme.
- **Home Network Public Key Identifier.** This represents the public key provisioned by the HN. In case of a null scheme, this field is set to null.
- **Home Network Identifier.** This contains the MCC and MNC part of the SUPI.
- **Protection Scheme Output.** This represents the output of the public key based protection scheme.

The subscriber identification mechanism allows the identification of a UE on the radio path by means of the SUCI. This mechanism is usually invoked by the SN by sending an **Identifier Request** to the UE, when the UE is not identifiable by means of a temporary identity. The UE then responds with the **Identifier Response**, containing the SUCI. Additionally, if the UE sends a **Registration Request** message of type "initial registration" to a mobile network for which it does not already have a 5G-GUTI, then the UE includes a SUCI to the **Registration Request**.

3.1 ECIES-Based Protection Scheme

We now provide an overview of the ECIES-based protection scheme as described in TS 33.501 (cf. Annex C.3) [11]. To compute a fresh SUCI, the UE generates a fresh ECC (Elliptic Curve Cryptography) ephemeral public/private key pair utilizing the HN public key. Processing on the UE side is done according to the encryption operation defined in [19] and as further illustrated in Fig. 2a. The final output of this protection scheme is the concatenation of the ECC ephemeral public key, the ciphertext value, the MAC tag value, and any other parameters, if applicable. The HN uses the received ECC ephemeral public key and its private key to deconceal the received SUCI. Processing on the HN side is illustrated in Fig. 2b.

---

[5] The null-scheme is used only if the UE is making an unauthenticated emergency session or if the HN has configured "null-scheme" to be used or if the HN has not provisioned the public key needed to generate SUCI.

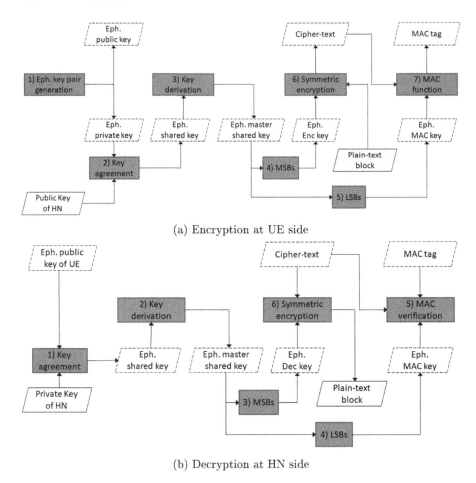

(a) Encryption at UE side

(b) Decryption at HN side

Fig. 2. Detail of ECIES-based protection scheme

3.2 Limitations of the 3GPP Protection Scheme

Although the ECIES-based scheme is oblivious to loss of synchronization between the UE and HN and provisions robust key management, both of which lead to significant reduction in connection failures, there still are aspects which require further improvement [4].

Post Quantum Vulnerability. As the ECIES-based scheme employs ECC to provision identity confidentiality, it relies on the hardness assumption of the Elliptic Curve Discrete Logarithm Problem (ECDLP). A quantum adversary capable of issuing quantum queries to an appropriate quantum computer can easily break this scheme employing Shor's quantum algorithm [21].

Chosen SUPI Attacks. Any arbitrary third party can always select a SUPI of his choosing and send the corresponding SUCI to the HN. Thereafter the adversary can look out for various responses from the HN, depending on whether the target user is present in that particular cell tower or not. Any noticeable variation in the perceived output would allow the adversary to confirm or deny the presence of the target in that particular cell. There is no mechanism in the ECIES-based scheme to prevent these kind of attacks.

Replay Attacks. Note that the ECIES-based scheme does not have any inherent mechanism to provide freshness guarantees to the HN and is thus susceptible to replay attacks. An adversary can always resend a previously encrypted SUPI to the HN and look out for various kinds of responses (an authentication challenge or a failure message). Based on the received response, a device whose SUPI is unknown to the attacker may be tracked with some confidence.

Bidding Down Attacks. An active adversary simulating a (false) base station can force the UE to use one of the previous generation (3G/4G) and then can get hold of the IMSI using an *identity request* message. Until all systems upgrade to 5G, nothing much can be done about these bidding down attacks. In the current 5G security specifications [11], the SUPI is derived directly from the IMSI, so these bidding down attacks also compromise the SUPI.

Update of HN Public Key. There could be situations which require the HN to have a robust way of quickly updating its public key to subscriber UEs. One such scenario could be a malware attack which tries to recover the home networks private key. Such situations enforce the need to have a quick way of updating the corresponding public keys.

4   Towards Quantum Resistant Identity Confidentiality

We now detail our proposal for an alternative protection scheme. Unlike the ECIES-based scheme, our proposal mostly requires the cryptographic primitives already provisioned by the current 5G specifications. We utilise the previously specified key derivation and message authentication functions of the 5G-AKA for our proposal. Specifically, we use function f_1 for message authentication and functions f_3, f_4, f_5 and f_5^* for key derivation. As elaborated in 3GPP TS 33.102, no valuable information can be inferred from the values of any of these functions about other functions [8]. Table 2 gives a summary of notations used in the proposed scheme and Fig. 3 provides an overview of the proposed scheme. Various phases of the scheme are explained further.

4.1   System Setup Phase

The *HN* generates a long-term secret key K_{HN} for the calculation of identification parameters for its subscribers. *HN* stores this value internally in some secure

Table 2. Notation used in the proposed scheme

Notation	Description
A and B	Identification parameters generated by HN
$SQNID$	Counter used for replay prevention
K_{HN}	Long term secret key of HN
K_N	Randomly generated ephemeral parameter
$RANDID$	Freshly generated random number
$CKID$	Confidentiality key
$AKID$	Anonymity key
$MACID$	MAC tag
f_1	Message authentication function
f_3, f_4, f_5, $f_5{}^*$	Key derivation functions
AE.Enc	Authenticated encryption function
AE.Dec	Authenticated decryption function
$f(K, X)$	Execution of keyed-function f upon input X with key K

way, allowing no other entity access. HN randomly chooses K_N during the UE registration and computes the (data) confidentiality key $CKID = f_4(K_{HN}, K_N)$ for the protection scheme as well as identification parameters $A = SUPI \oplus CKID$ and $B = K_{HN} \oplus K_N$. In addition to the $SUPI$, the AKA sequence number SQN and the shared key K (which are all from the original 5G-AKA), the UE also stores identification parameters A and B along with an additional 48 bit identification sequence number $SQNID_{UE}$ with initial value set to 1. HN initialises a corresponding identification sequence number $SQNID_{HN}$[6] with initial value of 0 and stores $SQNID_{HN}$ in its database. An algorithmic description of the computations of HN during this phase can be found below:

1. $K_{HN} \xleftarrow{\$} \{0,1\}^\lambda$
2. For each UE:
   $K_N \xleftarrow{\$} \{0,1\}^\lambda$
   $SQNID_{UE} \leftarrow 1$
   $SQNID_{HN} \leftarrow 0$
   $CKID \leftarrow f_4(K_{HN}, K_N)$
3. $A \leftarrow SUPI \oplus CKID$
4. $B \leftarrow K_{HN} \oplus K_N$
5. $K \xleftarrow{\$} \{0,1\}^\lambda$
6. $UE \leftarrow (SUPI, K, A, B)$

---

[6] Note that HN will maintain a separate distinct value of $SQNID_{HN}$ for each UE in its database.

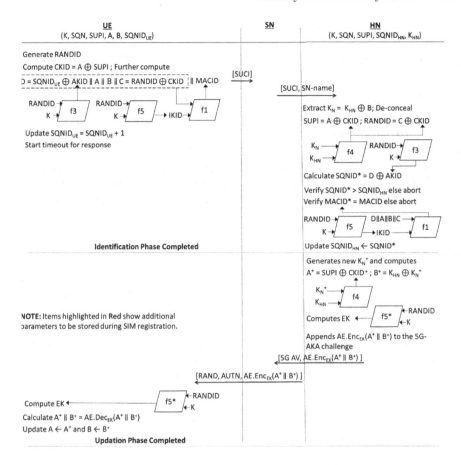

Fig. 3. Our proposed protection scheme PQID

4.2   Identification Phase

An algorithmic description of the operations of *UE* and *HN* during this phase are presented below. Note that the output of $f_3(K, RANDID)$ is truncated to get a 48 bit *AKID*. The UE prepares the $SUCI = (\text{label}_{\text{ps}}, \emptyset, \text{label}_{HN}, (D\|A\|B\|C\|MACID))$ using various data fields[7] as explained in Sect. 3 and forwards *SUCI* to *SN*. The *SN* appends its "SN-name" (cf. Clause 6.1.1.4 of [11]) to the received SUCI and forwards the resulting message to *HN*. Upon successful MAC verification, *HN* accepts the extracted *SUPI* as valid for subsequent processing.

---

[7] Note that label_{ps} is a constant value indicating the protection scheme, and label_{HN} is a constant value identifying the *HN*.

Description of UE's operations:

1. $RANDID \xleftarrow{\$} \{0,1\}^{\lambda}$
2. $CKID \leftarrow A \oplus SUPI$
3. $AKID \leftarrow f_3(K, RANDID)$
4. $IKID \leftarrow f_5(K, RANDID)$
5. $C \leftarrow RANDID \oplus CKID$
6. $D \leftarrow SQNID_{UE} \oplus AKID$
7. $MACID \leftarrow f_1(IKID, D\|A\|B\|C)$
8. $SUCI \leftarrow (\texttt{label}_{\texttt{ps}}, \epsilon, \texttt{label}_{HN},$
   $D\|A\|B\|C\|MACID)$
9. $SQNID_{UE} \leftarrow SQNID_{UE} + 1$

Description of HN's operations:

1. $K_N \leftarrow K_{HN} \oplus B$
2. $CKID \leftarrow f_4(K_{HN}, K_N)$
3. $SUPI \leftarrow A \oplus CKID$
4. $RANDID \leftarrow C \oplus CKID$
5. $AKID \leftarrow f_3(K, RANDID)$
6. $IKID \leftarrow f_5(K, RANDID)$
7. $SQNID^* \leftarrow D \oplus AKID$
8. **if** $SQNID^* \leq SQNID_{HN}$ **abort**
9. $MACID^* \leftarrow f_1(IKID, D\|A\|B\|C)$
10. **if** $MACID \neq MACID^*$ **abort**
11. $SQNID_{HN} \leftarrow SQNID^*$

4.3   Update Phase

An algorithmic description of the operations of UE and HN during this phase can be found below. The output of the encryption scheme $\mathsf{AE.Enc}_{EK}(A^+\|B^+)$ gets appended to the 5G-AKA authentication vector AV and is forwarded to the SN as part of the *authenticate response* message (Step 4 in Fig. 1) of the 5G-AKA. The SN upon receipt of the response message undertakes the required steps necessary for 5G-AKA and forwards the encrypted identification parameters to the UE along with the 5G-AKA authentication challenge parameters $RAND$ (note that $RAND$ is unrelated to $RANDID$) and $AUTN$ (Step 5 in Fig. 1).

Algorithmic description of HN's operations in the Update Phase:

1. $K_N^+ \leftarrow \{0,1\}^{\lambda}$
2. $CKID^+ \leftarrow f_4(K_{HN}, K_N^+)$
3. $A^+ \leftarrow SUPI \oplus CKID^+$
4. $B^+ \leftarrow K_{HN} \oplus K_N^+$
5. $EK \leftarrow f_5^*(K, RANDID)$
6. $EKID \leftarrow \mathsf{AE.Enc}(EK, A^+\|B^+)$

Algorithmic description of UE's operations in the Update Phase:

1. $EK \leftarrow f_5^*(K, RANDID)$
2. $A^+\|B^+ \leftarrow \mathsf{AE.Dec}(EK, EKID)$
3. $A, B \leftarrow A^+, B^+$

5   Security Framework

In this section, we introduce our *Symmetric Updatable Private Authentication* (SUPA) experiment, that follows in the long tradition of standard Bellare-Rogaway key-indistinguishability games. Essentially, a SUPA protocol is a protocol that authenticates an end-user to a central node via a shared symmetric key in a private way. In comparison to similar BR-styled mutual authentication games, our SUPA framework diverges by considering *identity confidentiality*. In particular, the SUPA security experiment asks the adversary to decide which of two parties attempted to authenticate itself to a centralised home network. In addition, SUPA distinguishes itself by considering a *multi-stage* authentication protocol - i.e. subsequent authentication attempts between the UE and the HN (after the first successful authentication) are not independent, but instead dependent on values derived from previous stages. This allows us to capture both *User Identity Confidentiality* and *User Untraceability* from the 3GPP requirements of user privacy. We can now turn to formally defining a SUPA protocol.

Definition 1 (Symmetric Updatable Private Authentication). *A Symmetric Updatable Private Authentication (SUPA) protocol is a tuple of algorithms* {SetupHN, SetupUE, Identify, Update}.

- SetupHN(λ) $\rightarrow K_{HN}$: SetupHN *takes as input some security parameter λ and outputs a long-term symmetric key K_{HN}.*
- SetupUE(λ, K_{HN}) $\rightarrow K, st$: SetupHN *takes as input some security parameter λ and a long-term symmetric key K_{HN}, and outputs some shared (between the UE and the HN) secret state st and a shared symmetric key K.*
- Identify($role, m, st, K_{HN}$) $\rightarrow (id, m', st')$: Identify *takes as input the role of the party in the protocol execution, a (potentially empty) message m, the internal state of the party st and (if role $=$ HN) the long-term HN key K_{HN}, and outputs an identifier id, a new (potentially empty) message m', and an updated state st'. Note that the identifier id doubles as a failure flag if the* Identify *algorithm is forced to abort.*
- Update($role, m, st, K_{HN}$) $\rightarrow (m', st')$: Update *takes as input the role of the party in the protocol execution, a (potentially empty) message m, the internal state of the party st and (if role $=$ HN) the long-term HN key K_{HN}, and outputs a new (potentially empty) message m', an updated state st'. As in* Identify, *the output message m' doubles as a failure flag if the* Update *algorithm is forced to abort.*

5.1 Execution Environment

Here we describe the execution environment of the SUPA security experiment. The experiment $\mathsf{Exp}^{\mathsf{SUPA}}_{\Pi, n_N, n_S, \mathcal{A}}(\lambda)$ is played between a challenger $\mathcal{C}$ and an adversary $\mathcal{A}$. The challenger $\mathcal{C}$ maintains a single *HN*, running a number of instances of the SUPA protocol Π, and a set of (up to) n_N users $UE_1, \ldots, UE_{n_N}$ (representing nodes communicating with the home network *HN*), each potentially running a single session executing (up to) n_S consecutive stages of Π. The protocol Π is represented as a tuple of algorithms SUPA $=$ {SetupHN, SetupUE, Identify, Update}. We abuse notation and use π_i^s to refer to both the identifier of the s-th stage of Π being run by node UE_i and the collection of per-session variables maintained for this stage. Each session maintains the following set of per-session variables:

- $i \in \{1, \ldots, n_N\}$ - the index of the party UE_i.
- $ltk \in \{0,1\}^\lambda$ - the long-term symmetric secret of UE_i, shared with *HN*.
- $id \in \{0,1\}^*$ - the identifier of party UE_i.
- $m_s \in \{0,1\}^* \cup \{\bot\}$ - the concatenation of messages sent by the session, initialised by $\bot$.

- $m_r \in \{0,1\}^* \cup \{\perp\}$ - the concatenation of messages received by the session, initialised by $\perp$.
- $st \in \{0,1\}^* \cup \{\perp\}$ - the per-stage secret state of the session, initialised by $\perp$.
- $s \in \{1,\ldots,n_S\}$ - the index of the most recently completed authentication stage, initialised by 1 and increased monotonically.
- $\alpha \in \{\texttt{active},\texttt{accept},\perp\}$ - the current status of the session, initialised by $\perp$.

Our experiment begins with the challenger $\mathcal{C}$ sampling the random test bit $b \xleftarrow{\$} \{0,1\}$. The challenger generates the long-term symmetric key of the *HN* K_{HN} and initialises its corruption registers (which maintain the list of secrets $\mathcal{A}$ has leaked). At this point, $\mathcal{A}$ now gains access to the queries listed in Sect. 5.2 and eventually terminates and outputs a single guess bit b'. If $\mathcal{A}$ has caused the challenger to either execute $\mathsf{Identify}(HN, m, HN.st, K_{HN}) \rightarrow (id, m', st')$ such that there exists some session $\pi_i^s.id = id$, but $m \not\subset \pi_i^s.m_s{}^8$ or; execute $\mathsf{Update}(UE, m, \pi_i^s.st, \epsilon) \rightarrow (m', st')$ such that $m' \neq \perp$ but there was no execution of $\mathsf{Update}(role^*, m^*, st^*, K_{HN}) \rightarrow (m, st'')$. If either of these are true and $\mathsf{fresh}(i,s) = \texttt{true}$ then $\mathcal{C}$ returns 1. Otherwise, if $\mathcal{A}$ issued a **Test**(i^*, s^*) query, then $\mathcal{C}$ computes $\mathsf{fresh}(i^*, s^*)$. If $\mathsf{fresh}(i^*, s^*)$ is $\texttt{true}$, then the challenger returns $(b = b')$, otherwise the challenger returns $b^* \xleftarrow{\$} \{0,1\}$.

5.2 Adversary Queries

Here we describe the intuition behind each query that $\mathcal{A}$ has access to during the SUPA experiment. For full details on each of these queries, see Fig. 4.

- **Create**(i): Allows $\mathcal{A}$ to initialise a new *UE* party with shared symmetric state and shared symmetric key with *HN*.
- **Send**$(i, s, m) \rightarrow m'$: Sends a message m to session π_i^s, which updates the per-session variables, returning a (potentially empty) message m'.
- **Corrupt**$(i) \rightarrow \pi_i.ltk$: Reveals to $\mathcal{A}$ the long-term symmetric key of UE_i.
- **Test**$(i, s, i', s') \rightarrow m$: Uses the random bit b sampled by $\mathcal{C}$ to begin a new Identify phase with either π_i^s (if $b = 0$) or $\pi_{i'}^{s'}$ (if $b = 1$). For ease of notation, we refer to the "test" session as π_b (and the other session as π_{1-b}). Note that $\mathcal{A}$ cannot issue this query if there exists some stage s such that either $\pi_i^s.\alpha = \texttt{active}$ or $\pi_{i'}^{s'}.\alpha = \texttt{active}$, nor can $\mathcal{A}$ issue **Send** queries to π_i^s or $\pi_{i'}^{s'}$ until π_b has either accepted or rejected the protocol execution.
- **SendTest**$(m) \rightarrow m'$: Allows $\mathcal{A}$ to send a message m to the test session π_b after $\mathcal{A}$ has issued a **Test** query. After $\pi_b.\alpha \neq \texttt{active}$, then the challenger responds to **SendTest** queries with $\perp$.
- **StateReveal**$(i, s) \rightarrow \pi_i^s$: Reveals to $\mathcal{A}$ the full internal state of π_i^s.

5.3 Security Definitions

Here we define the security of a Symmetric Updatable Private Authentication Protocols, and additionally show that the PQID protocol described in Fig. 3 executes correctly in the presence of a passive adversary.

---

[8] Note that here we are using $\subset$ to indicate substrings.

$\mathsf{Exp}^{\mathsf{SUPA,clean}}_{\Pi,n_N,n_S,\mathcal{A}}(\lambda)$:

1: $b \xleftarrow{\$} \{0,1\}$
2: $K_{HN} \xleftarrow{\$} \mathsf{SetupHN}(\lambda)$
3: $\mathsf{LSKflag}_i, \ldots, \mathsf{LSKflag}_{n_N} \leftarrow \mathbf{clean}$
4: $\mathsf{PSSflag}^1_1, \ldots, \mathsf{PSSflag}^{n_N}_{n_S} \leftarrow \mathbf{clean}$
5: $ctr \leftarrow 0$
6: $b' \xleftarrow{\$} \mathcal{A}^{\mathsf{Send}\star,\mathsf{Create},\mathsf{Corrupt},\mathsf{StateReveal}}(\lambda)$
7: **if** $\exists \quad (i^*, s^*) \quad$ s.t.
   $((\mathsf{Identify}(HN, m, HN.st, K_{HN}) \rightarrow$
   $(id, m', st) \quad$ s.t $\quad \pi^{s^*}_{i^*}.id = id,$
   $m \neq \pi^{s^*}_{i^*}.m_r) \wedge (\mathsf{clean}(\pi^{s^*}_{i^*})))$
   $\vee \quad ((\mathsf{Update}(UE, m, \pi^{s^*}_{i^*}.st, \epsilon) \rightarrow$
   $(m', st') \quad$ s.t. $\quad m' \neq \perp,$
   $\nexists \mathsf{Update}(HN, m^*, HN.st, K_{HN}) \rightarrow$
   $(m, HNst'))) \wedge (\mathsf{clean}(\pi^{s^*}_{i^*})))$ **then**
8: $\quad$ **return** 1
9: **end if**
10: **if** $\mathsf{clean}(\pi_b) \wedge \mathsf{clean}(\pi_{1-b})$ **then**
11: $\quad$ **return** $(b' = b)$
12: **else**
13: $\quad$ **return** $b' \xleftarrow{\$} \{0,1\}$
14: **end if**

$\underline{\mathsf{Test}((i,s),(i',s'))}$:

1: **if** $(\pi^s_i.\alpha = \mathbf{active}) \vee (\pi^{s'}_{i'}.\alpha = \mathbf{active})$
   then
2: $\quad$ **return** $\perp$
3: **end if**
4: **if** $(b = 0)$ **then**
5: $\quad \pi_b \leftarrow \pi^s_i$
6: $\quad \pi_{b-1} \leftarrow \pi^{s'}_{i'}$
7: **else**
8: $\quad \pi_b \leftarrow \pi^{s'}_{i'}$
9: $\quad \pi_{b-1} \leftarrow \pi^s_i$
10: **end if**
11: $m \leftarrow \Pi.\mathsf{Identify}(UE, \perp, \pi_b.st, \perp)$
12: **return** m

$\underline{\mathsf{StateReveal}(i,s)}$:

1: **if** $\pi^s_i.st = \perp$ **then**
2: $\quad$ **return** $\perp$
3: **end if**
4: $\mathsf{PSSflag}^i_s \leftarrow \mathbf{corrupt}$
5: **return** $\pi^s_i.st$

$\underline{\mathsf{Create}(\lambda)}$:

1: $ctr \leftarrow ctr + 1$
2: $\pi.s \leftarrow 1$
3: $\pi.ltk, \pi.st \leftarrow \Pi.\mathsf{SetupUE}(\lambda, K_{HN})$
4: $\pi.i \leftarrow ctr$
5: **return** $\pi.i$

$\underline{\mathsf{SendTest}(m)}$:

1: $\mathsf{Send}(\pi_b, m) \rightarrow m'$
2: **return** m'

$\underline{\mathsf{Send}(role, i, m)}$:

1: **if** $role = HN$ **then**
2: $\quad (HN.st', m') \leftarrow \Pi.F(\lambda, HN, m)$
3: **end if**
4: **let** $s = max\{s : \pi^s_i.\alpha \neq \perp\}$
5: **if** $\pi^s_i.\alpha \neq \mathbf{active}$ **then**
6: $\quad$ **return** $\perp$
7: **end if**
8: $\pi^s_i.m_r \leftarrow \pi^s_i.m_r \| m$
9: $(\pi^s_i, m') \leftarrow \Pi.F(\lambda, \pi^s_i, m)$
10: $\pi^s_i.m_s \leftarrow \pi^s_i.m_s \| m'$
11: **return** m'

$\underline{\mathsf{Corrupt}(i)}$:

1: $\mathsf{LSKflag}_i \leftarrow \mathbf{corrupt}$
2: **return** $\pi_i.ltk$

Fig. 4. An algorithmic description of the SUPA security experiment. We assume the existence of a function F that is capable of taking as input a message m and the current internal state $\pi^s_i.st$ of the protocol execution and forwarding the inputs to either Update or Identify as appropriate. We refer to the "test" session in the description of the SUPA experiment as π_b (and the other session as π_{1-b}).

Definition 2 (Private Authentication Security). *Let Π be a* SUPA *proto-col, and n_N, $n_S \in \mathbb{N}$. For a given cleanness predicate* clean, *and a PPT algorithm $\mathcal{A}$, we define the advantage of $\mathcal{A}$ in the* SUPA *game to be:*

$$\mathsf{Adv}^{\mathsf{SUPA,clean}}_{\Pi,n_N,n_S,\mathcal{A}}(\lambda) = |\Pr[\mathsf{Exp}^{\mathsf{SUPA,clean}}_{\Pi,n_N,n_S,\mathcal{A}}(\lambda) = 1] - \frac{1}{2}|.$$

We say that Π is SUPA-*secure if, for all $\mathcal{A}$, $\mathsf{Adv}^{\mathsf{SUPA,clean}}_{\Pi,n_N,n_S,\mathcal{A}}(\lambda)$ is negligible in the security parameter λ.*

We also need to define *Identification Correctness* as well as *Update Correctness*, to ensure that we only capture protocols that are actually useful.

Definition 3 (Identification Correctness). *Let Π be a* SUPA *protocol. We say that Π has* identification correctness *if after an execution of* Identify$(HN, m'$, $HN.st, K_{HN}) \rightarrow (id', m^*, st')$ *in the presence of a passive adversary $\mathcal{A}$ such that for some session $\pi_i^s.m_s = m'$, then $\pi_i^s.id = id'$.*

It is fairly straightforward to see that the proposed protocol in Fig. 3 has iden-tification correctness: The fields $A = SUPI \oplus CKID$ and $B = K_{HN} \oplus K_N$ sent by the UE contains all the information necessary to recompute the identifier $SUPI$ of the UE. HN first computes $K_N = B \oplus K_{HN}$ and then $CKID = f_4(K_{HN}, K_N)$. Retrieving $SUPI$ is then simply a matter of $SUPI \leftarrow A \oplus CKID$.

Update correctness is a little different to identification correctness. We only require that the session executing an Update using output from HN simply updates their state without aborting the protocol execution, instead of having to agree to some shared updated state. This is to capture stateless HN sessions that simply regenerate per-session state when required, usually by processing client-maintained tokens. In this sense, the A and B values sent by the UE during our PQID protocol are tokens that allow HN to recover per-session state.

Definition 4 (Update Correctness). *Let Π be a* SUPA *protocol. We say that Π has* update correctness *if after an execution of* Update$(UE, m', \pi_i^s.st, \epsilon) \rightarrow (m^*, \pi_i^s.st')$ *in the presence of a passive adversary $\mathcal{A}$ such that for some execution of* Update$(HN, m, HN.st, K_{HN}) \rightarrow (m', HN.st')$, *then $m^* \neq \perp$ and $\pi_i^s.st' \neq \pi_i^s.st$.*

Similarly to identification correctness, it is straightforward to see that the proposed protocol in Fig. 3 has update correctness: The fields $A^+ = SUPI \oplus CKID^+$ and $B^+ = K_{HN} \oplus K_N^+$ encrypted under $EK = f_{5^*}(K, RANDID)$ sent by the HN contains all the information necessary to update the values A, B and $CKID$. UE computes $EK = f_{5^*}(K, RANDID)$ (where $RANDID$ was sampled initially by UE and K is the long-term symmetric key shared by UE and HN, so both are known to UE), and decrypts A^+ and B^+. Afterwards, UE updates $A \leftarrow A^+$, $B \leftarrow B^+$, $CKID \leftarrow A^+ \oplus SUPI$.

Finally, we require a cleanness predicate, in order to disallow combinations of **Corrupt** and **StateReveal** queries that allow an adversary to trivially break $SUPA$ security. We do not capture notions of forward secrecy, so our cleanness predicate is very simple: $\mathcal{A}$ is not allowed to break sessions that it has issued either a **Corrupt** or a **StateReveal** query to.

Definition 5 (SUPA-clean). *A session π_i^s in the* SUPA *experiment defined in Fig. 4 is* clean *if* $\mathsf{LSKflag}_i \neq \mathsf{corrupt}$ *and* $\mathsf{PSSflag}_i^s \neq \mathsf{corrupt}$.

6   Analysis of the Proposed Protection Scheme

In this section we discuss and analyse our proposed 5G identification scheme within the SUPA security framework, and show that it achieves the notion of *Symmetric Updatable Private Authentication* protocols.

6.1   Formal Analysis

Theorem 1. *The SUPA protocol* PQID *given in Fig. 3 is* SUPA-*secure under cleanness predicate* clean *and assuming all hash functions are random oracles. For any PPT algorithm $\mathcal{A}$ against the* SUPA *experiment,* $\mathsf{Adv}_{\mathsf{PQID},n_N,n_S,\mathcal{A}}^{\mathsf{SUPA,clean}}(\lambda)$ *is negligible under the* AuthEnc, kdf *and* eufcma *security assumptions of the* AE, KDF *and* MAC *schemes, respectively.*

Proof. Before we begin our analysis in earnest, we show that an adversary $\mathcal{A}$ is unable to recover the long-term symmetric-key of the home network K_{HN} (with non-negligible probability) even if $\mathcal{A}$ reveals all long-term secrets K of all nodes and all per-stage secret states st assuming underlying hash functions are random oracles. In our proof we work within the random oracle model, and $\mathcal{A}$ cannot learn anything about K_{HN} from hash outputs $\mathsf{H}(K_{HN}, X)$ (where X is any concatenation of arbitrary values). We turn to $\mathcal{A}$ attempting to learn K_{HN} that has been "blinded" through exclusive-or (XOR) operations, which are only sent in the following values: $B = K_{HN} \oplus K_N$ and $B^+ = K_{HN} \oplus K_N^+$. K_N and K_N^+ are acting as one-time-pads encrypting the long-term symmetric key of the home network HN, and each K_N/K_N^+ is a value internal to the home network that *cannot* be compromised via $\mathcal{A}$ issuing a **Corrupt** or **StateReveal** query. $\mathcal{A}$ therefore cannot recover K_{HN} in this way, but can attempt to guess and verify the guess by first querying **StateReveal** to any *UE* party, recovering *CKID* and B, and querying the random oracle with $(K_{HN}', B \oplus K_{HN}')$ and comparing the output of the random oracle with *CKID*. The probability of $\mathcal{A}$'s success in this strategy is $q_r/2^{\lambda-1}$. (where q_r is the number of queries that $\mathcal{A}$ makes to the random oracle and λ is the bit-length of K_{HN}). During our analysis then, we assume that in each stage of a protocol execution K_{HN} is indistinguishable from a uniformly-random value K_{HN}^* from the same distribution.

In our analysis, we split our proof into three cases:

1. $\mathcal{A}$ has caused a session π_i^s to reach a status accept when calling $\mathsf{Update}(UE, m, \pi_i^s.st, \epsilon)$ such that m is not the output of HN and $\mathsf{clean}(\pi_i^s) = \mathsf{true}$.

2. $\mathcal{A}$ has caused HN to call $\mathsf{Identify}(HN, m, HN.st, K_{HN}) \rightarrow (id', m', HN.st')$ such that $\exists \pi_i^s.id = id'$, but m was not the output of some $\mathsf{Identify}(UE, \epsilon, \pi_i^s.st, \epsilon)$ and $\mathsf{clean}(\pi_i^s) = \mathtt{true}$.
3. $\mathcal{A}$ has output a guessed bit b' after issuing a $\mathbf{Test}(i, s, i', s')$ query.

We show that $\mathcal{A}$ has negligible advantage in causing the first two cases to occur, and thus $\mathcal{A}$ also has negligible advantage in winning the SUPA experiment in the third case. Due to space constraints we instead provide a proof sketch.

Case 1. We begin by guessing the session π_i^s such that π_i^s has reached a status $\mathtt{accept}$ when calling $\mathsf{Update}(UE, m, \pi_i^s.st, \epsilon)$ and m is not an output of the home network HN. Next, we replace the keys $AKID$, $IKID$ and EK computed in the session π_i^s with uniformly-random values $AKID^*$, $IKID^*$ and EK^* from $\{0,1\}^{|\mathsf{KDF}|}$ where $|\mathsf{KDF}|$ represents the output length of KDF, by interacting with a challenger implementing a KDF security game. Finally, we define an abort event $\mathsf{abort}_{\mathsf{dec}}$ that occurs when π_i^s sets $\pi_i^s.\alpha \leftarrow \mathtt{accept}$ during a call to $\mathsf{Update}(UE, m, \pi_i^s.st, \epsilon)$ and m is not the output of the home network HN. We do this by constructing a simulator $\mathcal{B}$ that interacts with an AE challenger, computing $\mathsf{AE.Enc}(EK^*, A^+\|B^+)$ by querying $(A^+\|B^+, A^+\|B^+)$ to the LoR AE challenger's AuthEnc oracle instead of computing it honestly. Thus, if $\mathsf{abort}_{\mathsf{dec}}$ occurs, then m is a ciphertext that decrypts correctly by the AE challenger, but was not the output of the query $(A^+\|B^+, A^+\|B^+)$ to the LoR AE challenger's AuthEnc oracle. Thus, when $\mathsf{abort}_{\mathsf{dec}}$ occurs, $\mathcal{B}$ has broken the AE security of the AE challenger, and we have bound the advantage of $\mathcal{A}$ in causing π_i^s to accept an Update when the received message was not the honest output of the HN.

Case 2. Similarly to Case 1 we begin by guessing the index of the session π_i^s and replacing the keys $AKID$, $IKID$ and EK computed in *any* stage s of the session π_i^s and the HN with uniformly-random values $AKID^*$, $IKID^*$ and EK^*. However, in Case 2 we interact with n_S challengers implementing n_S KDF security games. Finally, we define an abort event $\mathsf{abort}_{\mathsf{mac}}$ that occurs when HN outputs $\pi_i^s.id = id'$ during a call to $\mathsf{Identify}(HN, m, HN.st, K_{HN})$ and m is not the output of some stage s of the sessions owned by UE_i. We do this by constructing a simulator $\mathcal{B}$ that interacts with an MAC challenger, computing $\mathsf{MAC}(IKID^*, D\|A\|B\|C)$ by querying $(D\|A\|B\|C)$ to the MAC challenger instead of computing it honestly within HN or any session owned by UE_i. Thus, if $\mathsf{abort}_{\mathsf{mac}}$ occurs, then $\mathcal{A}$ has managed to produce a MAC tag under a key $IKID^*$ that verifies correctly, but was not the output of a query to the MAC challenger and has broken the eufcma security of the MAC challenger. Thus we have bound the advantage of $\mathcal{A}$ in causing HN to accept an Identify phase when the received message was not the honest output of the π_i^s.

Case 3. In this case we show that the advantage that $\mathcal{A}$ has in guessing the test bit b is negligible. We begin by guessing the session π_i^s such that $\mathcal{A}$ issues a $\mathbf{Test}(i^*, s^*, i', s')$ query and $\pi_i^s = \pi_b$. Next, we replace the key K_{HN} used in the test session π_i^s with a uniformly random values K_{HN}^* from the same distribution $\{0,1\}^\lambda$, following the argument at the beginning of Sect. 6, incurring a loss of $q_r/2^{\lambda-1}$. Following this, we replace the value $CKID^+$ computed in the *previous stage* of the test session π_i^{s-1} with a uniformly-random value $CKID^{+*}$ from $\{0,1\}^{|KDF|}$ as in the previous cases. Similarly, we replace that the keys $AKID$, $IKID$ and EK computed in the *previous stage* of the test session π_i^{s-1} with uniformly-random values $AKID^*$, $IKID^*$ and EK^*. We now interact with an AE challenger, computing AE.Enc($EK^*, A^+\|B^+$) by querying $(A^+\|B^+, A^{+*}\|B^{+*})$ to the LoR AE challenger's AuthEnc oracle instead of computing it honestly. At this point, the A^{+*}, B^{+*} values sent in the ciphertext in the previous stage are *independent* of the A^+, B^+ used in the test session. Similarly we replace the value $CKID$, and keys $AKID$, $IKID$ and EK computed in the *test stage* the test session with uniformly-random values via two KDF assumptions. Next, we hide the $SQNID_{UE}$ value with uniformly random value from the same distribution, to prevent linking it with values used in previous stages of the test session. Since $SQNID_{UE}$ is sent as the first field $D = SQNID_{HN} \oplus AKID$ in the *SUCI* message during the Identification Phase, and by previous replacement of $AKID$ as a uniformly random and independent value, we argue that $AKID$ acts as a one-time-pad perfectly hiding the replaced $SQNID_{UE}$ value. Finally, we interact with an AE challenger, computing AE.Enc($EK, A^+\|B^+$) (sent by the HN to the test session in the *test stage*) by querying $(A^+\|B^+, A^{+*}\|B^{+*})$ to the LoR AE challenger's AuthEnc oracle. At this point, the A^{+*}, B^{+*} values sent in the ciphertext are *independent* of the A^+, B^+ used in the *next stage* of the test session. We conclude that all values sent in the tested session π_i^s are independent of any value sent in previous and future sessions, and thus the adversary has negligible advantage in distinguishing between test sessions. Thus we have:

$$\mathsf{Adv}_{PQID,n_N,n_S,\mathcal{A}}^{SUPA,clean}(\lambda) \leq n_N n_S \cdot \left(\mathsf{Adv}_{KDF,\mathcal{A}}^{KDF}(\lambda) + \mathsf{Adv}_{AE,\mathcal{A}}^{AuthEnc}(\lambda)\right)$$
$$+ n_N n_S \cdot \left(\mathsf{Adv}_{KDF,\mathcal{A}}^{KDF}(\lambda) + \mathsf{Adv}_{MAC,\mathcal{A}}^{eufcma}(\lambda)\right)$$
$$+ n_N n_S \cdot \left(q_r/2^{\lambda-1} + 4 \cdot \mathsf{Adv}_{KDF,\mathcal{A}}^{KDF}(\lambda) + 2 \cdot \mathsf{Adv}_{AE,\mathcal{A}}^{AuthEnc}(\lambda)\right)$$

Now we discuss how our proposal prevents certain attacks and motivate our proposals to change aspects of the 3GPP specification.

Update of Long-Term Secret Parameters. As elaborated in Sect. 3.2, it may be required for HN to update its long-term secret key. In the current ECIES-based mechanism this is a difficult proposition as it requires a suitable mechanism to transport the updated public key of the HN to all of its subscribers and also an update-confirmation mechanism used by the subscribers. With our proposal, no such mechanism is required as the secret key is internal to HN. However, updating the K_{HN} will require an interim period during which the HN has to operate with both the new and old key, but this would be handled within domains of the Identification Scheme itself.

Migration to Authenticated Encryption in 5G. Our proposal uses authenticated encryption to update identification parameters. Currently, the 3GPP specifications do not list authenticated encryption algorithms, but instead separate encryption and integrity algorithms, ascribed to historical reasons. Previous generations of mobile telephony used to avoid integrity protection of user traffic (voice/data) because of the substantial errors during the radio channel propagation. Only the signalling traffic used to be integrity protected. But as the quality of radio traffic improved, provisions for integrity protection of user traffic were also created. Though we could have achieved the requisite security guarantees in our scheme using the currently specified primitives by following the "Encrypt-then-authenticate" paradigm, we stress that our approach is clearer and suggest that the 3GPP specifications should introduce such primitives.

Replay Prevention. We include and authenticate sequence numbers *SQNID* in our protection scheme to prevent replay attacks. Moreover, they also provide appropriate resilience to desynchronization between the *UE* and *HN* as now an arbitrary third party cannot initiate an identification request without access to the shared secret key K.

Chosen SUPI Attacks. Our scheme is resilient to *chosen SUPI attacks* (Sect. 3.2), due to inclusion of the shared secret key K as the keying input for the computation of the MAC tag *MACID*.

Multiple Identification Parameters. In the case of an unexpected interruption, the *UE* will re-attempt identification using the same parameters A and B. Although this does not violate the session unlinkability criterion (as it is effectively the same session), one could imagine the *UE* storing multiple pairs of identification parameters in these cases.

7   Conclusion

In this work we introduced a new private identification scheme for the 5G specification, a quantum-secure alternative to the current public-key based solution. We describe the limitations of the existing solution, and discuss how our proposal mitigates these drawbacks. We introduce a security model for *Symmetric Updatable Private Authentication* protocols, and prove the security of our proposal. We require minimal changes to the current 5G messages, mostly utilise the same underlying cryptographic primitives, with minimal computational overhead. As Release 15 (Phase 1 of 5G specifications planned to be finalized by September, 2018) is not closed yet, now is the correct time to incorporate and evaluate such additions. However, if such inclusions seem difficult in Release 15 then appropriate provisions need to be created in this Release to facilitate such changes in the future Release 16 (Phase 2 of 5G). Such actions would ensure that subsequent migration to quantum-resistant alternatives will be smooth after the 5G infrastructure gets deployed.

For 5G, the most cryptographically relevant quantum algorithms are Grover's searching algorithm [13] (quadratically faster than any classical brute force searching scheme) and Shor's factoring algorithm [21] (exponentially faster than the best known classical factoring algorithm - the number field sieve). It is worth noting, however, that if a quantum-resistant alternative was suggested that utilises the symmetric-key primitives offered by the current 3GPP specification (and their associated parameter sizes), then this may not achieve post-quantum security. For example, the output of the MAC algorithm (referred to as f_1, see Table 2) is 64 bits. For such a proposal to realize resilience against quantum algorithms [3], the standard technique to achieve this would be to increase the length of the classical-secure key-size, preferably to 256 bits. As regards the effects of bidding down attacks, in the current 3GPP specifications, the *SUPI* gets derived directly from the IMSI and thus is susceptible to bidding down attacks (Sect. 3.2) by an active adversary. To thwart such attacks, it is suggested to 3GPP that the derivation of *SUPI* should be independent of the previous generations' IMSI.

For future work, we suggest a security analysis of the combined 5G-AKA protocol and our proposal in an Authenticated Key Agreement security model. Another interesting direction may be to augment our SUPA security experiment to capture quantum adversaries, to show post-quantum security of our scheme.

References

1. Arkko, J., Lehtovirta, V., Eronen, P.: Improved extensible authentication protocol method for 3rd generation authentication and key agreement (EAP-AKA'). RFC **5448**, 1–29 (2009). https://doi.org/10.17487/RFC5448
2. van den Broek, F., Verdult, R., de Ruiter, J.: Defeating IMSI catchers. In: Ray, I., Li, N., Kruegel, C. (eds.) Proceedings of the 22nd ACM SIGSAC Conference on Computer and Communications Security, Denver, CO, USA, 12–16 October 2015, pp. 340–351. ACM (2015). https://doi.org/10.1145/2810103.2813615
3. Chen, L., et al.: Report on post-quantum cryptography. US Department of Commerce, National Institute of Standards and Technology (2016)
4. ETSI-SAGE: First response on ECIES for concealing IMSI or SUPI, October 2017. https://portal.3gpp.org/ngppapp/CreateTdoc.aspx?mode=view& contributionId=832160
5. Fox, D.: Der imsi-catcher. Datenschutz und Datensicherheit **26**(4), 212–215 (2002)
6. 3rd Generation Partnership Project: Rationale and track of security decisions in Long Term Evolution (LTE) RAN/3GPP System Architecture Evolution (SAE) (3GPP TR 33.821 Version 9.0.0 Release 9), June 2009. http://www.3gpp.org/DynaReport/33821.htm
7. 3rd Generation Partnership Project: Study on the security aspects of the next generation system (3GPP TR 33.899 Version 1.3.0 Release 14), August 2017. http://www.3gpp.org/DynaReport/33899.htm
8. 3rd Generation Partnership Project: 3G Security; Security Architecture (3GPP TS 33.102 Version 15.0.0 Release 15), June 2018. http://www.3gpp.org/DynaReport/33102.htm

9. 3rd Generation Partnership Project: Generic Authentication Architecture (GAA); Generic Bootstrapping Architecture (GBA) (3GPP TS 33.220 Version 15.2.0 Release 15), June 2018. http://www.3gpp.org/DynaReport/33220.htm
10. 3rd Generation Partnership Project: Mobile Application Part (MAP) Specification (3GPP TS 29.002 Version 15.3.0 Release 15), March 2018. http://www.3gpp.org/DynaReport/29002.htm
11. 3rd Generation Partnership Project: Security Architecture and Procedures for 5G Systems (3GPP TS 33.501 Version 15.0.0 Release 15), March 2018. http://www.3gpp.org/DynaReport/33501.htm
12. 3rd Generation Partnership Project: System Architecture for the 5G System (3GPP TS 23.501 Version 15.1.0 Release 15), March 2018. http://www.3gpp.org/DynaReport/23501.htm
13. Grover, L.K.: A fast quantum mechanical algorithm for database search. In: Miller, G.L. (ed.) Proceedings of the Twenty-Eighth Annual ACM Symposium on the Theory of Computing, Philadelphia, Pennsylvania, USA, 22–24 May 1996, pp. 212–219. ACM (1996). http://doi.acm.org/10.1145/237814.237866
14. Kelly, J.: A Preview of Bristlecone, Google's New Quantum Processor. https://ai.googleblog.com/2018/03/a-preview-of-bristlecone-googles-new.html. Accessed 08 June 2018
15. Khan, M.S.A., Mitchell, C.J.: Improving air interface user privacy in mobile telephony. In: Chen, L., Matsuo, S. (eds.) SSR 2015. LNCS, vol. 9497, pp. 165–184. Springer, Cham (2015). https://doi.org/10.1007/978-3-319-27152-1_9
16. Khan, M.S.A., Mitchell, C.J.: Trashing IMSI catchers in mobile networks. In: Noubir, G., Conti, M., Kasera, S.K. (eds.) Proceedings of the 10th ACM Conference on Security and Privacy in Wireless and Mobile Networks, WiSec 2017, Boston, MA, USA, 18–20 July 2017, pp. 207–218. ACM (2017). https://doi.org/10.1145/3098243.3098248
17. Lilly, A.: IMSI catchers: hacking mobile communications. Netw. Secur. **2017**(2), 5–7 (2017). https://doi.org/10.1016/S1353-4858(17)30014-4
18. Mattsson, J.: Post-quantum cryptography in mobile networks (2017). https://www.ericsson.com/research-blog/post-quantum-cryptography-mobile-networks/
19. SECG SEC 1: Recommended Elliptic Curve Cryptography, Version 2.0 (2009). http://www.secg.org/sec1-v2.pdf
20. Shaik, A., Seifert, J., Borgaonkar, R., Asokan, N., Niemi, V.: Practical attacks against privacy and availability in 4G/LTE mobile communication systems. In: 23rd Annual Network and Distributed System Security Symposium, NDSS 2016, San Diego, California, USA, 21–24 February 2016. The Internet Society (2016). http://wp.internetsociety.org/ndss/wp-content/uploads/sites/25/2017/09/practical-attacks-against-privacy-availability-4g-lte-mobile-communication-systems.pdf
21. Shor, P.W.: Algorithms for quantum computation: discrete logarithms and factoring. In: 35th Annual Symposium on Foundations of Computer Science, Santa Fe, New Mexico, USA, 20–22 November 1994, pp. 124–134. IEEE Computer Society (1994). https://doi.org/10.1109/SFCS.1994.365700
22. Shoup, V.: A proposal for an ISO standard for public key encryption. IACR Cryptology ePrint Archive **2001**, 112 (2001). http://eprint.iacr.org/2001/112

Great Expectations: A Critique of Current Approaches to Random Number Generation Testing & Certification

Darren Hurley-Smith$^{(\boxtimes)}$ and Julio Hernandez-Castro

University of Kent, Canterbury, Kent, UK
{d.hurley-smith,jch27}@kent.ac.uk

Abstract. Random number generators are a critical component of security systems. They also find use in a variety of other applications from lotteries to scientific simulations. Randomness tests, such as the NIST's STS battery (documented in SP800-22), Marsaglia's Diehard, and L'Ecuyer et al.'s TestU01 seek to find whether a generator exhibits any signs of non-random behaviour. However, many statistical test batteries are unable to reliably detect certain issues present in poor generators. Severe mistakes when determining whether a given generator passes the tests are common. Irregularities in sample size selection and a lack of granularity in test result interpretation contribute to this. This work provides evidence of these and other issues in several statistical test batteries. We identify problems with current practices and recommend improvements. The novel concept of *suitable randomness* is presented, precisely defining two bias bounds for a TRNG, instead of a simple binary pass/fail outcome. *Randomness naivety* is also introduced, outlining how binary pass/fail analysis cannot express the complexities of RNG output in a manner that is useful to determine whether a generator is suitable for a given range of applications.

1 Introduction

Random number generators (RNGs) are critical in security systems, for example in generating nonces, seeds and keys. Schindler and Killmann discussed the concept of an *ideal random number generator* [1], stating that such a generator is a fiction. They grouped real random number generators (RNGs) into three classes: true or physical RNGs (TRNGs), PRNGs, and *hybrid* RNGs. TRNGs, the focus of this work, are characterised by their reliance on some form of physical effect that can be used as a source of random noise.

Small-scale implementations, such as the TRNGs of NXP's DESFire EV1 and EV2 [2,3] are now commonplace and used in a variety of client-facing and cash-bearing roles (such as loyalty and pay-as-you-go cards). A variety of USB-connected or 'on board' TRNG designs using emitted noise from integrated circuitry represent the next step, with ChaosKey [4] providing an example of such a device. At the upper end of the spectrum, IDQ and Comscire have both

© Springer Nature Switzerland AG 2018
C. Cremers and A. Lehmann (Eds.): SSR 2018, LNCS 11322, pp. 143–163, 2018.
https://doi.org/10.1007/978-3-030-04762-7_8

developed commercial quantum RNGs (QRNGs) using optical and shot noise sources, respectively.

The output of an RNG must be tested to determine whether it possesses any undesirable characteristics. An ideal random number generator will provide sequences of outputs that are independent of each other and unpredictable. Test batteries such as Dieharder [5], NIST SP800-22 [6], Ent [7], and TestU01 [8] have been developed to test the null hypothesis: *the sequence under observation is random*. If this hypothesis is rejected, the generator is determined to be non-random.

We use results collected over two previous projects (Authenticated Self[1] and RAMSES[2]), in which the output of a variety of RNGs was evaluated using statistical tests. We will discuss the limitations of current testing regimens and the need for expanded test batteries to identify specific issues. This work critiques current randomness testing procedures, identifying critical areas in which statistical testing is found to be unreliable as a measure of RNG suitability. We also discuss common practices adopted by manufacturers and standards (NIST SP80090B/22, AIS 31/20) and their impact on the integrity of reported results. Independent experiments are reported, which show failings in the procedures engaged in during certification - institutional or independent - of RNGs.

The rest of this paper is organised as follows: Sect. 2 provides background on the key topics of this paper. Section 3 outlines the methodology used to collect data for the experimental evidence presented in this work. Section 4 provides a critique of the fundamental areas in which current testing and standards have been observed to fail. Section 5 suggests improvements to mitigate current issues. Section 6 provides our concluding remarks and a brief discussion of future work.

2   Background

A random sequence, from a computational perspective, should contain values that are independent and unpredictable. Insufficient entropy can cause repeating sequences to appear in RNG output, making them predictable. Biased output can have a similar effect. Incorrectly implemented or damaged hardware may also introduce weaknesses which may not be detected by some statistical tests. Poorly configured post-processing and data handling modules (software or hardware) can also cause biased or predictable sequences to occur. Crypto-systems must avoid predictability [9]. PRNGs, which are initialised using seed values, can employ hardware and software protection to ensure that this value is never observed by outsiders. If the seed becomes known, the output of a PRNG can be predicted. True Random Number Generators (TRNGs) provide random bit-streams using a variety of ostensibly random phenomena and do not require seed values.

---

[1] The Authenticated Self project has received funding from InnovateUK under reference number 102050.

[2] The RAMSES project has received funding from the European Union's Horizon 2020 research and innovation program, under grant agreement No. 700326.

Establishing whether a sequence of bits is random is far from trivial. Diehard [10], followed by Dieharder, and Tufftests [5], are early examples of statistical tests of randomness. NIST SP800-90B and SP800-22 documented the composition and use [6] of their Statistical Test Suite (SP800-22). Both SP800-22 and Dieharder are commonly used by TRNGs manufacturers to test their devices and add supporting evidence to *prove* their adequacy for cryptographic use.

But devices that perform well under both batteries can fail tests as simple as the χ^2 test [11]. More recent (2007) batteries, such as L'Ecuyer and Simard's TestU01 [8], have shown similar results for smart card integrated RNGs [12] and QRNGs.

Weak RNGs have been identified as the root cause of many security issues in computer systems. Garcia et al. [13,14] discovered in 2008 that the Mifare Classic, an RFID card manufactured by NXP, had an exceptionally weak PRNG which facilitated attacks against its supposedly secure communications channel. Kasper et al. [15] published attacks showing how a real-world payment system can be abused due to a weak random number generator, describing pre-play and man-in-the-middle attacks.

Bernstein et al. reported an attack against Taiwan's national *Citizen Digital Certificate* database, caused by a poor TRNG implementation in the BSI certified [16] *Renesas AE45C1 v.01*. These smart cards are used to sign official documents and perform other security-critical tasks, such as registration of residence and opening bank accounts. That so many can be compromised due to a weak RNG implementation is a cause for immediate concern and calls for further analysis and the modification of certification and testing schemes to mitigate the possibility of similar attacks in the future.

2.1 Certification, Standards, and Testing

NIST is a United States standards institute, concerned with the advancement of measurement science, standards and technology. SP800-90B [17] details specific test requirements of entropy sources for both PRNGs and TRNGs. It provides recommendations, outlining best practice and the minimum requirements of RNGs for security applications. IDQ and Comscire (two manufacturers of quantum RNGs) reference SP800-90B as the main source for their test and evaluation process. SP800-22 [18,19] provides a statistical test battery, developed by Rukhin et al.

Common Criteria [20] is an international standard (ISO/IEC 15408) for computer security certification. The scope of this standard is broad, covering such topics as the construction, function and assurance requirements of security-critical devices. These standards are intended to *permit comparability between the results of independent security evaluations, by providing a common set of requirements for security functions.* Evaluation Assurance Levels (EAL) are used to differentiate between levels of certification, with seven distinct tiers indicating the degree of vetting given to the design, production, and performance of a device. The EALs relevant to this work are 4 and 5, awarded, for example, to the DESFire EV1 and 2, respectively. Both EALs recommend testing of entropy sources as outlined in BSI's AIS-31 [21], with AIS 20 providing test recommendations specifically aimed at TRNG evaluation.

Statistical test batteries can consist of various individual tests with specific configurations depending on the aims of their developers. Marsaglia's Diehard battery [10] is one of the first of its kind. This battery has been expanded to include NIST SP800-22 tests and some independently developed tests over the years, resulting in a battery [22] known as Dieharder. Thirty tests (with 76 variants in total) are provided, requiring a large body of data to run in the default configuration. Test parameters can be changed to suit the target sample(s). It is crucial to avoid rewinds (where files reset to their first values after reaching the end) as such behaviour may easily introduce type 1 errors.

SP800-22 provides a suite of randomness tests that Rukhin et al. [19] suggested as a good starting point for the evaluation of RNGs. There are 15 tests defined in this document. SP800-22 evaluates p-values for both uniformity and the proportion of tests passed. Some tests, particularly the non-overlapping template matching and random excursions (variant) tests, have multiple iterations for a single execution of the battery. This leads to a total of 188 p-values at the conclusion of the test. Marton et al. [23] provided a more accurate number of failed tests that may be tolerated based on the NIST suggested confidence threshold of $a = 0.01\%$. The SP800-22 rev.1a document indicates that any failure is a cause for further testing, but leaves such testing to the discretion of those conducting the evaluation.

Ent [7] is a simple battery, intended to test the output of an RNG and provide some assurance that it is working as expected. It incorporates an entropy test, a chi-square test, a serial correlation test, a Monte-Carlo estimate of π test, and an arithmetic mean calculation test. This battery can be performed over bits or bytes, and runs for the whole length of any given sample file.

L'Ecuyer and Simard [8] have developed TestU01. It provides a variety of different test batteries incorporating classical tests, new ones identified in the academic literature, and some original tests developed by the L'Ecuyer and Simard.

2.2   Test Correlations

Statistical tests of randomness focus on checking for specific evidence of non-randomness. Batteries of tests use a variety of schemes to determine whether a sequence is seemingly random, by checking for as many potential non-random behaviours as possible. There is a large body of literature that details how statistical tests may be correlated, and the misleading effect this can have on the results of existing test batteries.

Hernandez-Castro et al. [24] identified that there is an undesirable degree of correlation between the Ent tests. They degenerated a random sequence over multiple iterations using a genetic algorithm, to control how the sequence transitioned from random to non-random states. This method allowed the observation of Ent's results for each degenerating sequence, and identified whether tests continued to share similar results regardless of the type of degeneration each sample exhibited.

Their results demonstrate that the tests in this battery are not wholly independent. The entropy and compression tests both measure similar features, resulting in closely matched results. The conclusion drawn is that two of the tests could be discarded with no impact on the ability of this battery to detect non-randomness.

NIST SP800-22 has also had the independence of its tests analysed internally and by other scholars. Soto [25] explicitly discussed the need for an analysis of test independence in SP800-22 as an open problem. He also mentioned the issue of test coverage: tests may be independent, but batteries may not test for sufficient features to be able to identify non-random behaviour in a given generator. Turan et al. [26] found that tests measuring frequency, overlapping templates (for input template 111), longest run of ones, random walk height and maximum order complexity produced correlated results. This is more of a problem with smaller sequences, or for small input block sizes when considering level 2 tests. Georgescu et al. [27] took this a step further, focusing on the open questions regarding the independence of SP800-22 tests. They comment on the complexity of the NIST test suite, and on methods for testing independence. They found that sample size has a significant effect on the dependency of various test statistics, reporting similar observations to those of Turan et al. They also commented that better tests may exist, and that the identification of such tests should be part of ongoing work in this field.

Zhu et al. did not comment specifically on the independence of SP800-22 tests, but they did identify that level 2 tests need improvements. They found that sequences may pass these tests while possessing clear statistical flaws, and propose a new *Q-value* which is computed using test statistics instead of p-values. This value is more sensitive to total variation distance and Kullback-Leiber divergence. A more in-depth analysis of sequences is possible as a consequence, that can help solve [28] some of the problems caused by the correlations between the non-χ^2 level 2 tests under SP800-22. The concept of *Randomness Naivety* is posited, building on the *Q-value* idea by highlighting how test suites favour binary pass/fail outcomes consisting of a p-value and confidence threshold, over more granular and complex test reports. All of the test batteries studied in this work exhibit this form of naivety.

As Dieharder shares many tests with NIST SP800-22, these criticisms apply to both batteries. Fan et al. [29] proposed a test methodology to identify correlations between tests in a suite, identifying that both SP800-22 (and by extension Dieharder) exhibit correlations in several tests. This is in contrast with the statement by NIST in revision 2 of SP800-22, that the tests have an acceptable degree of independence. More work needs to be done on deciding what constitutes an acceptable degree of independence.

Discussion of the test correlations in the TestU01 battery is limited and should be a focus of future work. This battery is better suited for the analysis of truly random sequences than Dieharder and SP800-22, both of which were developed with a focus on PRNGs. Turan et al. [26] commented that the tests that they find to be correlated are also present in this battery, reinforcing the need for further analysis. It has, however, been shown to identify issues with TRNGs that both Dieharder and SP800-22 have been unable to notice.

3   Data Collection

Table 1 provides an overview of the devices studied in this work. The DESFire cards have estimated prices per card based on batch purchasing prices. Their entropy sources are unknown at this time, as the public documentation does not provide any insight into their TRNG design. All data collection and testing was performed on an Ubuntu workstation with an Intel i7 3770k processor and 16 GB of RAM. Table 2 provides a summary of the data collection concerning the number of samples, the sample size and (where possible) the average data rate of the devices.

Table 1. Certifications and/or test recommendations achieved by target devices prior to this study

Manufacturer	Device	Cost €	Entropy source	Certifications/Tests
NXP	DESFire EV1	0.59	Not disclosed	CC EAL4+
NXP	DESFire EV2	1.25	Not disclosed	CC EAL5+
IDQ	Quantis 16M	2,900	Beam splitter	NIST SP800-22, METAS, CTL
IDQ	Quantis 4M	1,299	Beam splitter	NIST SP800-22, METAS, CTL
IDQ	Quantis USB 4M	990	Beam splitter	NIST SP800-22, METAS, CTL
Comscire	PQ32MU	1211	Shot noise	NIST SP800-90B/C NIST SP800-22 Diehard
Altus Metrum	ChaosKey	45	RBSJ[a]	FIPS 140-2

[a]Reverse biased semiconductor junction

Entries marked with an asterisk reflect unique samples taken from individual devices. For example, all DESFire EV1 and 2 samples were taken from different cards to determine whether errors were specific to a given card or batch, or systemic problems. The Quantis, Comscire, ChaosKey and urandom samples were all taken from a single device of each listed type. Speed tests were not performed for DESFire cards: benchmarking was not possible as it does not reflect the actual speed of the TRNG but of the authentication process. Urandom was not benchmarked either, as its output is limited by the write-speed of storage hardware in the PC, not the generator itself.

Data was collected from each device with no additional post-processing. Quantis devices were accessed through a command-line application provided by IDQ. The Comscire device's output was read via the inbuilt *dd* application under Ubuntu 16-04 LTS. A chaotic (classical) TRNG named ChaosKey was

Table 2. Number of samples and size with speed collection in target RNGs

	No. samples	Sample size MB	Mean data rate (Mbit/s)
DESFire EV1	3*	64	-
	100*	1	-
DESFire EV2	1*	64	-
Quantis 16M	100	2100	15.87
Quantis 4M	100	2100	3.86
Quantis USB 4M	100	2100	3.96
Comscire PQ32MU	100	2100	30.99
ChaosKey	10	2100	3.80
Urandom	10	2100	-

used to provide a small sample of sequences as a control. This device is known to pass the TestU01 batteries, which the other generators have not been evaluated with, providing a valuable comparison. Urandom, a version of the Linux PRNG, has been provided as a control to all of the above.

DESFire EV1 and EV2 presented a more significant challenge. There is no way to interface with the TRNG on either type of card directly. There is, however, an authentication function using a three-pass handshake method that exposes RNG output in 16-byte chunks. By repeatedly authenticating (successfully) with each card, data could be extracted from the TRNG. Due to the slow capture speed, 64 MB samples were collected from three DESFire EV1 cards and one DESFire EV2. A further 100 samples of 1 MB each coming from 100 unique DESFire EV1 cards were collected.

We were not able to verify whether the values retrieved were directly sourced from the TRNG, or whether they had undergone post-processing. After the responsible disclosure of our findings to NXP, they opened a dialogue in which they discussed potential flaws in the *whitening function* as a possible explanation.

4   Critique

4.1   Testing Diversity

The diversity of a test battery is related to, but separate from, the degree of correlation between its tests. A common theme in the literature is that observation of p-values is insufficient to identify all of the potential issues that may arise in sequences that pass testing. In this work, the results of testing over 8 RNGs are presented to demonstrate the need for a wider variety of tests. For example, TestU01's Alphabits, Rabbit, Small Crush, and Crush reveal issues with generators that pass Dieharder and SP800-22. Ent is also found to be effective at detecting flaws that other batteries fail to identify.

Table 3 provides a simple pass/fail output for Dieharder, NIST SP800-22, and 2 TestU01 results for the DESFire EV1 and DESFire EV2. We have presented these results in previous work [12] but replicate them here for reference in the following discussion. The results computed over 64 MB samples for 3 DESFire EV1s and 1 DESFire EV2 are shown. Data collection for these cards is very time-consuming, and hence we only had access to three 64 MB samples and a hundred 1 MB samples. The 100 MB samples were of insufficient size for reliable testing using Dieharder and NIST tests.

Table 3. Dieharder, NIST and TestU01 Results for the Mifare DESfire EV1 and 2 cards

Device	Size MB	Dieharder	NIST SP800-22	TestU01 Alphabits	TestU01 Rabbit
DESFire EV1	64	Pass	Pass	Fail	Fail
	64	Pass	Pass	Fail	Fail
	64	Pass	Pass	Fail	Fail
DESFire EV2	64	Pass	Pass	Pass	Pass

The DESFire EV2 passes all tests, but the 3 DESFire EV1s fail TestU01 Alphabits and Rabbit batteries. Furthermore, the DESFire EV1 demonstrated exceptionally poor performance on simple χ^2 tests. Only 21 out of 100 1 MB DESFire EV1 samples [12] (from 3 different batches) passed this basic uniformity test. When sample sizes was increased to 5MB for the cards that passed, they all failed the χ^2 test. This demonstrates that sample size plays a significant role in hiding flaws. A small sample may appear to be random, when in fact it possesses undesirable characteristics that only become more apparent with longer sequences. Full results for the Ent test can be found in Appendix B.

Table 4 shows the pass rates for output generated by three different Quantis generators, a Comscire PQ32MU, a ChaosKey and Linux's */dev/urandom*. Only 10 files were collected from the ChaosKey during our experiments. The randomness-testing-toolkit (rtt) was used to evaluate files of size 2 GB, for each of the selected generators.

Table 4. Dieharder, NIST and TestU01 Results for full Quantis, Comscire, ChaosKey, and urandom samples as reported by the rtt-randomness-test suite (https://github.com/crocs-muni/randomness-testing-toolkit)

Device	Samples #	Dieharder % Passed	NIST SP800-22 % Passed	TestU01 Alphabits % Passed	TestU01 Rabbit % Passed	TestU01 Small crush % Passed	TestU01 Crush % Passed
Quantis 16M	100	100	100	54	60	93	47
Quantis 4M	100	100	100	3	7	91	3
Quantis USB	100	100	100	3	21	89	3
Comscire PQ32MU	100	100	100	91	86	93	84
ChaosKey	10	100	100	90	90	90	80
urandom	100	84	100	96	85	92	79

Preliminary work reported in [30] showed similar results for a smaller selection of devices and samples. Dieharder and NIST tests were passed by Quantis devices.

TestU01 is divided into multiple test batteries. It is possible to define custom batteries of tests, but a variety of default batteries are pre-defined as part of the TestU01 API. These batteries are Alphabits, Rabbit, Small Crush, Crush and Big Crush. Big Crush has been excluded from our tests, as it requires more data that we have been able to collect. Exceptionally poor performance is reported on the Alphabits and Rabbit batteries. Small Crush and Crush also report failures across all RNGs tested, but to a lesser degree. The results of these tests are shown in Table 4.

Dieharder and NIST SP800-22 are successfully passed by the Quantis, PQ32MU, and ChaosKey generators. Unexpectedly, urandom appears to fail rtt's implementation of Dieharder 16 times, but upon closer inspection of the test results it was found that the reported failures were caused by a combination of rewinds and an overly stringent failure threshold in this implementation.

The rtt Dieharder implementation appears to classify weak results (p-values less than 0.5% or over 99.5%) as failures. Retesting of suspect files using the default Linux Dieharder implementation found no issues with the 16 urandom files that reportedly failed under rtt-Dieharder. This is an important consideration, as the selection of appropriate confidence thresholds and implementation is critical to the execution of a meaningful RNG analysis.

All devices pass NIST SP800-22 [23] within the threshold defined by Marton et al. The Quantis 4M does show a worryingly borderline set of results for its second sample, but over 92% of its 100 samples pass by a significant margin, with only 8% reporting borderline (within 0.001 of confidence threshold) passes.

TestU01 Alphabits is failed by the all of the tested RNGs to some degree. This is expected because of the definition of confidence intervals and the large number of samples tested. DESFire EV1 samples show multiple test failures, with the Multinomial Bits Over test reporting a 100% error rate for the three samples given. One sample also fails the Random Walk 1 test, and two others the Hamming Independence test. The DESFire EV2 demonstrates no such failures, passing all tests.

Quantis devices, especially the 4M and USB, fail Alphabits around 97% of the time. The Quantis 16M performs better (failing less tests) but still fails for 46% of its samples. The Multinomial Bits Over test reports the majority of these failures, with 100% of 4M failures being attributed to this test.

PQ32MU, urandom and ChaosKey report few failures for Alphabits. Solitary failures are reported in most cases, and different tests fail for each battery. The urandom generator fails the Hamming Correlation test twice. In isolation, the repeated failure of this test across a diverse array of different samples may indicate that it is prone to false positives. However, further testing using other TestU01 batteries shows that this is far from the only test failed.

TestU01's Rabbit battery reports fewer failures for Quantis and Comscire QRNGs, but urandom has worse performance on this battery (more failed tests) than on Alphabits.

The DESFire EV1 and Quantis (4M and USB) RNGs fail in the majority of their samples. The failure of urandom for the Multinomial Bits Over test is a cause for concern, and may indicate that this test is prone to false positives or possesses a dubious default configuration. On the other hand, this may indicate that the results themselves are consistently bad. Further experiments will be required solve this question.

The Multinomial Bits Over test uses different parameters under Rabbit, compared to its Alphabits implementation. As other tests account for the majority of failures over the other devices, these must also be explored to identify whether there may be configuration issues. As previously mentioned, output block size can have an effect [23] on TestU01 results.

The DESFire EV1 samples consistently fail Multinomial, Fourier3, Autocorrelation and Run tests. The 4M and USB also fail these (and many other) tests, but the primary test failed is the Autocorrelation test. For the 4M and USB, this accounts for more than 90% of battery failures. The tests that fail alongside the Autocorrelation tests vary between samples. The Autocorrelation test is the only constantly recurring failure throughout all Quantis 4M and USB samples. The failure of some tests for Quantis 4M and USB samples may be caused by statistically tolerable type-1 errors, but Fourier3 (42% of sample fail) and Run tests (67% of samples fail) fail for a significant portion of 4M samples. Quantis USB samples fail Fourier3 36% of the time, and Run tests 61% of the time. This is a significant result that shows that several non-random characteristics may be present with varying probability of expressing themselves in a given sample. The Quantis 16M doesn't share this trend, instead showing a high proportion of failures for Multinomial and Hamming Weight tests. This may be caused by the different structure of the 16M, which uses four entropy sources and a simple mixing function, instead of the one raw entropy stream generated by the 4M and USB. Issues with an individual entropy source may be masked, or the entropy *stretched* by the concatenation of consecutive bits as they are output by each source.

PQ32MU failures mostly occur in the Multinomial Bits Over test. ChaosKey also fails this test. This is its only failure for the Rabbit battery.

TestU01 Small Crush shares many tests with Dieharder, SP800-22, FIPS 140-2, and tests recommended under AIS-31 (via appended recommendations documents). The 2.1 GB samples tested with this battery have an 11% (Quantis USB) failure rate at most.

TestU01 Crush reports abysmal performance by Quantis devices. PQ32MU, ChaosKey and urandom also show many (but fewer) failures. A new trend is identified in Quantis devices, which fail the Runs test for 100% of their samples for the 4M and USB. The 16M shows over 60% of its failures having the Runs test in common. No such trends were observed in the other devices, which mostly failed individual tests with occasional multiple test failures in a sample.

The Crush results for Quantis devices show consistent failures with significant repetition of specific tests. The Run test consistently fails for all Quantis RNGs. Other tests fail to much smaller degrees (RandomWalk1 for the 16M, Fourier3 for the 4M).

These results reinforce the observation made at the beginning of this section: the two most commonly used test batteries (Dieharder and SP800-22) do not have sufficient breadth of tests to identify issues that Ent and TestU01 detect. A different combination of batteries may provide a short-term solution. Identifying batteries that expand on Dieharder and SP800-22 with minimal repetition of tests and parameters between batteries is a simple, if naive, method of expanding on current randomness test methodologies. Identification and removal of correlated tests is an essential part of such a process. This should be the target of future research.

A longer-term and more rigorous solution will be to develop new tests and create a new test battery taking the strengths of Dieharder, SP800-22, TestU01, Tufftests [5], and many more. A next-generation test battery should be application specific, with test selection and configuration controlled by the user with detailed guidelines to assist in analyzing RNGs for specific tasks (gambling, cryptography, etc.). Our research touches on the general requirements of randomness testing, in an effort to provide suggestions as to what form a next-generation statistical test battery for randomness may take.

4.2 Sample Size

SP800-90B states [31] that an entropy source must provide 1,000,000 bits of sequential output for testing. Concatenation of smaller sequences is allowed if the generator is not capable of such contiguous output, but each of these smaller sequences must be at least 1,000 samples in length. SP800-22 recommends [19] a similar sample size but extends it by suggesting that tests are performed over at least 100 such samples. AIS-31 does not stipulate a specific testing sample size but does suggest minimum entropy and internal state lengths via the AIS 20 TRNG developer guidelines.

As outlined in their self-published test reports[3], IDQ's Quantis devices pass the Diehard and NIST SP800-22 batteries with no failures. The SP800-22 test was conducted over 1,000 bit-streams of 1,000,000 bits each, at a significance level of 1%. Diehard was performed over a single bit-stream of 1 billion bits. A further series of 7 tests, all conforming to NIST SP800-22, are run before shipment of each device. The results reported in Tables 3 and 4 agree with these practices. While issues are identified in other test batteries, this is not due to the sample size being insufficient for identification under Dieharder and SP800-22. A brief report of Diehard and NIST SP800-22 tests is provided with each device, alongside a certificate *guaranteeing* the quality of the product.

---

[3] https://marketing.idquantique.com/acton/attachment/11868/f-004c/1/-/-/-/-/ Randomness%20Test%20Report.pdf.

An interesting observation in the PQ32MU NIST-Diehard validation report[4] is that they have reduced the number of tests, and have only analysed two samples, one of 80 million bits and the other of 1 million bits. Due to insufficient data, the Random Excursions, Random Excursions Variant, and Spectral DFT tests were omitted. This is an unexpected deviation from the procedures outlined in SP800-22, resulting in 148 test results (including permutations of tests) instead of 188. They also state that Diehard requires a *large* number of bits, citing the value 80Mb. This is a relatively small file, and John Walker states [7] that in their default configuration the Diehard tests should be run over 10-100MB at least. This is a substantially smaller sample than what is recommended under SP800-22.

The Mifare DESFire EV1 and EV2 documentation[5] details the evaluation process and results. These RFID cards are EAL4+ and 5+ rated, respectively. The specific sample size and number of devices tested is not mentioned in any documentation associated with either device. Due to the volume of devices produced, individual test reports are out of the question. The TRNG test process is unclear for the most part, as the TRNG implementation itself is black-boxed in all publicly accessible NXP information. This includes publicly available data sheets.

The statistical tests performed in this work tend to use significantly larger samples than advised by the developers of Diehard, NIST SP800-22, and TestU01. Further testing on various sample sizes will be required in future work to more comprehensively analyse the effect of differing sample sizes on test correlation and the accuracy of results even when tests are independent of each other.

It is well-known that at least $N = k/\epsilon^2$ samples are needed to reliably detect a bias of ϵ, for some constant k. This highlights the importance of selecting an appropriate minimum sample size. Even more important is the clear communication of such requirements and the attempt to identify new tests that are more sensitive (or statistical powerful) at smaller sample sizes. This latter consideration is important, as time is a limited resource for most companies seeking to evaluate the performance of their RNGs. If a test requires too large a sample size, it is likely that less robust tests that work on smaller samples will be selected. Identifying tests that meet both requirements would be of immense value to this field of research.

4.3 Number of Devices Tested

Ambiguous reporting on the number of devices tested is a concern, especially as it appears to be a recurring issue with three of the manufacturers of products analysed in this work. By only testing a small number of devices, a manufacturer ignores the possibility of identifying a representative bias brought by a particular

---

[4] https://comscire.com/files/cert/comscire-pq32mu-nist_diehard-validation-tests.pdf.

[5] https://www.commoncriteriaportal.org/files/epfiles/0712a_pdf.pdf.

product batch. Manufacturing flaws are common, though usually have a minimal effect on the resulting product. In some cases, such *flaws* are used as the basis of further security features, Physically Unclonable Functions (PUF) being an example [32] of this. However, it is vital to understand whether the results reported by a manufacturer are representative of a large and random selection of devices, or represent an exemplary (and potentially not representative) demonstration of their products.

The lack of detailed test reports for the DESFire EV1 is compounded by the abysmal performance it shows in test batteries (Tables 3 and 4) not used as a part of its certification. Comscire and IDQ provide in-depth test results while avoiding any mention of the number of items tested per batch. As with testing a single sequence, testing a single device can provide very misleading information.

4.4 Closed Source vs. Open Source

Closed-source development is understandable for the protection of intellectual property but harms the trustworthiness of security products. NXP, IDQ, and Comscire do not disclose the full schematics for their products in any public material. What is even more shocking, they do not have to do so as part of the certification processes they went through.

ChaosKey, however, discloses the circuit schematic for their generator. Figure 1 shows the diagram, which is part of a complete set of documentation available [33] through Altus Metrum's website.

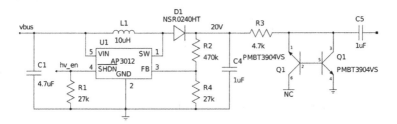

Fig. 1. ChaosKey noise-source circuit [4] diagram

This design has been found to pass the majority of the tests presented in this paper and also in our previous [11,12,30] work. The expectation of independent and unpredictable output is maintained despite knowledge of the structure of the generator (under normal operating conditions - the device has not been manipulated in any way).

Security through obscurity offers little protection against a determined and resourceful attacker. Sufficient experimentation can reveal flaws [12,13,34] in black-boxed functions and hardware. DESFire EV1's TRNG design is not disclosed in the publicly available documentation [12] but this knowledge is not needed to find it to be extremely biased. The security community has been through this discussion before: AES is the result of a NIST competition that aimed to standardise cryptographic algorithms in a way that made them secure even when the algorithm itself is known. This was a successful way to combat fears of back doors, which were suspected to be present in DES due to the less transparent nature [35] of its development. The AES standard is used to this day and has proven robust against attacks while fostering trust through its open design.

We suggest that RNGs follow a similar approach, with an open and critical development process to standardise noise sources and post-processing algorithms for security-critical applications. The process could also be used to establish more robust guidelines for non-security-critical RNGs that are nonetheless expected to be trustworthy, such as those used in gaming and gambling.

5   Recommendations

We have identified multiple ways in which randomness testing can be unreliable or misleading. This section discusses two areas of improvement identified during this work: the need to avoid naive approaches to statistical RNG testing, and a new and more realistic definition of suitable randomness that aims for an application-focused definition of a given RNG assessment.

5.1   Randomness Naivety

We make use of the term *randomness naivety* when discussing randomness test procedures that make sweeping assumptions, or fail to adhere to the documented requirements of statistical tests.

We characterise *randomness naivety* as:

- The use of simplified test statistics, such as p-values, over the analysis of full test statistics [28]
- The improper implementation or use of tests, for example using sample sizes that are too small, or testing too few [12] devices before reaching a final assessment
- Ignoring that self-certification is misleading at best and useless at worst, and that tests should be presented 'as is' instead of wrapped in manufacturer specific or PR terminology
- Pretending that closed-source entropy sources can be fully trusted and ignoring that they are a security issue by itself. Closed design force users to be naive as they have no choice but to trust the accompanying test results and manufacturer statements, especially when devices are novel or non-standard
- Assuming that *one size fits all* when assessing a generator. This is a fallacy because only sufficiently large sample sizes can offer guarantees about bias bounds. The sample sizes employed in testing should be reported in the literature, which is not common practice, and minimum sample sizes should be explicitly required for each statistical test.

One size fits all is an assumption that leads to dangerous conclusions regarding the quality of a random number generator. RNGs can exhibit over very large sample sizes, in the order of Gigabytes, issues that are concerning to cryptographers while still being suitable for non-security related uses. Gaming, gambling, and simulation are examples of applications that require good randomness, but do not generally require such stringent features as cryptographic applications.

5.2   Suitable Randomness

Suitable randomness refers to the detailed evaluation not only of an RNG but also of the precise context in which it will be used and the concrete requirements in such context.

A *suitably random* generator cannot be identified as such unless one defines as well a clear range of applications for which it has been designed and evaluated. An RNG used to generate cryptographic private keys will require far more rigour in the testing process than one merely used to generate playing cards or bidimensional points in space. It is hence critical to identify the precise range of uses for which one is testing an RNG. The RNG may be (ab)-used for other purposes, but the manufacturer or evaluating body can claim that it has been evaluated appropriately for only a list of very specific uses and that any usage outside those is risky and discouraged.

We posit that a result of any randomness test or evaluation should be a *bias bound* of the tested generator, computed over a sufficiently large and representative sample of sequences and devices. The EV1 has a *bias bound* of approximately 10^{-5} while Quantis devices show, on the other hand, biases on the order of 10^{-6} (summarised in Appendix B). By knowing the range of highest and lowest biases, one can decide whether the occurrence of values in a sequence is sufficiently uniform for the application at hand. For example, an online casino could be satisfied with a fast generator offering a bounded bias guaranteeing that any advantage, even if optimally exploited, will lead to profits of less than £1 per year per player.

However, uniformity is only one requirement of randomness: the predictability of sequences based on observed values must also be studied to compute a maximum bound. Following with the online casino example, even if the generator offers perfect uniformity it could suffer from very high predictability (e.g. a counter) so a study of the predictability bias is also important and complementary and should be taken into account in any risk modeling.

To summarize, a pass result from a randomness test or battery should never be used as a proof that a generator is random; only that its bias is bounded by a figure that should be precisely computed as a function of the test or battery statistical power, the size of the input, and possibly other features. No serious scientific claim should read "The TRNG X is random, as shown by passing all the tests in battery Y" but instead "The uniformity bias of TRNG X is below δ and its predictability bias is below γ, as shown by passing battery Y with size Z".

6   Conclusion

This work has provided a critical analysis of current randomness testing strategies. We have discussed a number of issues, such as sample size and number of tested devices, among others. These can and usually do lead to misleading results or wrong conclusions about the randomness characteristics of a given RNG.

Randomness naivety has been defined as the use of a reductionist definition of randomness: accepting a simple pass or fail outcome instead of characterising tested devices as *suitably random* for a given application. Furthermore, we suggest that bias bounds should be established and publicised for any tested device, over a sufficiently large number of representative samples and devices. This could be useful when realistically modeling a source of randomness in a real-world implementation or protocol, so that any known biases are put into the appropriate equations, and taken into account when evaluating risks, attack vectors, and countermeasures.

We need more scrutiny of the behaviour, characteristics and limitations of statistical test batteries. By defining test performance in terms of target applications, it will be possible to make more clear and valuable statements about the tasks for which a given RNG has been deemed appropriate.

Dieharder, NIST SP800-22, Ent, and TestU01 all demonstrate some degree of correlation in some of their tests. Dieharder and SP800-22 also have a high degree of duplication in their test selection. Future statistical test batteries should be thoroughly analysed for correlation in their tests before being released. A continuous review of new tests should be performed to ensure that efficient, statistical powerful and robust tests are integrated if they are uncorrelated with or superior to existing tests.

We find that the current recommendations for RNG testing are useful in identifying egregious departures from randomness, but are an unsubtle set of instruments that require a radically new approach able to characterise tested RNGs instead of merely declaring a reductionist pass/fail or random/not-random result.

Acknowledgements. This project has received funding from Innovate UK, under reference number 102050 (authenticatedSelf) and from the European Union's Horizon 2020 research and innovation programme, under grant agreement No. 700326 (RAMSES project). This article is based upon work from COST Action IC1403 CRYPTACUS, supported by COST (European Cooperation in Science and Technology). We would like to thank NXP Semiconductors Ltd. for their timely and professional communication following the responsible disclosure of our findings.

A   Appendix: Test Battery Configuration

The Randomness Testing Toolkit (RTT)[6] was used to conduct the Dieharder, NIST SP 800-22 and TestU01 experiments. Ent was used as provided in the Ubuntu 16.04 LTS distribution. Modified parameters are discussed below.

---

[6] https://github.com/crocs-muni/randomness-testing-toolkit.

A.1   Dieharder

The DESFire cards required some modification of the test parameters, due to their small sample size. The following modifications were made:

- Overlapping Permutations: 125,000 t-samples
- Binary rank 32x32: 4,750 t-samples
- Binary rank 6x8: 25,000 t-samples
- Craps: 20,000 t-samples

Four fewer tests (23 instead of 27) are conducted over 64 MB DESFire sequences. Tests that rewind during a single run are omitted. Rewinds are tolerated so long as the sequence does not reach the end of the file during a single test. 1 MB sequences are not tested with Dieharder, due to insufficient file size. All other devices use default settings over 2.1 GB.

A.2   NIST SP800-22 (revision V3)

The DESFire EV1 and DESFire EV2 cards were tested using the full NIST SP800-22 statistical test suite, but only for their 64 MB samples. The 1 MB samples were too small to allow the minimum recommended test parameters outlined in SP800-22 and so are omitted. 200 bit-streams of 1,048,576 bits were tested for each sample of every device (Quantis 16M, 4M, USB, Comscire PQ32MU, ChaosKey, urandom, DESFire EV1, and DESFire EV2). The suggested minimum for tests [6] is 100 bit-streams of at least 1,000,000 bits in length.

A.3   Ent

Ent runs for the full length of all samples. Both byte and bit tests were performed. All tests were run over all samples, without exception.

A.4   TestU01

Due to their small size, the DESFire EV1 and DESFire EV2 samples were only tested with the Alphabits and Rabbit batteries. Both batteries take an argument representing the size of the input stream, in this case the full 64MB of the samples in question.

The first $2 \cdot 10^9$ bits of the Quantis, Comscire, ChaosKey, and urandom samples were tested using Alphabits and Rabbit. Small Crush was executed using its default parameters. Crush was executed using a reduced set of tests to allow for testing 2.1 GB files (test numbers provided in brackets next to each test):

- smarsa CollisionOver (3–10)
- smarsa BirthdaySpacings (11)
- snpair ClosePairs (18–20)

- snpair ClosePairsBitMatch (21 and 22)
- sknuth Max0ft (43)
- svaria SampleProd (45)
- svaria SampleMean (47)
- svaria AppearanceSpacings (49 and 50)
- smarsa MatrixRank (56)
- smarsa MatrixRank (58)
- smarsa MatrixRank (60)
- smarsa GCD (63–64)
- swalk RandomWalk1 (65–70)
- scomp LinearComp (71–72)
- scomp LempelZiv (73)
- sspectral Fourier3 (74 and 75)
- sstring HammingIndep (90)
- sstring Run (91)

Big Crush was omitted, as it requires substantially more data than was included in the sample files.

B   Appendix: Ent Results

See Table 5 and Figs. 2, 3.

Table 5. ENT results for the first 3 samples from each device

	X^2	Serial corr.	Bytes	X^2	Serial corr.	Bits
DESFire EV1	2709.10	$8.00 \cdot 10^{-6}$	$6.4 \cdot 10^7$	2.3451	$8.04 \cdot 10^{-4}$	$5.1 \cdot 10^8$
	973.07	$4.50 \cdot 10^{-5}$	$6.4 \cdot 10^7$	0.2901	$4.53 \cdot 10^{-4}$	$5.1 \cdot 10^8$
	2470.32	$9.32 \cdot 10^{-5}$	$6.4 \cdot 10^7$	0.6942	$7.31 \cdot 10^{-4}$	$5.1 \cdot 10^8$
DESFire EV2*	256.21	$1.60 \cdot 10^{-4}$	$6.4 \cdot 10^7$	1.1603	$4.50 \cdot 10^{-5}$	$5.1 \cdot 10^8$
Quantis 16M	373.13	$-2.40 \cdot 10^{-5}$	$2.1 \cdot 10^9$	107.72	$1.26 \cdot 10^{-5}$	$1.7 \cdot 10^{10}$
	302.60	$8.52 \cdot 10^{-6}$	$2.1 \cdot 10^9$	74.43	$1.17 \cdot 10^{-5}$	$1.7 \cdot 10^{10}$
	354.93	$5.4 \cdot 10^{-5}$	$2.1 \cdot 10^9$	99.40	$1.35 \cdot 10^{-5}$	$1.7 \cdot 10^{10}$
Quantis 4M	553.77	$1.41 \cdot 10^{-5}$	$2.1 \cdot 10^9$	141.80	$9.36 \cdot 10^{-5}$	$1.7 \cdot 10^{10}$
	489.71	$-3.88 \cdot 10^{-5}$	$2.1 \cdot 10^9$	103.55	$8.43 \cdot 10^{-5}$	$1.7 \cdot 10^{10}$
	514.28	$-1.63 \cdot 10^{-5}$	$2.1 \cdot 10^9$	140.01	$8.73 \cdot 10^{-5}$	$1.7 \cdot 10^{10}$
Quantis USB	436.95	$3.20 \cdot 10^{-5}$	$2.1 \cdot 10^9$	46.036	$8.88 \cdot 10^{-5}$	$1.7 \cdot 10^{10}$
	426.65	$5.03 \cdot 10^{-6}$	$2.1 \cdot 10^9$	61.399	$8.98 \cdot 10^{-5}$	$1.7 \cdot 10^{10}$
	472.57	$6.25 \cdot 10^{-5}$	$2.1 \cdot 10^9$	70.272	$9.07 \cdot 10^{-5}$	$1.7 \cdot 10^{10}$
Comscire PQ32MU	266.50	$-1.07 \cdot 10^{-6}$	$2.1 \cdot 10^9$	0.3669	$-1.16 \cdot 10^{-6}$	$1.7 \cdot 10^{10}$
	213.33	$-7.06 \cdot 10^{-6}$	$2.1 \cdot 10^9$	1.2088	$1.49 \cdot 10^{-5}$	$1.7 \cdot 10^{10}$
	236.59	$1.39 \cdot 10^{-5}$	$2.1 \cdot 10^9$	0.0035	$5.85 \cdot 10^{-7}$	$1.7 \cdot 10^{10}$
ChaosKey	238.29	$-2.13 \cdot 10^{-4}$	$2.1 \cdot 10^9$	0.7668	$1.29 \cdot 10^{-5}$	$1.7 \cdot 10^{10}$
	295.64	$6.40 \cdot 10^{-6}$	$2.1 \cdot 10^9$	0.0044	$2.72 \cdot 10^{-6}$	$1.7 \cdot 10^{10}$
	238.29	$1.14 \cdot 10^{-5}$	$2.1 \cdot 10^9$	1.1845	$1.22 \cdot 10^{-6}$	$1.7 \cdot 10^{10}$
urandom	270.79	$2.59 \cdot 10^{-5}$	$2.1 \cdot 10^9$	6.0520	$3.62 \cdot 10^{-6}$	$1.7 \cdot 10^{10}$
	234.63	$-1.96 \cdot 10^{-5}$	$2.1 \cdot 10^9$	0.1386	$-2.61 \cdot 10^{-6}$	$1.7 \cdot 10^{10}$
	229.11	$-6.96 \cdot 10^{-6}$	$2.1 \cdot 10^9$	0.0148	$-1.18 \cdot 10^{-5}$	$1.7 \cdot 10^{10}$

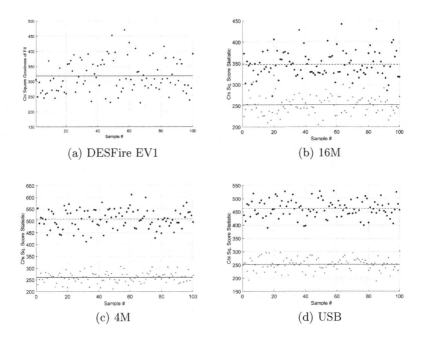

Fig. 2. Distribution of chi-square scores for devices that fail Ent

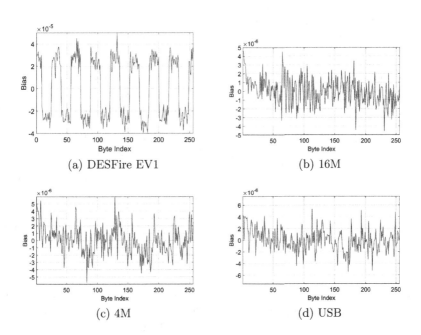

Fig. 3. Bias observed in the distribution of byte values for the first samples of devices that fail the chi-square test

References

1. Schindler, W., Killmann, W.: Evaluation criteria for true (physical) random number generators used in cryptographic applications. In: Kaliski, B.S., Koç, K., Paar, C. (eds.) CHES 2002. LNCS, vol. 2523, pp. 431–449. Springer, Heidelberg (2003). https://doi.org/10.1007/3-540-36400-5_31
2. NXP Semiconductors Ltd. MF1PLUSx0y1 Public Datasheet. NXP Semiconductors, 21 February 2011
3. NXP Semiconductors Ltd. MF3D(H)x2 MIFARE DESFire EV2 contactless multi-application IC, 2 edn. NXP Semiconductors Ltd., February 2016
4. Altus Metrum. ChaosKey True Random Number Generator, June 2008
5. Marsaglia, G., Tsang, W.W., et al.: Some difficult-to-pass tests of randomness. J. Stat. Softw. **7**(3), 1–9 (2002)
6. National Institute of Standards and Technology. NIST SP800-22 Revision 1a A Statistical Test Suite for Random and Pseudorandom Number Generators for Cryptographic Applications. https://nvlpubs.nist.gov/nistpubs/Legacy/SP/nistspecialpublication800-22r1a.pdf. Accessed 21 May 2018
7. Walker, J.: Ent. A pseudo-random number sequence testing program. https://www.fourmilab.ch/random/. Accessed 07 Aug 2018
8. L'Ecuyer, P., Simard, R.: TestU01: a C library for empirical testing of random number generators. ACM Trans. Math. Softw. (TOMS) **33**(4), 22 (2007)
9. Dodis, Y., Ong, S.J., Prabhakaran, M., Sahai, A.: On the (im)possibility of cryptography with imperfect randomness. In: Proceedings of 45th Annual IEEE Symposium on Foundations of Computer Science, pp. 196–205. IEEE (2004)
10. Marsaglia, G.: DIEHARD, a battery of tests for random number generators. CD-ROM, Department of Statistics and Supercomputer Computations Research Institute, Florida State University. http://stat.fsu.edu/Ageo
11. Hurley-Smith, D., Hernandez-Castro, J.: Bias in the mifare DESFire EV1 TRNG. In: Hancke, G.P., Markantonakis, K. (eds.) RFIDSec 2016. LNCS, vol. 10155, pp. 123–133. Springer, Cham (2017). https://doi.org/10.1007/978-3-319-62024-4_9
12. Hurley-Smith, D., Hernandez-Castro, J.: Certifiably biased: an in-depth analysis of a common criteria EAL4+ certified TRNG. IEEE Trans. Inf. Forensics Secur. **13**(4), 1031–1041 (2018)
13. Garcia, F.D., et al.: Dismantling MIFARE classic. In: Jajodia, S., Lopez, J. (eds.) ESORICS 2008. LNCS, vol. 5283, pp. 97–114. Springer, Heidelberg (2008). https://doi.org/10.1007/978-3-540-88313-5_7
14. Garcia, F.D., Van Rossum, P., Verdult, R., Schreur, R.W.: Wirelessly pickpocketing a Mifare Classic card. In: 2009 30th IEEE Symposium on Security and Privacy, pp. 3–15. IEEE (2009)
15. Kasper, T., Silbermann, M., Paar, C.: All you can eat or breaking a real-world contactless payment system. In: Sion, R. (ed.) FC 2010. LNCS, vol. 6052, pp. 343–350. Springer, Heidelberg (2010). https://doi.org/10.1007/978-3-642-14577-3_28
16. Renesas AE45C1 and Smartcard Integrated Circuit. BSI-DSZ-CC-0212-2004 (2004)
17. Barker, E., Kelsey, J.: Recommendation for the entropy sources used for random bit generation (DRAFT) NIST SP800-90B (2012)
18. Rukhin, A., Soto, J., Nechvatal, J., Smid, M., Barker, E.: A statistical test suite for random and pseudorandom number generators for cryptographic applications. Technical report, DTIC Document (2001)

19. Rukhin, A., Soto, J., Nechvatal, J.: A statistical test suite for random and pseudo-random number generators for cryptographic applications. NIST DTIC Document. NIST SP800-22 (2010)
20. Mellado, D., Fernández-Medina, E., Piattini, M.: A common criteria based security requirements engineering process for the development of secure information systems. Comput. Stan. Interfaces **29**(2), 244–253 (2007)
21. Killmann, W., Schindler, W.: AIS 31: functionality classes and evaluation methodology for true (physical) random number generators, version 3.1. Bundesamt fur Sicherheit in der Informationstechnik (BSI), Bonn (2001)
22. Brown, R.G., Eddelbuettel, D., Bauer, D.: Dieharder: a random number test suite. Open Source software library, under development (2013)
23. Marton, K., Suciu, A.: On the interpretation of results from the NIST statistical test suite. Sci. Technol. **18**(1), 18–32 (2015)
24. Hernandez-Castro, J., Barrero, D.F.: Evolutionary generation and degeneration of randomness to assess the indepedence of the Ent test battery. In: 2017 IEEE Congress on Evolutionary Computation (CEC), pp. 1420–1427. IEEE (2017)
25. Soto, J.: Statistical testing of random number generators. In: Proceedings of the 22nd National Information Systems Security Conference, vol. 10, p. 12. NIST, Gaithersburg (1999)
26. Turan, M.S., DoǦanaksoy, A., Boztaş, S.: On independence and sensitivity of statistical randomness tests. In: Golomb, S.W., Parker, M.G., Pott, A., Winterhof, A. (eds.) SETA 2008. LNCS, vol. 5203, pp. 18–29. Springer, Heidelberg (2008). https://doi.org/10.1007/978-3-540-85912-3_2
27. Georgescu, C., Simion, E., Nita, A.-P., Toma, A.: A view on NIST randomness tests (in)dependence. In: 2017 9th International Conference on Electronics, Computers and Artificial Intelligence (ECAI), pp. 1–4. IEEE (2017)
28. Zhu, S., Ma, Y., Lin, J., Zhuang, J., Jing, J.: More powerful and reliable second-level statistical randomness tests for NIST SP 800-22. In: Cheon, J.H., Takagi, T. (eds.) ASIACRYPT 2016. LNCS, vol. 10031, pp. 307–329. Springer, Heidelberg (2016). https://doi.org/10.1007/978-3-662-53887-6_11
29. Fan, L., Chen, H., Gao, S.: A general method to evaluate the correlation of randomness tests. In: Kim, Y., Lee, H., Perrig, A. (eds.) WISA 2013. LNCS, vol. 8267, pp. 52–62. Springer, Cham (2014). https://doi.org/10.1007/978-3-319-05149-9_4
30. Hurley-Smith, D., Hernandez-Castro, J.: Quam Bene Non Quantum: Bias in a Family of Quantum Random Number Generators. Cryptology ePrint Archive, Report 2017/842 (2017). https://eprint.iacr.org/2017/842
31. National Institute of Standards and Technology. NIST SP800-90B Reccommendation for the Entropy Sources used for Random Bit Generation. https://nvlpubs.nist.gov/nistpubs/SpecialPublications/NIST.SP.800-90B.pdf. Accessed 21 May 2018
32. Verbauwhede, I., Maes, R.: Physically unclonable functions: manufacturing variability as an unclonable device identifier. In: Proceedings of the 21st edition of the Great Lakes Symposium on VLSI, pp. 455–460. ACM (2011)
33. Altus Metrum. https://altusmetrum.org. Accessed 11 Sept 2018
34. Langheinrich, M., Marti, R.: Practical minimalist cryptography for RFID privacy. IEEE Syst. J. **1**(2), 115–128 (2007)
35. Burr, W.E.: Selecting the advanced encryption standard. IEEE Secur. Priv. **99**(2), 43–52 (2003)

The New Randomness Beacon Format Standard: An Exercise in Limiting the Power of a Trusted Third Party

John Kelsey[1,2(✉)]

[1] National Institute of Standards and Technology, Gaithersburg, MD, USA
john.kelsey@nist.gov
[2] Department of Electrical Engineering, ESAT/COSIC, KU Leuven, Leuven, Belgium

Abstract. We discuss the development of a new format for beacons–servers which provide a sequence of digitally signed and hash-chained public random numbers on a fixed schedule. Users of beacons rely on the trustworthiness of the beacon operators. We consider several possible attacks on the users by the beacon operators, and discuss defenses against those attacks that have been incorporated into the new beacon format. We then analyze and quantify the effectiveness of those defenses.

1 Introduction

A randomness beacon is a source of timestamped, signed random numbers; randomness beacons (among other kinds) were first described by Rabin in [11].

At high level, a randomness beacon is a service that regularly outputs random values, with certain cryptographic guarantees and with associated metadata, including a timestamp and a cryptographic signature. Each output of a beacon is called a *pulse*, and the sequence of all associated pulses is called a *chain*. An individual pulse from a given beacon can be uniquely identified by its timeStamp, and a pulse must never become visible before its timestamp.

In 2013, NIST set up a prototype beacon [8] service. Recently, a new beacon format has been developed with a number of new security features. Several independent organizations are currently planning to adopt this format, which offers the opportunity to have multiple independent beacon operators (in different countries) supporting an identical format, and supporting the generation of random values using multiple beacon inputs.

A beacon is a kind of *trusted third party*(TTP)–an entity which is trusted to behave properly, in order to get some cryptographic protocol to work securely. It's very commonly the case that we need a TTP to get a cryptographic protocol to work, or to make it efficient. However, this introduces a new security concern: the TTP is usually in a position to violate the security guarantees of the system. In the case of a beacon, users of a beacon gain the benefits of a convenient source of public random numbers, but must now worry that the beacon operator may reveal those random numbers in advance to favored parties, manipulate the

C. Cremers and A. Lehmann (Eds.): SSR 2018, LNCS 11322, pp. 164–184, 2018.
https://doi.org/10.1007/978-3-030-04762-7_9

public random numbers for his own purposes, or even "rewrite history" by lying about the value of previous beacon pulses.

The design of the new beacon format was largely an exercise in trying to limit the power of a TTP (the beacon) to violate its users' security. We believe this effort has some lessons for anyone trying to design a cryptographic protocol or standard that requires a trusted third party.

In the remainder of this document, we first propose a few principles for designing protocols with trusted third parties to minimize their potential harm. We then discuss the current NIST beacon and the general applications of public randomness. Next, we illustrate our TTP-limiting principles with specific aspects of the design of the NIST beacon format. We conclude by considering the ultimate effect of our efforts, and consider some possible improvements for the future.

2   Trusted Third Parties

A trusted third party (TTP) is an entity in some cryptographic protocol who must behave properly, in order for the protocol to meet its security goals. For example, in a public key infrastructure, a certificate authority (CA) is a TTP. The CA's job is to verify the identity of users, and then to issue users a certificate that binds their identity to a public key. A CA which is careless or malevolent can issue certificates to the wrong users–for example, giving an attacker a certificate that lets him impersonate an honest user. In most currently-used voting systems, the voting hardware is a kind of trusted third party; if it misbehaves, it may undermine the security of the election. A good discussion of the downsides of TTPs appears in [16].

Many important real-world cryptographic systems require TTPs to function. However, a TTP in a system is always a source of vulnerabilities to attack–if the TTP misbehaves, the security of the system will be violated. Because of this, anyone designing or standardizing a cryptographic system with a TTP should try to minimize the potential for abuse or misbehavior of the TTP. In general, this requires going through a few steps:

1. Enumerating each way that the TTP might misbehave so as to undermine the security claims of the system.
2. For each such potential attack, adding features to mitigate the attacks as much as possible.
   (a) In some cases, the attack may be possible to eliminate entirely. This essentially means removing one area of required trust from the TTP.
   (b) Sometimes, it may not be possible to eliminate the attack, but it may still be possible to limit its power or scope.
   (c) In other cases, the design of the TTP or protocol can be altered so that misbehavior creates evidence that can be shown to the world.
   (d) In still other cases, the design may be altered so that misbehavior is at least likely to be *detected* when it is attempted, even if this produces no solid evidence that can be shown to others.

(e) Sometimes, an external or optional auditing step can be added that makes the misbehavior likely to be detected. (For example, having multiple users compare transcripts of their interaction with the TTP might allow them to detect misbehavior.)

(f) In the worst case, it may be impossible to make this kind of misbehavior impossible or even detectable–in that case, we can at least document the risk of this kind of misbehavior.

Each of these steps is valuable. Once the designer of a system realizes that the TTP could misbehave in some way, it is often possible to work out mechanisms to move up the list–to make an undetectable attack detectable, or to make some kind of misbehavior by the TTP leave evidence that can be shown to the world. Even the final step, documenting the risk of misbehavior, is worthwhile, as it allows users of the TTP to understand exactly what risks they are accepting.

When there is some auditing step added to the protocol to keep the TTP honest, it is very important to consider how practical the auditing step is. If it is extremely computationally expensive or otherwise inconvenient, it may never be done even if it is, in principle, possible.

2.1   Incentives for the Honest TTP

An entity that wants to run an honest TTP has many strong incentives to try to reduce its own scope for abuse.

Fear, Uncertainty, and Doubt. When silent, undetectable misbehavior is possible, there will always be suspicions swirling around that it is being done. This can undermine the TTP's reputation, or even convince people to avoid the system that relies on the TTP. Sometimes, this will happen even when the alternative is obviously less secure.

Insider and Outsider Attacks. An organization trying to run a TTP honestly must deal with the possibility of both insider and outsider attacks. An insider might cause the TTP to misbehave in some way, despite the good intentions of the organization running the TTP. Or an outsider might subvert the security of the TTP in some way. Both of these have the potential to damage the reputation of the organization running the TTP.

Coercion. The organization running a TTP must also worry about the possibility that they will be coerced in some way to misbehave. This might be done via legal means (such as a national security letter), or extralegal ones (a mobster threatening the head of the organization if some misbehavior isn't done). It might involve financial pressure (a business partner threatening some dire reprisals if the misbehavior isn't done), or a change in management of the organization in the future. It could even involve some intense short-term temptation to do the wrong thing that might be hard to resist in the future. The best way to resist this coercion is to have bad behavior simply be unworkable; what you cannot do, you cannot be coerced to do.

This follows the general pattern noted in [13], in which it is sometimes possible to improve one's position by limiting one's options. When it comes to the design and operation of a TTP, both the users and the operators of a TTP benefit from having a TTP and surrounding system designed to minimize the scope for abuse, and to make any abuse instantly detectable.

3   Public Randomness and the NIST Beacon

As described in Sect. 1, a beacon is a source of *public random numbers*, released in self-contained messages called *pulses*. The numbers should be random–unpredictable and impossible for anyone to influence. Each pulse contains a timestamp, and neither the pulse nor its random values may be released before the time indicated in the timestamp. Pulses are digitally signed and incorporated into a hash chain to guarantee their integrity. In order to be useful, a beacon should issue pulses on a fixed schedule, and should keep a database of all old pulses which it will provide on request.

3.1   Public Random Numbers?

Most discussions of random numbers in cryptography involve secret random numbers, such as those used to generate keys. However, there are many places where it is more useful to have *public* random numbers–numbers which are not known by anyone until some specific time, and then later become known (or at least available) to the whole world.

Why would we want *public* random numbers?

– Demonstrate we did something randomly (outside our own control).
– Guarantee that some event could not have happened before time T, by making the event dependent on the value of the pulse from time T.
– Coordinate a random choice among many parties.
– Save messages in a crypto protocol.

The added value of a beacon is that these random numbers can be shown even to parties who were not present or involved at the time some event occurred. For example, if the random numbers from a beacon pulse are used to select a subset of shipping containers to open for inspection, then people who weren't present and weren't participating can verify that the selection was random–assuming they trust the beacon.

There are a number of properties that users need from public random numbers:

– Genuinely random.
– Unpredictable to anyone until they become public.
– Verifiable by everyone after they become public.
– Impossible for anyone to control or manipulate.
– Impossible to alter past values.

3.2   A Beacon as a TTP

All these applications work well with a beacon[1]. However, a beacon is a kind of trusted third party, as described in Sect. 2, above. Users of the beacon (including anyone trusting the randomness of the choices made) need to trust that the beacon is behaving correctly. A corrupt beacon might do all kinds of bad things, such as:

– Reveal future random values early to favored people.
– Control or influence random values to undermine the security of some user.
– "Rewrite history" by altering old pulses, thus changing claimed historical results.

4   The NIST Beacon

The NIST beacon is a practical source of public random numbers that has been running continuously (with occasional downtime) for five years. The NIST beacon consists of several parts:

– Engine: the device that actually generates the pulses.
– Multiple independent cryptographic RNGs used to generate random values.
– A commercial hardware security module (HSM) used both as one source of random bits, and also to sign pulses.
– Frontend–the machine talking to the world, providing the random numbers. The frontend must support various requests from users.

The beacon format used since 2013 had only a few fields:

– version
– timeStamp
– Frequency (renamed period)
– Seed Value (renamed localRandomValue)
– Previous Output (renamed previous)
– Signature (renamed signatureValue)
– Status (renamed statusCode)
– OutputValue

The new format has added many new fields. In Fig. 1, the new fields appear in red boldface.

Despite the complexity of the new format, there are only a few fields in each pulse which are actually important for users:

– timeStamp – the timestamp (UTC) at which the value will be released.
– localRandomValue – the internal random value produced once a minute.

---

[1] There are other ways to get public random numbers. Many also depend on some trusted third party; others introduce other practical problems–ambiguity about correct values, lack of a fixed schedule, etc. Overall, we believe beacons are the best way to get practical public randomness for real-world applications.

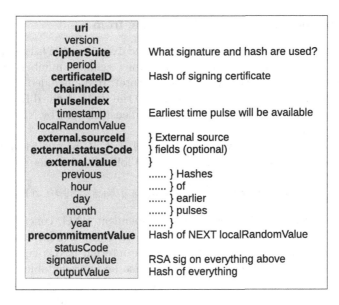

Fig. 1. The new pulse format

- `signatureValue` – a digital signature on the pulse contents.
- `outputValue` – the output of the pulse–the hash of all other fields of the pulse[2].

The other fields (including all the new fields) add security or improve convenience in using the pulses.

4.1   Timestamps

The `timeStamp` in the new pulse format is always in UTC, so that the time at which a pulse is created is easy for any user to determine, without the need to determine time zone or daylight savings time rules. The beacon promises never to release a pulse (or any information about the `localRandomValue` or `outputValue` field from the pulse) before the time in the timestamp, and never to issue more than one pulse with a given timestamp. The beacon also issues pulses on a fixed timetable–each timestamp is separated by `period` milliseconds[3]. In the new format, `timeStamp` always appears as a string in RFC3339 [7] format.

---

[2] The `localRandomValue` is the locally-produced random value, but the actual random value of the pulse is `outputValue`–this is what almost any application should use, as discussed below.

[3] It's possible for a beacon to suffer an outage, during which scheduled pulses are not produced. Gaps in a sequence of pulses are reflected in the `statusCode` of the first pulse produced immediately following an outage.

4.2   Where the Random Numbers Come from

Each pulse contains a new random value, called `localRandomValue`. This value is generated using multiple independent, strong random number sources. At present, the NIST beacon uses two RNGs–the Intel[4] RNG included in the Beacon Engine machine, and the hardware RNG inside the HSM. A third RNG based on quantum phenomena (single-photon detection), custom built by NIST scientists, will soon be added.

Suppose the beacon has k different RNGs. Let R_i be the 512-bit random output from the i-th RNG. Then, we have the following formula:

$$\text{localRandomValue} \leftarrow \text{SHA512}(R_0 \parallel R_1 \parallel \ldots \parallel R_{k-1}) \tag{1}$$

That is, we take 512 bits from each independent RNG, concatenate them, and then hash them with SHA512 [14]. The resulting 512-bit value becomes `localRandomValue` in the pulse. If *any* of the internal RNGs generate unpredictable, random values, then the result will also be unpredictable and random. Even if one of the RNGs is flawed or backdoored, the value of `localRandomValue` will still be secure, as long as at least one of the RNGs is good.

However, there is no way for any outside observer to verify `localRandomValue` is generated in this way; if the beacon were compromised or malfunctioning, the contents of `localRandomValue` could be produced in some entirely different and non-random way, and this would not be detectable from looking at the pulse.

4.3   Signing Pulses

At any given time, the beacon is using a particular signing key. The beacon also has a corresponding certificate, issued by a well-known commercial CA. (The beacon frontend has an entirely different certificate and key used so that it can support TLS; there is no relationship between these keys.)

In the new format, each pulse contains:

- `signatureValue` is an RSA [15] signature over the entire contents of the pulse.
- `certificateId` contains the `SHA512()` of the X.509 [4] certificate of the signing key used for pulses. (The full X.509 certificate is available from the beacon frontend.)

Having each beacon pulse digitally signed accomplishes two security goals: First, it ensures that impersonating the beacon will be difficult. Second, it ensures that a beacon which issues invalid pulses is creating permanent evidence of its misbehavior–a recipient of an improperly formed pulse with a valid

---

[4] The use of brand or company names does not imply any endorsement on the part of NIST; they are included only to clearly explain how the NIST beacon operates at present.

signature can demonstrate to the world that the beacon is releasing improperly-formed pulses.

In the current NIST beacon, the RSA key used for signing the pulse is kept inside a commercial hardware security module (HSM). The HSM is designed to prevent even the beacon engine from extracting the RSA key. This limits the ability of some attackers (both insiders and outsiders) to carry out certain attacks, as discussed in detail below.

CA Attacks. Note that the use of certificates introduces another kind of attack based on a trusted third party–the CA could issue a certificate to some other entity, allowing that entity to impersonate the beacon. Such behavior would be visible and would damage the reputation of the CA, but still could lead to problems for the beacon's users until the impersonation was detected. Attacks on the CA are outside the scope of this paper, but might be mitigated by the use of Certificate Transparency [5].

4.4   The Output Value

The current beacon format (like the previous one) defines the output value of the pulse as the final field in the pulse, labeled `outputValue`. The output value is defined as

$$outputValue \leftarrow SHA512(\text{all other fields in the pulse}) \tag{2}$$

Because this includes the value of `localRandomValue`, `outputValue` contains the all the randomness in the pulse. However, users of the beacon can always verify that `outputValue` was computed correctly. As described below, the fact that users of the beacon will normally use `outputValue` has important security consequences.

5   Limiting the Beacon's Power to Misbehave

5.1   Attacks

Above, we noted the sorts of bad behavior possible for a corrupt beacon operator[5]:

- Reveal future random values early to favored people.
- Control or influence random values to undermine the security of some user.
- "Rewrite history" by altering old pulses, thus changing claimed historical results.

A good design of the beacon format and the normal operations of a beacon should ideally make such violations impossible; if not, it should make them harder; at the very least, it should make them detectable. In this section, we discuss mechanisms in the new beacon format which either add difficulty to misbehavior by the beacon, or which support users of the pulses protecting themselves from misbehavior.

---

[5] While these are not the only possible ways for a beacon to misbehave, they are the ways that undermine the security guarantees of a beacon service.

5.2   Prediction: Revealing the Value of `outputValue` in the Future

The first way a beacon operator can misbehave is to reveal future outputs to selected people.

A beacon that is operating correctly generates a new random value very soon[6] before issuing a given pulse, and so can't possibly tell anyone a value of the pulse very far into the future. However, a misbehaving beacon operator can, in principle, generate its pulses far in advance. All the computations needed to compute a pulse are relatively cheap, so computing a year's worth of pulses in advance can easily be done in an hour.

There are two limits on the ability of a corrupt beacon to reveal future pulses:

The Certificate ID. The `certificateId` is the `SHA512()` of the certificate currently being used to sign pulses. Certificates normally have a fixed validity period–for example, one year. A corrupt beacon operator cannot predict the value of a certificate until he has seen it. Therefore, the validity period of the certificate imposes a (very generous) limit on the ability of the beacon to precompute future pulses.

Suppose each certificate has a validity period of one year, and is issued one month ahead of its validity period. Then the beacon is limited to precomputing pulses no more than 13 months in advance.

The External Source. The new format allows beacons to optionally incorporate an *external source* into pulses. For example, a given beacon could incorporate the winning Powerball [10] lottery numbers twice per week, or the Dow Jones Industrial Average [17] at the close of each trading day. By incorporating an external source that is outside the control of the beacon, the beacon operator can demonstrably lose a huge amount of power.

Each pulse contains a field called `external.value`, which contains the `SHA512()` of the current external value. It is updated only when a new external value appears; otherwise, it retains the value it had previously.

Each pulse also contains a field called `external.sourceId`, which contains the `SHA512()` of a text description of the external source and how and when the external value will be updated. This should almost never change, and it's important that the beacon should announce any changes to this field well in advance.

Suppose a beacon incorporates a lottery drawing which occurs once per day as its external source; the result is incorporated six hours after the result is made public. In this case, the beacon is limited to precomputing future values no more than 30 h in advance.

A beacon might store old external source values for the convenience of its users. However, the only way external values can add security is if they are

---

[6] There must be some lag time between when the random value is generated and when the pulse is output, since the beacon engine must sign its pulse, compute `outputValue`, and propagate the pulse to the frontend.

independently verified. A corrupt beacon operator can easily change the value it reports for last week's closing stock market prices; he cannot change the value stored in financial records, old newspapers, etc.

Prediction: Summary

1. A corrupt beacon can precompute its pulses far in advance and reveal the output values to friends.
2. Incorporating an optional `external.value` into the pulse limits the precomputation (and thus the ability to reveal future outputs) to the time between updating the `external.value`.

5.3   Influencing Outputs

Recall that the output of the pulse is computed as:

$$\text{outputValue} \leftarrow \text{SHA512}(\text{all other fields of the pulse})$$

Further, the recipient of the pulse can verify that this value is correct by recomputing the hash. This means that, while the beacon operator can completely control the value of `localRandomValue`, he cannot directly control the value of `outputValue`. Instead, in order to exert control over this value, he must try many different inputs; each input leads to a different random output value.

For concreteness, in the rest of this discussion, we will assume that the beacon operator wants to force the least significant bits of a given pulse's `outputValue` to be zeros. Thus, with 2^k work, he can expect to force the low k bits to zero. This generalizes; an output value with any property that has a 2^{-k} probability can be found about as easily.

From [1], we get benchmarks for an 8-GPU desktop machine doing brute-force hashing[7]. The listed system can do about 8.6 million SHA512 hashes per second, which is about 2^{23} hashes per second. An attacker with such a system could do about 2^{39} hashes per day, or 2^{47} hashes per year. Because the whole process is parallelizeable, spending N times as much money will get an N-way speedup. However, in order to add one bit of control of `outputValue` with the same hardware, an attacker must double the time taken for the computation.

At the time of this writing, the most powerful attacker imaginable might conceivably have the computing resources to compute 2^{90} SHA512 hashes in a year. This puts an upper bound on the beacon operator's control of `outputValue`. However, for concreteness, we will assume in the rest of this discussion that the attacker has the 8-GPU desktop machine described in [1], and is trying to control bits of `outputValue` using it.

There are several components of the new pulse format which limit the attacker's control of the output bits.

---

[7] That system is doing password cracking attacks. Trying to control some bits of the output of the beacon is very similar to password cracking.

The Certificate ID. As described above, the beacon operator can't predict the value of its next certificate, incorporated into every pulse in `certificateId`. This limits the attacker to no more than about 13 months of precomputation– with only about a year to do his attack, he is limited to controlling 47 bits of `outputValue`.

The Signature. Each pulse contains an RSA signature, `signatureValue`, over all fields except the `outputValue`. This affects the attack in two ways: First, it means that each new value of a pulse will require a new RSA signature–adding slightly to the work needed per new output value computed. This probably reduces the attacker's ability to control `outputValue` by a small number of bits.

More importantly, in the NIST beacon, the RSA signing key is stored inside an HSM, and should be very difficult to extract. If the attacker doesn't have access to the signing key[8], then the attacker must involve the HSM in every new computation of an output value.

Suppose the HSM can do 100 RSA signatures per second. Then, the attacker is limited to only about 2^{32} trial values for the output in a year of trying, and so can control only about 32 bits of `outputValue` with a year of precomputation.

`external.value`. As described above, the new format allows beacons to optionally incorporate an *external source* into pulses.

Once again, suppose the external source is updated from a lottery drawing carried out each day. The lottery drawing results become public six hours before the value is incorporated into the `external.value` field. (This must be described precisely in the text whose hash appears in `external.sourceId`.) The attacker's ability to control outputs is now enormously diminished–his precomputations can now run for at most 30 h.

An attacker who has extracted the RSA key from the HSM and has the 8-GPU system can thus carry out no more than 2^{40} computations, and so can control about 40 bits of `outputValue`. An attacker who hasn't extracted the RSA key from the HSM can control only about 23 bits of the output value.

This makes a pretty good argument for the idea that the private key for the beacon should be generated inside the HSM once and never released to anyone, even encrypted. In the best case, we'd have some kind of guarantee that even the beacon operator could never see the private key.

Influence: Summary. Consider an attacker trying to control `outputValue`:

1. A vastly powerful and well-funded attacker might be able to control as many as 90 bits given a year of computation.
2. An attacker with a powerful setup for password cracking can control 47 bits in a year of computation.

---

[8] This might be an outsider who has compromised the beacon engine, or an insider with access to the engine but not the HSM or RSA keys.

3. When the attacker is unable to extract the RSA key from the HSM, his attack is limited by the speed of RSA signatures from the HSM. If the HSM can do 100/s, then the attacker can control about 40 bits of the output value with a year of computation.
4. If the beacon incorporates external values, the attacker's power is massively diminished. Assuming an external value known to the attacker for only 30 h:
   (a) With the RSA key from the HSM, the attacker can control 40 bits.
   (b) Without the RSA key from the HSM, the attacker can control 23 bits.

It is important to note that there is no way for any user to detect these attacks from the outside–as far as the user is concerned, the beacon is behaving normally, and the pulses look just like any other pulses.

5.4   Combining Beacons to Block Prediction and Influence Attacks

Having multiple beacons operating at the same time gives users a choice of which beacon to trust. However, multiple beacons allow a user to *combine* outputs from two or more beacons. The goal of combining beacons is to reduce trust in the beacon operators: if we combine pulses from N beacons and at least one is honest, then the resulting random value should be random, unpredictable, and outside anyone's control. Instead of having to trust a single beacon operator, the user can end up needing to trust that any one of two or three operators is honest. Note that in the rest of this discussion, we will assume all beacons are operating on the same schedule–for example, releasing pulses once per minute, and releasing them at the same time.

Notation for Talking About Beacons. In order to discuss combining of beacons, we need to introduce some notation: Suppose A and B are beacons:

- $A[T]$ is beacon pulse at time T from A.
- $B[T]$ is beacon pulse at time T from B.
- $B[T+1]$ = next pulse, $B[T-1]$ = previous pulse.
- $B[T]$.localRandomValue is the localRandomValue field of the pulse at time T from beacon B.

Combining Beacons: What Doesn't Work?. A natural approach would be to XOR the outputValue fields from two beacons, getting

$$Z \leftarrow A[T].\texttt{outputValue} \oplus B[T].\texttt{outputValue}$$

For simplicity, let's suppose A is a corrupt beacon and B is an honest one.

Combining the beacons even in this simple way prevents the prediction attack: A can't know what random number B will produce at time T, so cannot reveal the future Z to his friends.

Unfortunately, A can still exert control over the combined output Z. A uses the following strategy to exert control over the bits of Z, despite B's genuinely random contribution:

1. A does a precomputation of 2^{32} possible values of $B[T]$.outputValue.
2. B sends pulse $B[T]$.
3. A observes $B[T]$.outputValue
4. A chooses $A[T]$ to control low 32 bits of

$$A[T].\text{outputValue} \oplus B[T].\text{outputValue}.$$

This attack led us to add a new field to the beacon format: precommitmentValue.

$$A[T-1].\text{precommitmentValue} = \text{SHA512}(A[T].\text{localRandomValue})$$

That is, $A[T-1]$ **commits** to localRandomValue in $A[T]$. Once a user has seen $A[T-1]$, A has **no choice** about the value of $A[T]$.localRandomValue.

Note that precommitmentValue requires that the beacon engine compute the value of localRandomValue one pulse in advance.

By forcing the beacon to commit up front to the next pulse's random value, we can construct a protocol for combining beacons that is much more secure.

Combining Beacons the Right Way. In order to combine beacons from A and B, the user does the following steps:

1. Receive $A[T-1]$ and $B[T-1]$.
2. Verify that both pulses:
   (a) Are valid (that is, the signatures and hash chains are intact)
   (b) Were received before time T
3. Receive $A[T]$ and $B[T]$.
4. Verify that the precommitmentValue fields are in agreement with the localRandomValue fields:

$$A[T].\text{precommitmentValue} = \text{SHA512}(A[T].\text{localRandomValue})$$
$$B[T].\text{precommitmentValue} = \text{SHA512}(B[T].\text{localRandomValue})$$

5. Compute combined value by hashing together:
   - outputValue fields from $T-1$
   - localRandomValue fields from T

$$Z \leftarrow \text{SHA512}(A[T-1].\text{outputValue} \,\|\, B[T-1].\text{outputValue}$$
$$\|\, A[T].\text{localRandomValue} \,\|\, B[T].\text{localRandomValue})$$

This is a somewhat more complex way of combining beacons, but the added complexity adds security:

1. By incorporating $A[T-1]$.outputValue and $B[T-1]$.outputValue, we incorporate the external value, RSA signatures, and other security mechanisms described above.

2. By incorporating $A[T]$.localRandomValue and $B[T]$.localRandomValue, we incorporate a fresh random number from each beacon. Any honest beacon will provide a completely unpredictable random value.
3. Thanks to the precommitmentValue fields in $A[T-1]$ and $B[T-1]$, neither beacon can change the value of their localRandomValue fields after they see the random value from the other beacon.

As long as the beacons output their values on time, the result is that if at least one beacon is honest, Z is random, it can't be predicted by anyone before time T, and it cannot be influenced by either beacon.

Hitting the RESET Button. Combining beacons massively improves security, but isn't quite perfect–a corrupt beacon still has a very small amount of influence.

Once again, suppose A is an evil beacon, and B is an honest one. The attack works as follows:

1. Both beacons send out pulses for time $T-1$.
2. At T, B sends out $B[T]$.
3. A computes combined output Z.
4. If it doesn't like Z, A simulates a failure.

Note that this attack follows a common pattern: simulating a failure that really could happen for innocent reasons. If the corrupt beacon is willing to do this once for a given attempt to combine beacons, then it gets a very small amount of influence on Z–it gets one opportunity to veto one value of Z it finds unacceptable. Along with massively decreasing the power of a corrupt beacon, this attack also forces a corrupt beacon trying to influence the combined output to take a visible action–it must simulate a failure and stop producing pulses for awhile. This is very visible to the user trying to combine beacon pulses, and also leaves a permanent record in its sequence of pulses.

Attacks by the Combining User. A user combining beacon pulses can protect himself and others relying on his combined pulse from corrupt beacons, but he gains a small amount of power of his own. Consider a user who commits to combining pulse T from beacons A and B. The user receives the pulses at time $T-1$, then at time T. He then computes the combined value Z. If he doesn't like this value, he can also "hit the RESET button"–by claiming that he did not receive $A[T-1]$ before he received $A[T]$, and so could not trust the precommitmentValue value in $A[T-1]$.

Other users trusting this combined value can protect themselves from this attack by requiring that the user send out a message, before time T, that he has received $A[T-1]$ and $B[T-1]$. However, for users trusting this combined value far in the future (for example, trying to verify that a published result used the right random pulse), blocking this attack seems quite difficult.

As with the attack described above, this gives the combining user only a very small amount of power over the combined value.

Summary: Combining Beacons

1. Combining beacons massively decreases the power of a corrupt beacon–as long as at least one beacon used is honest, the user's security is massively improved.
2. Prediction attacks become impossible–a corrupt beacon cannot reveal the value of a future combined value to a friend even one minute in advance.
3. Influence attacks become much harder–a corrupt beacon can veto one combined value, but must do so in a way that is obvious and leaves a permanent record in the chain of pulses.

5.5   Rewriting History

Both the old and new beacon pulse format have two fields that make it impossible for a beacon operator to "rewrite history" without leaving permanent evidence that it has done so.

First, each pulse has a `signatureValue` field, signing the pulse with a key for which the beacon operator has the key and certificate. Second, each pulse contains the `outputValue` of the previous pulse, in its `previous` field. Since the output value is the hash of the contents of the pulse, this means that a sequence of pulses forms a *hash chain*.

A hash chain has the property that introducing a change anywhere in the chain requires changing every block *after the chain*. Fig. 2 shows the hash chain (with most fields omitted for clarity) when a change is made to a pulse.

The result of this is that if the beacon operator makes such a change to some pulse in the past, then that pulse's output value becomes inconsistent with the later pulses in the chain–pulses that users have already seen and stored, and that have valid signatures from the beacon operator. A change to any pulse leaves an inconsistency in the chain. Examining the chain will always detect the inconsistency.

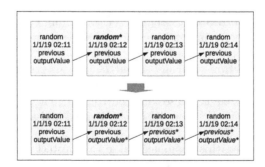

Fig. 2. Altering a pulse affects every future pulse in the hash chain

The result of this is that any attempt to "rewrite history" by changing the value of some past pulse creates permanent evidence of the beacon's misbehavior.

Unfortunately, verifying that the beacon hasn't rewritten history can be expensive. Consider the situation where a user knows the value of 2022-10-04 17:35, and wants to use this to verify the value of 2019-11-29 22:58. There are about 1.5 million pulses between these two, so a user wanting to do this verification would have to request 1.5 million pulses from the beacon, and then verify the entire hash chain.

Showing Different Pulses to Different Users. The hash chain running through the pulses also prevents a corrupt beacon from showing a different sequence of pulses to two different users. Once the beacon has shown a different pulse to Alice than to everyone else, he must prevent Alice ever seeing any pulse provided to the rest of the world. Once Alice sees a single such pulse, she can verify that the hash chain is invalid, and this plus the signatures on the beacon pulses provides permanent, public evidence of the beacon's misbehavior. If Alice has been shown a different value for pulse T than the rest of the world, then she can detect this fact by seeing the value of pulse $T + 1$ shown by the rest of the world.

In general, trying to show different users different sequences of pulses can be seen as a variant of trying to change history.

Skiplists. An auditing step that is unworkably complex and expensive will seldom be done. In order to make this auditing step more efficient, we added several fields to the pulse format, in order to support a much more efficient way to verify that a given pulse has not been changed, by returning a sequence of pulses we refer to as a *skip list*. A skiplist[9] between two pulses, TARGET and ANCHOR, guarantees that pulse TARGET is consistent with the value of pulse ANCHOR–the beacon cannot construct a valid skiplist if the value of TARGET has been changed.

A hash chain used to verify the value of the pulse at 2019-11-29 22:58 given knowledge of the value of the pulse at 2022-10-04 17:35 would require about 1.5 million pulses; the skiplist requires nine pulses. More generally, when the known (ANCHOR) pulse and the pulse to be verified (TARGET) are Y years apart, the skip list will be about $Y + 46.5$ pulses long on average.

Skiplists: How They Work. In order to support skiplists, we added four additional fields to the pulse format which contain the `outputValue` of previous pulses. (`previous` was defined in the old beacon format.)

`previous`	`outputValue` of previous pulse.
`hour`	`outputValue` of 1st pulse in the *hour* of previous pulse.
`day`	`outputValue` of 1st pulse in the *day* of previous pulse.
`month`	`outputValue` of 1st pulse in the *month* of previous pulse.
`year`	`outputValue` of 1st pulse in the *year* of previous pulse.

---

[9] A skiplist [3] is a data structure for efficiently accessing and maintaining sorted records; the data structure in this section is a cryptographic one using a hash function, which is based loosely on the original skiplist. A hash skiplist bears the same relationship to a skiplist as a Merkle tree does to an ordinary binary tree.

By adding these fields, we ensure that instead of a sequence of pulses having a single hash chain, any long sequence of pulses has a huge number of different hash chains running through them, of varying lengths, as shown in Fig. 3.

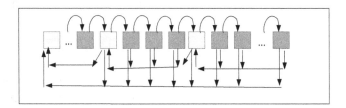

Fig. 3. A long sequence of pulses has a huge number of different hash chains

The algorithm for extracting a minimal chain (what we call a skiplist) is illustrated in Fig. 4.

Fig. 4. Constructing a skiplist from TARGET to ANCHOR

A more precise description of the algorithm appears in Algorithm 1.

In this case, the result is that instead of needing to verify a chain of 1.5 million pulses, the user requests a skiplist of nine pulses from the beacon frontend, and verifies them very efficiently. If the beacon has altered the TARGET pulse, it will not be able to provide a valid skiplist from TARGET to ANCHOR.

In general, a skiplist between a value of TARGET and ANCHOR that are Y years apart will be about $Y + 46.5$ pulses long.

Algorithm 1. Construct a skiplist from TARGET to ANCHOR.

1: **function** MAKE_SKIPLIST(TARGET, ANCHOR)
2:      path ← []
3:      current ← TARGET
4:      **while** current< ANCHOR **do**
5:          path ← pp ‖current
6:          **if** current is first pulse in its **year then**
7:              current ← first pulse in NEXT **year**
8:          **else if** current is first pulse in its **month then**
9:              current ← first pulse in NEXT **month**
10:         **else if** current is first pulse in its **day then**
11:             current ← first pulse in NEXT **day**
12:         **else if** current is first pulse in its **hour then**
13:             current ← first pulse in NEXT **hour**
14:         **else**
15:             current ← NEXT pulse
16:     path ← path ‖ANCHOR
17:     **return** (path)

---

6 Conclusions and Open Issues

In this article, we have described the design of the new NIST beacon format from the perspective of minimizing the power of a beacon operator to misbehave. By adding fields to the pulse format, and defining a protocol for combining pulses from multiple beacons, we have massively decreased the power of the beacon operators to misbehave without detection. In the case where a user can combine pulses from two independent beacons, he can be extremely secure from misbehavior by any one beacon operator.

The table below shows how various ways for the beacon to operate and be used affects the vulnerability of the users to attacks by a corrupt beacon operator. The important points from this table are:

1. A beacon that includes an external value *enormously* reduces its own scope for misbehavior.
2. Combining pulses from multiple beacons gives very high security, assuming at least one beacon is honest. (If all the combined beacons are corrupt, then it makes no difference.)

There are two possible directions for further work: we can make changes to future versions of the beacon format, and we can add new recommended protocols for users of the beacon.

6.1 Improving the Beacon Format

The influence attacks described above are computationally expensive. If the output value were computed using a memory-hard function designed to foil password

Attack	Resources and modifications	Vulnerability
Prediction[a]	Original format	Unlimited
	No external value	13 months
	External value	30 h
	Combined pulses	Attack blocked
Influence[b]	Original format	At least 47 bits
	No external, RSA key known	47 bits
	No external, RSA key unknown	32 bits
	External, RSA key known	40 bits
	External, RSA key unknown	23 bits
	Combined pulses	1 bit, but attack visible
Rewriting history	Original format	Permanent evidence, Expensive verification
	New format	Permanent evidence, Cheap verification

[a] Assuming an external value that updates every 24 h with six hours of lead time.
[b] Assuming an 8-GPU machine capable of 2^{23} hashes per second, an HSM capable of 100 RSA signatures per second, and an external value that updates every 24 h with six hours of lead time.

cracking attacks, such as scrypt [9] or Argon 2 [2], these attacks would become enormously less practical. Even implementing scrypt with a minimal set of hardness parameters would easily cut ten or more bits off the ability of an attacker to influence outputs. However, there is a hard limit on how much difficulty can be added to the computation of outputValue–the beacon engine must be able to compute each pulse in time to output it on time!

The "hitting the RESET button" attack exploits the fact that when a beacon commits to its next pulse's localRandomValue field, it can still refuse to disclose that. In [6], the authors propose a number of techniques to foil this attack, including the use of time-lock puzzles [12] for the random value in each pulse, and the use of "Merlin chains" to take away any ability for a beacon operator to simulate a failure without permanently shutting down the beacon. We could consider adding these to a future beacon format.

6.2   Improving Protocols and Recommendations for Users

A simple way for a user to protect itself from a corrupt beacon is simply to pre-commit to how it will use the beacon pulse at time T, and also to pre-commit to a secret random number kept by the user. The user reveals his random number at the same time the pulse is revealed, and derives a seed by hashing the pulse's output value and his own random number together. Note that this completely blocks any influence or prediction by the beacon operator, assuming the user is honest.

Instead of adding a memory-hard function to the calculation of the outputValue, we could also recommend using a memory-hard password-hashing function for the computation of the final seed. This has the advantage that the user could set the hardness parameter to a larger value than would be practical for the beacon. For example, the user might choose a hardness parameter that would require five minutes to compute on a high-end desktop computer; this would be unworkable for a beacon that needed to produce pulses once per minute.

Acknowledgements. The author would like to thank René Peralta, Luís Brandão, Harold Bloom, Paul Black, Carl Miller, and the participants of the Vail Computer Elements Workshop and COSIC Seminar, for many useful comments, questions and conversations about this work. The author would also like to thank the anonymous referees, for many useful comments and requests for clarification.

References

1. 8x Nvidia GTX 1080 Hashcat Benchmarks. Accessed 09 July 2018
2. Biryukov, A., Dinu, D., Khovratovich, D.: Argon2: new generation of memory-hard functions for password hashing and other applications. In: IEEE European Symposium on Security and Privacy, EuroS&P 2016, Saarbrücken, Germany, 21–24 March 2016, pp. 292–302 (2016). https://doi.org/10.1109/EuroSP.2016.31
3. Black, P.E.: Skip List. Dictionary of Algorithms and Data Structures. [online], Pieterse, V., Black, P.E. (eds.) https://xlinux.nist.gov/dads/HTML/skiplist.html. Accessed 17 Nov 2017
4. Cooper, D., et al.: Internet X.509 Public Key Infrastructure Certificate and Certificate Revocation List (CRL) Profile. In: RFC 5280, pp. 1–151 (2008). https://doi.org/10.17487/RFC5280
5. Laurie, B., Langley, A., Käsper, E.: Certificate transparency. In: RFC 6962, pp. 1–27 (2013). https://doi.org/10.17487/RFC6962
6. Mell, P., Kelsey, J., Shook, J.M.: Cryptocurrency smart contracts for distributed consensus of public randomness. In: Stabilization, Safety, and Security of Distributed Systems - 19th International Symposium, SSS 2017, Boston, MA, USA, 5–8 November 2017, pp. 410–425 (2017). https://doi.org/10.1007/978-3-319-69084-1_31
7. Newman, C., Klyne, G.: Date and Time on the Internet: Timestamps. RFC 3339, July 2002. https://doi.org/10.17487/RFC3339. https://rfc-editor.org/rfc/rfc3339.txt
8. NIST Randomness Beacon (2018). https://www.nist.gov/programs-projects/nist-randomness-beacon. Accessed 09 July 2018
9. Percival, C., Josefsson, S.: The scrypt password-based key derivation function. In: RFC 7914, pp. 1–16 (2016). https://doi.org/10.17487/RFC7914
10. Powerball. https://www.powerball.com/games/home. Accessed 19 Sep 2018
11. Rabin, M.O.: Transaction protection by beacons. J. Comput. Syst. Sci. **27**(2), 256–267 (1983). https://doi.org/10.1016/0022-0000(83)90042-9
12. Rivest, R.L., Shamir, A., Wagner, D.A.: Time-lock Puzzles and Timed-release Crypto. Technical report Cambridge, MA, USA (1996)
13. Schelling, T.C.: The Strategy of Conflict. Oxford University Press, Oxford (1960)
14. National Institute of Standards and Technology. FIPS 180–4, Secure Hash Standard, Federal Information Processing Standard (FIPS), Publication 180–4. Technical report. Department of Commerce (2015). http://nvlpubs.nist.gov/nistpubs/FIPS/NIST.FIPS.180-4.pdf

15. National Institute of Standards and Technology. FIPS 186–4, Secure Hash Standard, Federal Information Processing Standard (FIPS), Publication 186–4 Digital Signature Standard (DSS. Technical report Department of Commerce (2013). http://nvlpubs.nist.gov/nistpubs/FIPS/NIST.FIPS.186-4.pdf
16. Szabo, N.: Trusted Third Parties are Security Holes (2001). Accessed 09 July 2018
17. Wikipedia contributors. Dow Jones Industrial Average—Wikipedia, The Free Encyclopedia (2018). https://en.wikipedia.org/w/index.php?title=Dow_Jones_Industrial_Average&oldid=860019957. Accessed 19 Sep 2018

Author Index

Printed in the United States
By Bookmasters